G000152849

Rich Law, Poor Law

Differential Response to
Tax and Supplementary Benefit
Fraud

DEE COOK

Open University Press
Milton Keynes · Philadelphia

Open University Press
12 Cofferidge Close
Stony Stratford
Milton Keynes MK11 1BY

and
242 Cherry Street
Philadelphia, PA 19106, USA

First published 1989

Copyright © Dee Cook 1989

All rights reserved. No part of this publication may be
reproduced, stored in a retrieval system or transmitted in
any form or by any means, without written permission from the
publisher.

British Library Cataloguing in Publication Data

Cook, Dee
  Rich law, poor law: differential response
  to tax and supplementary benefit fraud
  1. Great Britain. Supplementary benefits.
  Fraud
  I. Title
  364.1'63

  ISBN 0-335-15878-1
  ISBN 0-335-15877-3 (pbk)

Library of Congress Cataloging-in-Publication Data

Cook, Dee.
  Rich law, poor law: differential response to tax and
  supplementary benefit fraud/Dee Cook.
    p.   cm.
  Bibliography: p.
  Includes index.
  ISBN 0-335-15878-1—ISBN 0-335-15877-3 (pbk.)
  1. Tax evasion—Great Britain.   2. Welfare fraud—Great Britain.
  I. Title.
  KD5410.C66   1989
  345.41'0233—dc20
  [344.105233]   89-9226
                                                         CIP

Typeset by GCS Limited, Leighton Buzzard
Printed in Great Britain

For Marston and Haydn

Contents

List of Relevant Statutes

Finance Act 1971
Finance Act 1982
Police and Criminal Evidence Act 1984
Social Security Act 1975
Social Security Act 1980
Social Security Act 1986
Supplementary Benefits Act 1976
Taxes Management Acts 1971
Theft Act 1968

List of Tables

Abbreviations

OVS denotes an official verbal source of information which, for reasons of confidentiality, cannot be named.
OWS denotes an official written (unpublished) source which cannot, for reasons of confidentiality, be attributed.

Acknowledgements

I am grateful to the Economic and Social Research Council for the Competition Award which funded the first year of this research (1984/5).

I should also like to thank all the (unnamed) people who made this study possible – DHSS and Inland Revenue staff, Trades Union officials from the CPSA and IRSF, and all the supplementary benefit claimants and taxpayers who allowed themselves to be interviewed.

Thanks too to my friends (particularly Jane Pearce) and my colleagues from the Keele Centre for Criminology (particularly Pat Carlen) whose support and practical assistance over the last four years has been much appreciated. But special thanks to my husband Marston and son Haydn whose help, love and sense of humour kept me going.

Preface

The research upon which this book is based was conducted between 1984 and April 1988 when I submitted a PhD thesis on 'Rich Law, Poor Law'. April was a notable month for both taxation and welfare policy: the euphoria (or despair) which greeted the March Budget had barely subsided when the full implementation of the Social Security Act 1986 heralded 'reforms' which, amongst other things, would replace supplementary benefit with 'Income Support'. Although it may appear that this moved the analytical goalposts of my research, the comparative analysis with tax fraud remains valid because the poor are still poor and the taxpayer is richer still.

None the less the benefits vocabulary has changed: 'supplementary benefit' claimants are now officially recipients of 'Income Support' payments. But they still refer to themselves in terms of the old labels: as being 'on social security', 'on the Social', 'the dole' or 'the club'. The official label has, thus far, rarely surfaced outside of official and parliamentary discourse. Moreover, emerging evidence suggests that claimants' material conditions will worsen under the new scheme, so accentuating the inequalities described here rather than eroding them (*Poverty* 1988b). I have therefore decided to use the term 'supplementary benefit' in the present tense, not only because it *was* the focus of my empirical research, but also because it is still (in September 1988) the term which most claimants use. However, where the new Social Security regulations would result in material changes (in procedures or rules of entitlement), I have referred to the relevant 'new' provisions and to Income Support by name.

Introduction

Two partners in a vegetable wholesalers business admitted falsifying accounts to the tune of £100,000. At their trial the judge said he considered they had been 'very wise' in admitting their guilt and they had paid back the tax due (with interest) to the Inland Revenue. They were sentenced to pay fines. A chartered accountant who defrauded taxes in excess of £8,000 was sentenced to pay a fine as the judge accepted, in mitigation, that his future income would be adversely affected by the trial.

An unemployed father of three failed to declare his wife's earnings to the Department of Health and Social Security (DHSS). He admitted the offence and started to pay back the £996 he owed them by weekly deductions from his supplementary benefit. He was prosecuted a year later and sentenced to pay fines totalling £210, also to be deducted from his benefit. Magistrates told him that 'this country is fed up to the teeth with people like you scrounging from fellow citizens'. A young woman defrauded the DHSS to the tune of £58: she served three months in custody as magistrates said she 'needed to be taught a lesson'.

These are examples of the possible eventual outcome of defrauding the public purse by two different means: by defrauding the Inland Revenue in evading tax, and defrauding the DHSS by falsely claiming supplementary benefit. On the face of it cases such as these are evidence of the old saying that 'there's one law for the rich, another for the poor'. But it is not as simple as that. Only the most 'heinous' cases of tax fraud ever even reach the courts, the vast majority being dealt with by financial settlement – a private system of justice, negotiated between Revenue and taxpayer (*Cmnd 8822* 1983). Moreover, these negotiations are conducted within a particular administrative, social and economic context. This context (and the interactions within it) reflects significant inequality in official responses to taxpayer and benefit claimant in general – inequality which is accentuated when taxpayer or claimant is suspected of fraud. For example, tax offices are reasonably well-furnished, interviews are conducted (with professional representatives encouraged to be present) in relative privacy, by Revenue staff who are well aware of the rights of the taxpayer and of the need to ensure taxpayers' compliance in order to recoup tax owed. By contrast, in the local offices where supplementary benefit interviews are held chairs are usually nailed to the floor (unless already uprooted by angry and frustrated claimants). Claimants may have to queue for several hours for an interview, which is then likely to be conducted through a shatter-proof screen because stress and desperation has led to soured and sometimes violent relations with DHSS staff (Mandla 1987).

The 'rich law, poor law' slogan therefore needs to be examined not only in relation to the law and the criminal process, but also in relation to the routine departmental responses to taxpayers and welfare recipients, through which differential response is articulated. But the Inland Revenue and DHSS policies which generate those responses are not produced in a political, economic and social vacuum: they must be located within a specific material and ideological context if we are to describe how and understand why tax and supplementary benefit fraud attract such different departmental and judicial responses.

This book therefore sets out to analyse the different social, political, departmental and judicial responses which the 'rich' and the 'poor' attract when they engage in similar forms of law-breaking – making false statements to government departments (Inland Revenue and DHSS), in order to gain financial advantage, illegally, from the state. The 'poor' who engage in such activities are supplementary benefit claimants who are, by definition, living on the poverty line. To enable a meaningful comparison with the frauds of the benefit claimant, my analysis of the (relatively) 'rich' focused on the offences of *individual* taxpayers who evade personal taxes. In this way the unit of comparison was, as far as possible, kept the same, and the focus of study more relevant: the social, administrative and judicial processes discussed here refer to *most* taxpayers and not merely a 'super-rich' few.

Part I deals with the question of 'rich law, poor law' as it is constituted in both common sense and in theory: Chapter 1 examines common-sense knowledge about tax evasion and supplementary benefit fraud in order to analyse how the problem of 'rich law, poor law' does or does not arise in popular discourse. Chapter 2 outlines not only the historical, administrative and legal preconditions for the commission of both these forms of fraud, but also the different opportunity structures which are thus available for tax and benefit fraud.

The focus of Part II is the fraudsters: it examines both the techniques and the motivations of those who defraud the Inland Revenue and the DHSS. (Yet despite many similarities in fraud techniques and self-justifications, the tax and benefit fraudster are attributed entirely different motives in popular rhetoric.)

Part III looks at the regulation of tax evasion and benefit fraud: first, in relation to *official* discourse on departmental enforcement policies, and second in relation to the *effective* rationales which underpin the practices of Revenue and DHSS investigators.

Part IV examines differential responses to the 'rich' and the 'poor' when they are suspected or convicted of defrauding the public purse: this often involves private justice for tax evaders, yet criminal justice for benefit 'scroungers'. The profoundly unequal responses to those who fiddle their taxes and those who fiddle the DHSS are then set in the context of current tax and social security policy: policies which have profound implications for 'social justice'.

Part I

One Law for the Rich, Another for the Poor

1

Defining the Problem

Tax evasion and supplementary benefit fraud may or may not be constituted as 'problems' within public discourse. As will be argued below, the former may be represented as a justifiable 'fiddle' or shrewd business practice, the latter as a despicable form of 'scrounging' from the state. These two forms of economic crime share the same basic characteristic (defrauding the public purse), yet may not be recognized as comparable in popular rhetoric. In order to analyse differential responses to tax and benefit fraud it is first necessary to examine how knowledges about these two forms are created.

But several problems emerge in attempting to disentangle everyday or 'common-sense' knowledge of tax and benefit fraud: for instance, upon what 'official' information are such knowledges based? Is the official information which the Inland Revenue and DHSS provide about fraud equally available, reliable and amenable to comparison? How is official discourse transformed (or reproduced) into the public idiom? In what ways do the mass media and interest groups respond differently to the 'problems' of tax and supplementary benefit fraud? These are the questions to be addressed in the first part of this chapter.

Official information

Fraud and the measures used to combat it are covert activities. Secrecy therefore surrounds the issues of Inland Revenue and DHSS counter-fraud practices: in order to deter fraud the two departments need to retain a degree of confidentiality concerning their techniques of fraud prevention and regulation. But the comprehensiveness (or otherwise) of departmental information made available to the public indicates the extent of openness (or otherwise) of a relatively secretive area of departmental activity. In turn, this may indicate the degree to which that department is seen to be accountable to the public it serves, and efficient in terms of its duty to safeguard public funds. In this respect the analysis of official publications is important not only for what information is provided, but also for what is *not* provided. The absence of certain types of data is thus significant as both the emphases and omissions of official discourse delineate the parameters (and the vocabulary) of public debate on tax and benefit fraud (Burton and Carlen 1979).

The Inland Revenue systematically collect and publish details on, for instance, prosecutions mounted, the yields gained from investigation work (and details of interest and penalties levied on tax found to be due), and statements on Revenue policy objectives. All such information is regularly available in the Board's Annual Report (Board of Inland Revenue 1987). By contrast, no similar systematic collection of information is published by the DHSS. Prior to its abolition in 1980, the Supplementary Benefits Commission (SBC) produced an annual report, but no current DHSS publication gives comparable information. The principal means for disseminating information on supplementary benefit fraud are now ministerial statements and press releases. The public's knowledge of the costs, scale and investigation of benefit fraud is therefore largely determined by the ministers who are themselves responsible for framing, directing, administering and evaluating DHSS policies. Under these circumstances there must be doubts as to the objectivity of such information.

The processes of collection and distribution of information have a direct effect on everyday knowledge about tax and supplementary benefit fraud. For example, the Revenue's prosecution policy and details of numbers and types of offences prosecuted are available in the Annual Report. This document can be seen to demonstrate the openness, clarity and professionalism of the Revenue's approach to informing both its staff and the public on issues such as counter-evasion measures. Such an approach is not adopted by the DHSS: for example, Mr Hugh Rossi outlined the DHSS's prosecution policy in a statement to the House of Commons on 7 February 1983 in response to questions arising from the 'Operation Major' anti-fraud swoop in Oxford. However, openness and clarity do not characterize ministerial statements on DHSS anti-fraud policy.

The reliability of official information on supplementary benefit fraud is also called into question when the processes of data collection are examined more closely. For example, figures of benefit 'saved' as a result of investigation efforts are calculated by multiplying the weekly amount of benefit received by suspected claimants by a number which represents the likely duration (in weeks) of their claim (see Chapter 6 for a further discussion of 'multipliers'). These 'multipliers' effectively introduce an element of guesswork into figures which purport to represent the costs and scale of supplementary benefit fraud. It is therefore difficult to establish the veracity of DHSS estimates of the scale of detected fraud as the amounts they refer to represent *notional* not *actual* losses. This contrasts with Inland Revenue figures of yields from investigation work which do refer to actual amounts.

Problems of reliability and availability of official information may directly affect common-sense public knowledge about fraud. Estimated 'benefit savings' may be accepted as indicating the 'real' extent of fraud, and so fuel the scrounger mythology. But equally important is the fact that the more reliable information provided by the Revenue (which indicates that tax fraud clearly dwarfs benefit fraud in costs and scale) remains largely absent in popular rhetoric. Difficulties are thus presented by the lack of systematic, clear and comprehensive information from the DHSS, which hinders analysis of benefit fraud and can also adversely affect public knowledge. But these problems are compounded when the information which *is* available is used and interpreted selectively by particular interest groups (as will be seen below).

A further problem in defining the problem of differential response in common-sense terms is the issue of comparability. One senior civil servant observed to me that examining the differential responses to tax and benefit fraud was like 'comparing apples and pears'. Although the end product of both forms of fraud remains the same (loss of state revenue), it may be argued that direct comparisons are inappropriate because of differences in the legal, administrative and social processes involved in evading taxes and in defrauding supplementary benefit. However, there are important justifications for a comparative approach. First, there are significant similarities and a high degree of overlap in the activities engaged in by both tax and benefit fraudsters: for instance, 'moonlighting' and other black economy activity often unites those who are evading taxes and those who are fiddling welfare benefits by working 'on the side'. Second, both forms of fraud involve false declarations of personal circumstances to government departments, motivated by the desire to maximize personal gain at the expense of the state: the criminal act is thus essentially the same (though, as argued in Chapter 2, issues of intent and standards of proof required differ widely). Third, a comparative approach is essential if the broader issues of (a) social justice in a mixed economy and (b) the differential criminalization of fraudsters according to their social and economic status are to be analysed. These issues are central concerns of this book.

In order to make a reasoned comparison between tax and benefit fraud it is first necessary to delineate what forms of tax fraud are being alluded to. Tax fraud may range in scale and scope from concealment of income by PAYE taxpayers to complex and massive corporate swindles. For the purposes of this book it is necessary to restrict the analysis to a level which is comparable to the experience of an individual supplementary benefit claimant. My analyses will therefore centre on tax frauds committed by individuals subject to PAYE, by self-employed people and by small businessmen. In this way a valid comparison with the commission of, and responses to, supplementary benefit fraud remains possible.

Comparability is not only a methodological problem, but also has wider implications for public conceptions of tax and benefit fraud. If comparisons between these two types of frauds are absent, then the injustice of differential response remains concealed. For instance, Franey (1983) notes a local case of tax evasion which came to court within a month of Oxford's Operation Major. The directors of The Bear Hotel, Woodstock ('by appointment to his Grace the Duke of Marlborough'), were found guilty of tax frauds to the tune of £330,000. However, national media coverage was minimal, being largely confined to the 'quality' press (*Guardian* 8.10.83; 11.1.84). As will be seen below, public knowledge of tax and benefit fraud is constructed in a way which does not encourage such critical comparisons (Golding and Middleton 1982; Franey 1983). A central task of this book is to examine the political, material and ideological conditions under which

1 public knowledge about benefit fraud is constructed in a way which emphasizes the social and economic threat it allegedly poses, yet
2 public knowledge about tax fraud is relatively underdeveloped, and fails to attract similar condemnation, and
3 the issues of tax and benefit fraud are rarely linked in the public rhetoric (except by certain campaigning groups), and thus the problem of differential response fails to surface in popular discourse as a 'problem' at all.

Competing perspectives on the problem

The 'problems' of tax and supplementary benefit fraud are constructed within an ideological context. This context is created by coincidences of particular economic and political ideas which inform the way in which tax and benefit fraud are perceived. Although such clusters of ideas are often complex (and internally contradictory), they will be examined under two broad categories:

1 Advocates of 'effort' (and Revenue critics)
2 Advocates of social justice (and DHSS critics)

Advocates of 'effort'

The effort school of thought is primarily concerned with the maintenance of incentives to work, and disincentives to 'idleness'. In so doing it invokes both the virtue of the work ethic and the vice of financial dependency on the state. Both personal taxation and welfare provision are therefore important elements in this school of thought. The alleged links between them are outlined by Hermione Parker (1982) in a monograph entitled *The Moral Hazards of Social Benefits:*

> A consequence of the widespread dependence on means-tested benefits is that the young in particular feel no stigma when they claim benefit. We are breeding a race which will regard dependence on the taxpayer as a normal state of affairs. Already the young claim social security without hesitation as a matter of right.

Clearly Parker implies that stigma *should* be attached to claiming benefits in order to deter 'dependence' (such views are reminiscent of the Poor Law's objective, to deter pauperism: see Chapter 2). But benefit claimants are being presented here as a 'species' apart from taxpayers, and as morally inferior. Rhodes Boyson makes a similar connection between the moral evil of dependency and the provision of welfare benefits by the state:

> If . . . the state always picks up the bill, there will be no moral growth at all. . . . It has been well said that 'the ultimate result of shielding men from the effects of folly is to fill the world with fools'. A further effect of too much welfare support is not only that individuals lose their independent character but that they actually enjoy their servitude.
>
> (Boyson 1978 : 110)

At the same time, Boyson sees the civil servants who administer the welfare system as both inefficient and as 'corrupting' the poor by increasing their dependency on the state. The effort school prefers the poor to depend on private charity, which is humbling and stigmatizing, but more efficient in targeting cash:

> As much as Lady Bountiful might be scorned, she also could distinguish between the deserving and the undeserving poor. Not so the state professional worker with his rule book.
>
> (ibid : 110)

Taken together, these views represent most welfare benefit claimants as wilfully idle, 'undeserving' and lacking in moral fibre. By contrast, taxpayers are represented as victims: victims of the idle poor (who are financed by the taxpayer) and victims of the state bureaucracy of taxation itself:

> Taxation has no merit in itself. It is but a necessary evil and should be limited to the lowest level possible.
>
> (ibid : 135)

Moreover, the use of taxation as a means of redistributing income is associated with 'envy' and not social justice. Those who manage to *avoid* paying their taxes are applauded by the effort school of thought:

Of course tax avoidance does thwart the efforts of egalitarians. It is perhaps the main defence of the rich against what some would call their right and proper taxation but what others would call their despoilation

(Shenfield 1968:25)

Shenfield continues to argue that it can be seen as 'heartening' that the rich have managed to save their wealth from their 'rapacious fellow citizens' (ibid:26).

The traditional British hatred of taxation (see Chapter 2) is implicit in the 'effort' ideology, and coincides with emphases on the positive virtues of entrepreneurialism, wealth creation and 'freedom' (personal and economic) through the operation of the market. This combination of ideas is a powerful one, tapping popular resentment at paying tax. Within such an ideological context it is not surprising that the Inland Revenue is subjected to intense criticism. For example, an accountant dealing mainly with small businesses argued 'For some time I have felt that the Inland Revenue is bashing the little man' (*The Times* 22.6.85). Another accountant protested that 'people trying to make a go of things get hounded by the taxman'. He further complained at the Revenue's 'assumption of guilt' and 'intrusion' into people's private lives (ibid.). In a similar vein the National Federation for the Self-Employed complained that the Revenue 'continues to pursue the hapless trader' (*Guardian* 12.4.85). It is significant that newspapers such as *The Times* refer to such views sympathetically, (in this example under the headline 'Tax Hounds'), yet call for *more* intrusion into the private lives of supplementary benefit claimants under headlines such as 'A life of luxury on the scrounge' (*The Times* 21.1.85). Clearly the tabloid press are not alone in using grossly exaggerated 'scrounger' stereotypes.

It is important to recognize the important influence of the effort school of thought in constructing public knowledge about taxation and welfare. These views have a long pedigree: the legacy of the 1834 Poor Law (discussed in Chapter 2) is evident in the assumptions of commentators such as Boyson and Parker. Although New Right ideology is based on similar assumptions about the value of what is now termed the 'enterprise culture' and the 'go-getting society', the effort school incorporates a broader spectrum of opinion which has long been influential in shaping public discourses on tax and welfare. Golding and Middleton identify three key ideas which have, historically, formed the basis of popular conceptions of welfare:

These were efficiency, morality and pathology: efficiency of the labour market and the economy; morality of the work ethic and self-sufficiency; and the pathology of individual inadequacy as the cause of poverty.

(Golding and Middleton 1982:48)

The twentieth century has seen the 'naturalizing' of these images about welfare (ibid.) and thus it can be argued that the political dominance of New

Right ideology can be seen as won, in part, through the successful incorporation of these 'common-sense' ('naturalized') critiques of the taxman and the scrounger.

To summarize, it can be argued that the effort school of thought constructs the abuse of supplementary benefit as a 'problem', but underplays the social and economic damage caused by fiddling taxes. Benefit 'scroungers' are thus seen as evidence of a wider problem of the cossetting effects of state welfare, individual idleness and lack of 'morality' among the undeserving poor. Tax fraudsters are seen as reacting to 'hounding' by the taxman, punitive rates of personal taxation and intrusive state regulation of individual taxpayer's affairs. The 'problem' of differential response to tax and benefit fraud does not, therefore, arise within such discourses.

Advocates of social justice

Commentators adopting a social justice perspective locate the problems of tax and supplementary benefit fraud within a very different economic and social framework. Benefit fraud is not linked with idleness and lack of work incentives, but with poverty and powerlessness (Field 1979; Ward 1985a). The problem is addressed in a less hyperbolic manner which does not focus on individual pathology:

> There is nothing wrong ... with a department responsible for the payment of some £6 billion in supplementary benefits each year being concerned that it goes only to those entitled. And, given the size of the undertaking, fraud and abuse are bound to occur – just as a degree of shoplifting is anticipated by any large department store. But the ways in which they are controlled needs examining.
>
> (R. Smith 1985:113)

The righteous moral indignation and contempt for the culpable poor which characterize the effort school's comments about benefit claimants are absent here. The social justice perspective shifts attention from the 'undeserving' poor to the activities of those who regulate their behaviour. This shift also focuses attention on government policy which shapes investigatory practice, and in this way invokes critical comparisons with policies directed towards tax fraud:

> Government policy towards the administration of the tax and social security systems is socially divisive. While it continues to give great emphasis to tackling alleged abuses of social security, the government consistently refuses to make extra resources available to tackle tax fraud.
>
> (TUC 1983:3)

To the social justice commentators, differential response *is* a problem, and, according to the Inland Revenue Staff Federation (IRSF) General Secretary, Tony Christopher, represents 'a duality of standards no civilized society could defend' (ITV *World in Action* 7.2.83).

The trade union movement has consistently attempted to inform public discourses on tax and supplementary benefit fraud (IRSF/AIT 1981; TUC 1983; CPSA 1984). They have attempted to deconstruct the scrounger mythology and at the same time indicate the unequal responses to tax and benefit fraud in terms of social policy, departmental manpower and societal reaction. These aims have also been shared by other interest groups and by academic commentators (see for instance Ward 1985a; Franey 1983; Scraton and South 1984; Golding and Middleton 1982; Levi 1987). But this task has presented several problems.

First, despite notable 'leaks' (such as the Fraud Investigators' Guide 1983) information concerning the operational guidelines and methods of investigation used to regulate benefit fraud emanates from ministerial statements. The secrecy surrounding the policing of benefit fraud thus concentrates the power to define the fraud agenda in the hands of the DHSS primary definers (Hall *et al.* 1978). This argument may help to explain why public knowledge on benefit fraud reflects the political priorities of 'scapegoating' the scroungers (Golding and Middleton 1982). However, it fails to explain adequately the lack of similarly consistent organized public resentment against the equally hidden activity of tax fraud.

Second, when advocates of social justice broaden the issue of 'scrounging' into a problem of structural social inequality, they render the whole issue more complex. Public resentment largely depends on lack of ambiguity: tax frauds are complicated and not easily distinguished from 'shrewd business practice' in popular rhetoric. Tax offences are not easily translated into the public idiom whereas restricted opportunity structures (discussed in Chapter 2) mean that most benefit frauds are relatively crass and so may be presented unambiguously (Cohen and Young 1973; Ericson *et al.* 1987).

Third, 'common-sense' knowledge is not unified and immutable. The problems of tax and benefit fraud can be represented from a variety of perspectives. But social justice commentators are faced with the problem of reconciling basic contradictions which have historically undermined British commitment to the Welfare State (Deakin 1987), and which are evident in the contradictory political goals of 'economic growth' and 'social justice' (discussed in the second part of this chapter).

Fourth, in drawing attention to differential responses to tax and benefit fraud the social justice school of thought is faced with the task of combatting powerful 'common-sense' notions of *whose* money is being fiddled. It is far easier to represent tax evaders as merely *keeping* their own money, than it is to represent them as *taking* money from the state (and fellow taxpayers). It is also simple to represent those who are already seen as *takers* (benefit claimants) as taking money from the hard-pressed taxpayer. The differing relations between taxpayer and the state, and benefit claimant and the state, are constructed within a particular material, historical and ideological context (see Chapter 2). Once the nature of these relationships has been 'naturalized' it becomes difficult to deconstruct the vocabularies of 'givers' and 'takers' which have become incorporated into public discourse as 'common sense'. One aim of this book is to begin the task of deconstructing this common-sense knowledge so as to reconstitute the 'problem' of tax and supplementary benefit fraud.

Media processes and products

Public knowledge of tax and supplementary benefit fraud is, in the absence of direct personal experience, likely to be shaped by images and vocabularies supplied by the mass media (Wilkins 1964). Although the national press is an infamous source of scroungermania (Golding and Middleton 1982; Franey 1983), television also reproduces similar imagery. Both press and television coverage reflect consensual ideas about 'how the world works' in relation to issues like unemployment, taxation, the Welfare State and the institution of the family (Glasgow University Media Group 1982). But, as already indicated, vocabularies about work, idleness, tax, welfare, morality, thrift, dependency, inequality, 'fiddling' and 'scrounging' are differentially invoked, depending on particular material and ideological preconditions. For instance, the domestic ideologies about 'woman's proper place' may be reversed when economic conditions (for instance, economic boom or wartime) require their services as a reserve army of labour (Braybon 1982). In the same way the rhetoric of 'incentives' may be suspended in favour of 'fair shares' following the levelling experiences of total war (see Chapter 2).

It cannot therefore be assumed that the construction of a consensus about tax and welfare is a simple process. And in addition to 'fitting' stories into a picture of the world which is by no means constant, journalists also fit stories within a set of assumptions about how their *job* works (Erikson *et al.* 1987). Yet in practice the discourses which result may show remarkable congruence as, for instance, reporters from 'quality' national newspapers agree with the commonly held view that stories concerning the provision and delivery of social security benefits are boring:

> I mean, who can understand it for a start? . . . It's to do with money. It's not picturesque, unlike health – patients, wards, that sort of thing. Cuts in social security are complex and difficult to portray, there are no picturesque images.
> (*Guardian* journalist, quoted in Golding and Middleton 1982 : 127)

This belief, that social security is not a 'sexy' subject, means that fascination or compulsion have to be introduced into stories, usually by the technique of personalization. This technique can be used in a variety of ways: for instance, in a story entitled 'A life of luxury on the scrounge' (*The Times* 21.1.85), a reader bemoans that her 21-year-old daughter (who lives with a middle-aged man), has 'never done a day's paid work in her life'.

Personalization is effected through assumed identification with the respectable mother who talks of her social embarrassment and personal disappointment at her daughter's failure (or 'lack of ambition'). Other elements are borrowed from the scrounger mythology, despite the fact that no fraud has been committed. The only crimes these 'scroungers' have committed are that they have 'chosen to live off government allowances' and that they are living happily:

> A comfortable faintly bohemian lifestyle – wholesome food, homemade wine, the odd cigarette – these two are happily content to rest among the statistics of the registered unemployed.
>
> (*The Times* 21.1.85)

This story clearly indicates the powerful ideology of the work ethic: in rejecting this ethic, the couple are labelled 'scroungers' and should thus be subjected to state regulation and punishment. But the story also includes another important element of personalization as the claimants' failure to adhere to the ideal of the nuclear family style is in itself implicitly criticized. Media attention often reinforces the familial ideal through its castigation (or gross stereotyping) of alternatives. The desire to maintain the ideal-type family is essentially political, and has assumed a renewed importance in New Right ideology (Levitas 1986; Fitzgerald 1983). Lone parent families are, in Minford's words, 'to be discouraged' (Minford 1987). They are thus presented as culpably deviant scroungers:

> Single parents have made their case so well that they have expanded their *subsidies* from the public purse from some £15 million in 1960 to £1 billion in 1983.... Low paid members of *normal* families are taxed at standard rate to subsidise not only those forced to be one-parent families by misfortune, but also to subsidise those who have specifically *chosen* to be one-parent families.
>
> (Boyson, quoted in *Guardian* 10.10.86, my emphasis added)

These comments, made at the 1986 Conservative party conference, appeared under the heading 'Boyson condemns "evil" single parents'. However, the picture which appeared immediately above this story showed, ironically, Cecil Parkinson (responsible for one such 'evil' family) and his wife at the conference.

It is significant that the issues of taxation and welfare are linked through the notion of taxpayers' *subsidizing* deviant families. An alternative agenda may have drawn attention to poorer taxpayers subsidizing those richer couples who live 'in sin' as a means of claiming double mortgage interest tax relief. The 1988 Budget which removed this subsidy merely referred to it as an 'anomaly', or a 'tax on marriage' (*Guardian* 16.3.88). Such discourses fail to invoke against the rich the same vocabulary of 'subsidy' or of righteous moral indignation which is regularly invoked against the poor. Public knowledge is therefore created through differential use of discourses on both morality and economics. In relation to economic vocabularies, these financial transfers (described above) are represented as taxpayers' 'subsidies' for the undeserving poor, but are represented as tax 'allowances' for the rich.

Personalization serves to render otherwise-boring social security stories 'sexy', this term being used to describe a high degree of fascination. Examples of this process are also found in local press coverage of benefit fraud, as evident in one story entitled 'Life on the scrounge' which followed court proceedings in which a couple were jailed for a £50,000 supplementary benefit fraud. But press coverage relied not upon the court proceedings (as both pleaded guilty), but on the comments of neighbours:

> Neighbours spoke today of the spend, spend, spend life-style of a Wolverhampton couple who fiddled £50,000 in social security handouts. Kathleen Smyth and her husband Tom were always rolling in money.... Kathleen Smyth known as the 'tattooed lady' admitted 12 charges.... While they were enjoying the good life Smyth, a 19 stone mother of six, drank much of the cash away in pubs and her husband bet heavily on horses.
> (*Express and Star* 15.2.85)

This coverage includes all the necessary ingredients of a scrounger story: massive amounts of cash, local gossip and disapproval, a 'sponging' life-style, heavy drinking, and gambling. The language is typical of similar stories which form an important source of local and national knowledge about benefit fraud. Here benefit payments are termed 'handouts' and the depravity of the fraudsters is evidenced in drinking, gambling and the recklessness associated with the 'spend, spend, spend' spree of pools winner Viv Nicholson. In addition there is an insidious sexualization of this particular story whereby the woman's name appears foremost (and hence attracts unusual prominence). This paves the way for a circus-like titillating exposé of her failure to conform to gender expectations concerning self-presentation, propriety and femininity. The woman's love for her six children is not doubted, but the moralizing tone of the story suggests that good mothers (and nice women) do not get drunk, have tattoos or engage in economic crime.

This story is a typical one in its focus on aspects which construct the offence or the offender as 'atypical' (Cohen and Young 1973). This technique makes the story 'sexy', but 'by scorning the commonplace as dull and unnewsworthy, the routine of life's pattern is rendered invisible' (Golding and Middleton 1982: 128). For supplementary benefit fraudsters life's pattern is characterized by poverty and degradation, but this is absent in popular discourses on the 'problem' of scrounging. Yet, as discussed in Chapter 4, these 'invisible' material conditions form the most important self-justification which benefit fraudsters offer for their actions.

Popular knowledge of tax and benefit fraud is constructed within ideological boundaries. Although shifts are possible (see Chapter 8), these boundaries encompass 'common-sense' ideas concerning the work ethic, hostility to taxation, economic success and failure. Politicians are important primary definers of such ideas;

> I was unemployed with debts of £400,000. I know what unemployment is like – and a lot of it is getting off your backside and finding yourself a job.
> (Jeffrey Archer, quoted in *Guardian* 7.10.85)

Archer goes on to describe the large group within the unemployed 'who find it convenient to collect every single benefit God can give' (ibid.). The views expressed by Archer and by Norman Tebbit (telling the unemployed to 'get on their bikes') support the imagery of the idle, undeserving poor (see Chapter 2). Public knowledge is currently being shaped by official discourse stressing 'genuine' availability for work, to be established by Restart interviews, Job Club attendance and other work-tests. The conflation of issues of 'availability' and 'scrounging' serves to cast unemployed people as by definition scroungers.

In summary, it has been argued that the journalist's adherence to 'news values' skews media attention towards the exceptional, but the problem is that the skew is towards 'certain marginal areas (social security abuse), and not others (. . . tax fiddles)' (Golding and Middleton 1982: 129). Journalists justify this unequal emphasis on the grounds that 'Mr Average' feels social security fraud is more important, yet research on attitudes indicates that public perceptions of right and wrong in public life are not so simplistic:

> if people break the law to help their children, we may judge matters more leniently. . . . If prominent or socially distant persons and organizations are perceived as breaking rules, judgements may be relatively strict.
> (Jowell and Witherspoon 1985: 137)

The issue of social distance therefore becomes an important factor in explaining differential response by journalists (and judiciary) to tax and supplementary benefit fraud. This is particularly relevant if the tax fiddles of journalists themselves (see Chapter 3) are also considered. It could therefore be argued that Mr or Ms Average is likely to feel that tax frauds committed by the better-off are *more* reprehensible than benefit frauds committed by the poor, but that s/he is less likely to be told about them. The problem is that media coverage, with skewed assumptions about clarity, importance and 'sexiness', feeds the Averages with the stories it thinks they want. Tax fraud stories will gain prominence only if they have other compelling aspects, as in the case of 'housewife's choice' jockey Lester Piggott or 'showbiz personality' Ken Dodd. The public are thus routinely denied the knowledge upon which to assess adequately the problems of tax fraud (or upon which to make comparisons with benefit fraud). Therefore media stories, and the official discourses they often reproduce, effectively foreclose on alternative interpretations of 'the problem' of tax and supplementary benefit fraud.

Defining the problem: in theory

Common-sense knowledge of the problem of differential treatment of tax and supplementary benefit fraud is grounded in a complex set of assumptions concerning the role of taxation and welfare in modern society. Complexity arises because the different histories of tax and welfare (discussed in Chapter 2) produced contradictory principles which still underpin current welfare and taxation policy. These principles, although antagonistic, are by no means mutually exclusive: existing ideas and social philosophies are never simply replaced by new and alternative ones, but rather they are challenged, incorporated and have an effect upon subsequent discourses (as, for instance, nineteenth-century distinctions between the deserving and undeserving poor still inform welfare provision in the 1980s).

Defining 'the problem' of differential response to tax and benefit fraud therefore involves identifying those contradictory principles which inform our current understanding of the role of the state in two interlocking areas: first in the collection of revenue *from* its citizens in order to finance the various activities of the modern state, and second in the provision of welfare services *for* those citizens (see Table 1). The relationship between these two areas is complex and not amenable to simple explanation. As a result the theoretical approach adopted here will assume that responses to tax fraud

Table 1 Contradictory principles underlying taxation and welfare

CONCEPTIONS OF THE STATE	Liberal minimalist	v	Democratic interventionist
FUNCTIONS OF THE STATE	Accumulation	v	Legitimation
SOCIAL PHILOSOPHY	Individualism	v	Collectivism
IDEOLOGY	Free market	v	Social justice
WELFARE POLICY EMPHASIS	Selectivism means testing 'needs'	v	Universalism citizenship 'rights'
IMAGERY, FOCUS ON	Entrepreneurial wealth creators	v	Social inequality Poverty
	'scroungers' 'undeserving' poor	v	'deserving poor'

cannot be reduced to a single explanation (for instance, to the operation of free market ideology) any more than responses to welfare benefit fraud can be reduced to the determinism of purely economic relations. The analyses in Parts II and III of the book show that similar justifications are often offered for both forms of fraud, and that investigators from both departments may use similar rationales for their regulatory activities. But although similar discourses are invoked, they are attributed different meanings and attract different kinds of judicial and societal reactions.

Differential responses to tax and benefit fraud thus derive from a series of contradictions in the political, economic and philosophical principles which form the basis of our understanding of personal taxation and the Welfare State.

The state

At the heart of the problem of differential response lies a fundamental contradiction between liberal and democratic conceptions of the state. Philosophically the 'ethos of liberalism and ethos of democracy are antithetical' (George and Wilding 1984: 238). Liberalism advocates a minimalist state which should intervene in the affairs of its citizens only to preserve law, order and justice. By contrast the democratic state implies positive state intervention to reduce the social inequalities which may affect the citizen's ability to exercise his/her democratic rights effectively. According to some commentators the contradiction between liberal and democratic conceptions of the state is itself an indication of fundamental contradictions within capitalism – the need to maintain consent and legitimacy while encouraging accumulation and profit (O'Connor 1973; Mishra 1984; George and Wilding 1984).

The tensions created by these two antagonistic functions of the modern Welfare State are the tensions which enable entirely contradictory discourses on taxation and welfare to be generated. For instance, free market ideology enables the individual to justify evasion of tax as a reaction against excessive state regulation and the consequent stifling of enterprise. As will be argued in Chapter 3, these justifications emphasize the entrepreneurial spirit and a 'sporting' view of tax evasion which together contribute to representations of tax evasion as socially acceptable and even quasi-legal. But the same representations do not result when similar entrepreneurial spirit is demonstrated by supplementary benefit claimants who 'work on the side', despite the fact that these fraudsters' economic motives are the same. Also, excessive state regulation is not perceived as an aspect of claimants' lives which would justify their fiddling, although it appears to excuse the fiddles of the small businessman.

Ideology

It can be argued that the problem of tension between free market and social justice ideologies is in essence the location of class struggle (George and Wilding 1984). It is equally evident that in Britain in the 1980s this struggle is centred upon the issues of the welfare state consensus (or lack of it), and the aims of current taxation policy. Taxation may be perceived as distributive or as stifling incentive to enterprise according to social justice and free market ideologies respectively. In a similar vein, welfare benefits may be seen as a redistribution of income from rich to poor, or as a subsistence level provision to maintain work incentives and thrift. But these perspectives are by no means determined by either class position or adherence to a single set of political principles, nor are they mutually exclusive (Taylor-Gooby 1985). For example, those who adhere to democratic principles may argue that they do not pay their taxes in order to benefit claimants to fiddle the system. Furthermore, many taxpayers I spoke to expressed concern at the lack of work incentives engendered by an (allegedly) bureaucratic and 'soft' Welfare State. Even those who appeared to pay their taxes willingly are still imbued with notions of incentives which owe much to free market technology. Their attitudes towards supplementary benefit claimants were also influenced by the individualism and free market ideology which enabled them to perceive the poor as being (to some extent) culpable – for allegedly lacking in the personal qualities of enterprise and effort needed to succeed in work.

Imagery

The poor are frequently represented in popular imagery as being at fault: for example in their familial relationships. Lone parents and large families in particular are often regarded as to blame for a variety of social ills, ranging from promiscuity and divorce to crime and delinquency. This, coupled with political critiques of a 'cosseting' Welfare State, has led to negative stereotyping of benefit claimants and ultimately to the scrounger mythology, a mythology deeply permeated by conceptions of the 'deserving' and 'undeserving' poor (Boyson 1978; Minford 1987; Golding and Middleton 1982).

Social policy

Imagery has been influenced too by a shift of emphasis in policy towards the poor since the later 1970s. A long-standing debate between advocates of universalism and of selectivity in welfare benefits has all but been won by the selectivists. Economic recession, the political rediscovery of individualism in the economics of monetarism and the political philosophy of the New Right have all eroded the universalist principle of 'rights' to benefit: the notion of *rights* has been replaced by the selective targeting of benefits according to demonstrable (and tested) *need*. Simultaneously an emphasis on the 'enterprise culture' together with a desire to privatize the production of goods and services has had an impact on taxation policy. De-regulation, rolling back the frontiers of the state and encouraging enterprise are the antithesis of redistributive taxation and the notion of paying tax as a civic duty. It is at this point that the contradiction between liberal and democratic ideology surfaces as of vital importance in understanding contemporary attitudes to both tax and welfare.

Summary

The first part of this chapter examined how everyday 'common-sense' knowledge about tax and supplementary benefit fraud was constructed. In addition to official discourses on taxation and welfare, the examination also focused on the different vocabularies used by interest groups, who approach the issues of tax and welfare (broadly) from the perspective of social justice or the promotion of 'effort'. Official discourse and the social justice and effort vocabularies have effects upon how popular knowledge is created by the mass media. Media personnel use these vocabularies selectively as they interpret and translate tax and welfare issues.

Journalists and other media personnel are subject to a variety of organizational constraints and hold work-based values which also influence the construction of knowledge about tax and benefit fraudsters. For example, the perceived public 'demand' for unambiguous, simple and personalized stories allegedly renders benefit fraud stories more popular with writers and readers. But the media are not merely *reproducers* of 'what the public want', rather they are *producers* of knowledge which the public does not 'already' have. The production of news and ideas is therefore a complex process, involving both external (contextual) influencing factors and internal (organizational) processes:

> Information does not lie around like pebbles on the sand, waiting to be picked up and turned into knowledge. Knowledge is interpretation in context, and all work of journalists involves interpretation in context as they transform the specialized and bureaucratic knowledge of sources into the common sense. What is required to do this is itself common sense, knowledge that seems natural, practical, simple, immethodical and accessible. The reporter seeks to illuminate, not to search; to borrow not to burrow. His is the power of news transformation, constructing as part of the common sense what most people do not know otherwise.
>
> (Ericson *et al.* 1987: 346)

The book will examine how certain discourses about tax fraud and its regulation are accepted as 'natural, practical and acceptable', whereas alternative discourses are not. At the same time, it will examine why the justifications which are offered by tax fraudsters (for instance, the desire to create wealth, or the belief that 'everyone is on the fiddle') are not successfully invoked by benefit fraudsters. This examination also involves analyses of why some discourses triumph and others fail, and why tax and benefit fraudsters are attributed different motives and so attract different responses.

The second part of this chapter outlined ideological and political contradictions and inconsistencies which have enabled the paradox of differential response to tax and benefit fraud (see Table 1). The analysis of these contradictions provides the conceptual framework within which to analyse the empirical reality of differential response.

2
Different Opportunities for Fraud

In order to describe how and explain why tax and supplementary benefit frauds attract such different social responses it is first necessary to examine the historical, political, administrative and legal contexts within which these two forms of economic crime are committed. Thereafter it may be possible to summarize the different opportunities which exist for individuals first, to engage in tax and benefit fraud, and second to be investigated, detected and punished by regulatory agents.

Different histories

Taxation

Historically the first function of income tax was to raise revenue for war: first the French Wars and later the Crimean (Sabine 1966). Direct income tax thereafter became an integral part of the fiscal system and continued under both Gladstone and Disraeli, despite a traditional British hostility to tax (evident in Disraeli's maxim that there are only two inevitabilities in life: death and taxation!). However, by the 1880s taxation was beginning to be seen as an instrument of social reform: importantly it was argued that tax should be set on a graduated scale, and although Gladstone considered such graduation 'tended to communism' (Sabine 1966: 125), a movement towards some redistribution in income had begun. But arguments still raged over the costs of administering a graduated income tax system as against its 'yield' in cash terms, and also over the dangers of capital 'emigrating' in the face of super-tax. These arguments are still invoked a century later (despite the fact that the greatest emigration of capital in recent times was not a result of increased taxation, but a consequence of the removal of exchange controls in 1979).

By the beginning of the twentieth century it was possible to distinguish two perspectives in relation to personal taxation, both of which were evident in the Select Committee on Income Tax (Dilke Committee). The 'old' view saw income tax as a 'harsh inquisitorial system eager to strengthen its powers by assuming the right to interrogate taxpayers', and contrasted with 'the new idea of a tax designed to serve public welfare' (Sabine 1966: 144). The alternative views of taxation as repressive or progressive lie at the heart of the contractions between the ideologies of liberalism and social justice (see Chapter 1), and underpin different responses to those who evade taxes.

Lloyd George's 'People's Budget' adopted the 'new' approach to the role of personal taxation, but in his budget speech he used irony to invoke an early justification for raising taxes – war: 'This is a War Budget. It is for raising money to wage implacable warfare against poverty and squalidness' (Fraser 1973).

Measures adopted to this end included increasing indirect taxation and death duties and, importantly, levying income tax on a progressive scale. Super-tax was to be levied at sixpence extra for all income over £3,000, and Land Duty and Capital Gains Tax were also introduced (ibid.). (The latter measures in particular gave rise to the rejection of the budget by the House of Lords and subsequently to a constitutional crisis.) In addition to the introduction of progressive rates of tax, the People's Budget was also important for its incorporation of manual wage-earners into the orbit of taxation. This meant that taxation policy became of personal relevance to all sections of society.

The Pay-As-You-Earn (PAYE) system of income tax collection was advocated in 1943 when, once again, the practicalities of collecting revenue for war were uppermost in the minds of policy-makers. The Income Tax Act 1945 which followed thus laid the foundations of the current Inland Revenue organization and the PAYE system itself (through which all employees still pay their taxes). Critics had argued that the new system of taxation would act as a disincentive to workers. But arguments defending PAYE in parliament epitomized the immediate post-war attitude to tax – that it came 'just as much from the tool room as the Boardroom' (Fraser 1973). The galvanizing effects of war on social policy are evident in such arguments which stress that in peace, as in war, all citizens were 'in it together' (Fraser 1973; Marwick 1965).

The era of post-war reconstruction was characterized by a (grudging) consensus between the major British political parties in relation to fiscal policy. This 'Butskellism' continued into the 1950s with economic growth and full employment supporting the notions that poverty was all but eliminated, and that economic prosperity was ensured for the future

(Mishra 1984). Such prosperity clearly encouraged the pursuit of still greater wealth by some, at times by dubious means as this period also saw the need for unprecedented anti-avoidance measures against 'dividend stripping', 'bond washing' and other such loopholes for tax avoidance (*British Tax Review* July 1960).

The Labour Government in 1965 returned briefly to the redistributive goals of the 1945 administration in the introduction of Capital Gains Tax and Corporation Tax. But these measures and more recent ones (for example, Capital Transfer Tax) have not succeeded in shifting either income or wealth from the rich to the poor. There has been no redistribution of income from the richer half of income-earners to the poorer half since 1949 (Byrne 1987) and although wealth has been redistributed differently *amongst* the richer 50 per cent of the population, there is no evidence of a redistribution of wealth *to* the poorer half (Reid 1981). Moreover, recent evidence suggests that the gap between rich and poor has widened since 1979 (Byrne 1987; CPAG 1988). Yet the myth of the redistributive 'Robin Hood' state remains ideologically powerful, and buttresses the allied myth of the over-taxed or 'harassed' taxpayer. This image, in turn, can be successfully used as a justification for fiddling taxes (see Chapter 3).

It is significant that in terms of social policy it is the issue of (over) taxation which has dominated the 'official' political agenda since the 1970s. Recent attempts to define an alternative political agenda in terms of the 'war against poverty' have failed (for instance, during the 1987 general election campaign) (CPAG 1987). This failure may be largely attributable to the ascendancy of New Right ideology which has fundamentally shifted popular attitudes and social policies in relation to both personal taxation and poverty. Such changes are evident in shifts from the notion of *collective* to *individual* responsibility, from *state* to *market* regulation and from the goal of *personal freedom* 'to be' towards an alternative *economic freedom* 'to get' (Gallie 1976; Levitas 1986). Taken together, these elements have been incorporated into New Right policies prioritizing reductions in personal taxation on the grounds of creating incentives, increasing personal economic freedom (freedom of choice in how to spend more disposable income), and advocating market (not state) regulation of economic and social life.

The results of such ideological principles when put into practice have been paradoxical: while officially espousing tax reductions and financial incentives, Thatcher governments have actually increased the burden of personal taxation for the lowest paid citizens (Esam *et al.* 1985; Byrne 1987). Financial incentives for the better-off (allegedly promoted by tax cuts) have produced a credit-driven consumer boom rather than a sound economic recovery. There is thus evidence that for the well-off the personal contentment of the 'income effect' may cancel out the alleged effort-inducing 'incentive effect' of reduced tax. At the same time ideologies of *freedom* (economic and individual) have been accompanied by dramatic trends towards centralized government *control* (for example in education and local government policy). That such contradictions can, for the present, be contained within the framework of New Right ideology may be regarded as a strength and a factor contributing to its dominance (Levitas 1986). It is in the context of these contradictions that current attitudes towards taxation in general (and tax evasion in particular) must be located.

But the history of taxation indicates other important elements which influence attitudes on the desirability and the goals of personal tax: first, Disraeli's saying (on the inevitability of death and taxation), demonstrates a *traditional British hatred of personal tax*. This attitude offers a rationale for those who fiddle their taxes and, at the same time, ensures that such justifications are popularly accepted (see Chapter 3). Second, debates concerning the ethics and the effectiveness of *progressive taxation* have long included arguments that such measures either 'tend to communism' or that progressive taxation is counter-productive in depriving the successful of financial incentives to create still more wealth. These arguments offer justifications for tax fraud on grounds of penally high rates of marginal tax, and the repressive nature (in practical terms) of any system of progressive tax. Third, history shows that when taxation is levied for war (or, in popular rhetoric, for 'defence'), it may be regarded as disagreeable but tolerable. The 'war' spirit has in the past been invoked to justify progressive taxation to finance social reform (for instance, by Lloyd George and later by Beveridge). But such justifications are successful only so long as 'fair shares' are seen to be 'won' (and so deserved). The winning of consent for social reform through progressive taxation can be seen as a process of struggle against deeply held traditional resistance to personal taxation, and also as a struggle against the (capital accumulative) logic of the British society within which the struggle takes place. The outcome of that struggle is determined by a combination of economic, political and ideological preconditions: in 1945 these conditions enabled tax and National Insurance financed social reforms to proceed, albeit in modified, compromised form (Deakin 1987). But any 'consensus' on tax and welfare had by the 1970s been dissipated by economic recession and ideological attack from both the left and the 'New Right' (Mishra 1986).

Welfare

When reviewing orthodox accounts of the development of the Welfare State it is important to question simplistic histories which see 'The Welfare State' as coming into being in 1948, the product of a unilinear social progression. Many critics of post-war British social policy argue that 1948 did not mark a revolution in policy towards the poor so much as a pragmatic response to the need for both post-war social and economic reconstruction, and for political compromise (Mishra 1977; Deacon and Bradshaw 1983; Deakin 1987). None the less, a historical perspective is necessary in order to trace important shifts in the assumptions underpinning social policy: for instance changes in definitions of who constitutes 'the poor', or in notions of individual culpability. Such issues are important because they illuminate attitudes towards those perceived as 'living off the state' (or parish) or as 'work-shy' (in former times, idle). Although the words used to denote attitudes to the poor may have changed, the meanings and attributes associated with state/parish, work-shy scrounger/idle pauper are essentially the same: past vocabularies indicate a remarkable consistency with some contemporary approaches to poverty, despite the lapse in years from the 1834 'New Poor Law' through to the 1980s.

At the beginning of the nineteenth century poor relief was 'selective, discontinuous and supplementary' and so offered a very different form of assistance from both later-nineteenth-century poor relief and late-twentieth-century social security (Williams 1981). Payment for relief of poverty was based upon the Elizabethan Poor Law which was modified in order to supplement the incomes of the 'able-bodied', usually unemployed or lowly paid men with families. This was known as 'outdoor relief' and such payments existed in tandem with indoor relief to the very young, old or sick housed in institutions (Fraser 1973; Williams 1981). Payments were financed at parish level by the poor rates: concern at increases in rates (arising from increased expenditure on poor relief) is often cited as a principal reason for the setting up of the Royal Commission which reported on the Poor Law in 1834. Commissioners Chadwick and Senior believed the key problem was that granting outdoor relief to able-bodied people had stifled ambition and effort, and had interfered with market forces which, they argued, determined wage levels. Such ideas had been pronounced forcibly by Reverend Joseph Townsend in 1786:

> What encouragement have the poor to be industrious and frugal when they know for certain that should they increase their store it will be devoured by the drones, or what cause have they to fear when they are assured, that if by their indolence and extravagance, by their drunkenness and vices, they should be reduced to want, they shall be abundantly supplied?
>
> (Fraser 1973: 35)

The legacy of such ideas is clear in the pronouncements of contemporary politicians who use similar imagery of 'the idle, feckless and failures' in order to mobilize resentment against the poor: the vocabulary of 'broiler hens' merely replaces 'drones' in such arguments, which stress that poverty is a problem of culpable, feckless individuals (Boyson 1971).

The 'New Poor Law' of 1834 thus sought to reduce 'abundant' expenditure on poor relief and to deter pauperism through the twin principles of less eligibility and the workhouse test. A nineteenth century economist summarized the role of the workhouse in putting 'less eligibility' into effect:

> The able-bodied tenant of a workhouse should be made to feel that his situation is decidedly less comfortable than that of the industrious labourer who supports himself.
>
> (McCullock, quoted in Fraser, 1973: 43)

Implicit within these principles is a form of incentives argument suggesting that allegedly high levels of poor relief (or benefits) are responsible for idleness. Consequently the conditions under which such relief is paid were to be made less attractive, and in the amounts paid out were to be reduced. Parallels can be drawn here with contemporary calls for an end to the 'anti-effort trap' and for reductions in expenditure on welfare benefits.

The Poor Law after 1870 presents a complex picture of a variety of strategies for dealing with poverty: often attempts to 'educate' the poor 'degenerated into more repression of pauperism' (Williams 1981: 92). But the separation of the able-bodied unemployed male from other groups claiming relief is highly significant. According to Bill Jordan this division remained important over a century later as it not only fails to deal with the structural problem of poverty, but also creates the possibility of antagonism between two clearly defined groups – workers and claimants. Such a division is firmly rooted in the operation of the Poor Laws and the mechanics of exclusion. For instance, Jordan cites DHSS re-establishment centres as an example of the practice of separation: compulsion to attend (under threat of withdrawal of benefit) and separation from wife and family are seen as firmly rooted in the nineteenth-century tradition of dealing with the male able-bodied pauper. The ideology of the workhouse thus remained manifest, in the later twentieth century, in the regulation of the recalcitrant unemployed.

At the beginning of the twentieth century pioneering social surveys, popular literature and the work of charitable organizations had all contributed to a growing awareness of poverty and so heightened popular demand for change. But change also derived from less humanitarian motives: for instance, in 1919 Addison argued that the First World War had shown 'hundreds of thousands of men who were physically unfit and could not pass the very moderate standard of physical fitness which the army required' (Marwick 1965: 242). Good performance in warfare began to be seen as contingent upon better conditions of welfare in peacetime. To this extent the promotion of health care, homes fit for heroes and financial protection against unemployment or sickness can be viewed as the logical and functional responses of the state to the need for a fit work-force and war-force.

Selectivity remained the theme dominating state provision for the poor in the 1930s. Benefits were targeted to meet the *needs* of those who could demonstrate such needs through means testing, and were not paid as of right (that is, 'rights' that were accorded to *all* those individuals within a specific category or group – Deacon and Bradshaw 1983). Public attitudes towards the poor were, however, changing: poverty was less likely to be attributed to personal failings and there was a far greater appreciation of the misery it caused (ibid.). In addition the Second World War had a profoundly levelling effect in terms of human experiences across the boundaries of social class. Titmuss noted that the 'fair shares' slogan was an inevitable consequence of the unity of the 'Dunkirk spirit'. Universalism thus began to replace selectivity as the desired theme of social policy because 'a people's war had to produce a people's peace' (Fraser 1973: 194). But the war-time goal of universal social provision was soon dissipated in the face of the problems of financing post-war social policy. Moreover, these principles (which ostensibly underpinned the Beveridge proposals in 'Social Insurance') never materialized:

> It is a misconception to describe these measures as protecting the individual citizen or family 'from the cradle to the grave', for the deficiencies in provision soon became apparent although for nearly two decades they were masked, or partially masked, by the fact of near-full employment.
>
> (Saville 1983: 15)

Not surprisingly, many critics of the Beveridge Report stressed that welfare benefits would undermine the work incentive and that a universal benefits system would prove too costly for the taxpayer. These concerns mirror many raised in relation to early-nineteenth-century poor relief: the encouragement of idleness and (unduly) high costs for the ratepayers. In turn, these ideas are still present in the 1980s, particularly in New Right critiques of the Welfare State (see Chapter 1).

Although the development of what is now termed the Welfare State cannot be seen in simplistic or causal terms, certain historical points of departure, for example in terms of changes in attitudes towards the poor, ideologies of poverty and strategies for dealing with poverty, are indicated by this brief historical outline. Despite the vagaries of war, social upheaval, economic boom and recession, certain consistencies remain in the rhetoric used by policy-makers relating to state provision of welfare. These consistencies may be summarized in the form of three themes which have emerged from this discussion of the historical development of welfare.

First, *the concern to maintain work incentives:* this resulted in the principles of less eligibility in 1834, by the imposition of the 'Wage-Stop' in the 1960s and early 1970s, and the abolition of Wages Councils in 1985. Also, the 1980s have seen effective reductions in benefits, particularly for young people, and stringent work-testing for unemployed people (Walker and Walker 1987). Second, *the distinction which is made (theoretically and practically) between the 'deserving' and the 'undeserving' poor:* elderly and sick people are not regarded as 'undeserving' in popular rhetoric to the same extent as are unemployed people (Furnham 1985). Once again, this ideological distinction demonstrates the potency of the attitudes dating back to the 1834 Poor Law. Third, *the social cleavage created by ideologies of poverty and pauperism:* in distinguishing worker from claimant (and, in the past, the worker from the idle pauper), antagonism is produced *within* what may be termed the 'working' class (Jordan 1973; Hall *et al.* 1978; Golding and Middleton 1982). The extent to which this feature is a conscious attempt by the powerful to 'divide and rule' (Jordan 1973) or the logical product of a competitive capitalist society is open to debate (Golding and Middleton 1982). None the less, the effect of such divisions is to open up the ideological space within which some groups who constitute 'the poor' may be both isolated and negatively stereotyped. This marginalization effectively enables differential responses to such groups, justified in terms of their status as undeserving 'scroungers' taking *from* the state: this response is amplified when such claimants engage in fraud.

The legal and administrative context

Taxation

British taxpayers usually pay their personal taxes in one of two ways: first, employees pay tax under Schedule E, through the PAYE system. Second, self-employed people and small businesses pay tax under Schedule D, direct to the Collector of Taxes (Inland Revenue IR 28, 1982). The administrative regulations concerning the collection of personal tax were consolidated in the Taxes Management Act 1970 which, together with the current Finance Acts, constitute the statutory basis for tax collection. Case law dating back to 1874 (M. Lewis 1977) also influences the drafting of tax statutes, but may lead to difficulties (and loopholes) in the administration of the Taxes Acts. Consequently debates over technicalities and 'loopholes' surround discussions of tax evasion and, as the Keith Committee Report noted, there are problems in establishing if anything illegal has taken place. Thereafter difficulties arise when attempting to explain such technicalities to judges and juries (*Cmnd 8822* 1983).

All taxpayers have statutory obligations to declare all income they receive, from whatever sources (S1, Taxes Management Act 1970) and to submit periodic returns of income (S7). In the case of self-employed taxpayers and companies, returns must be completed annually, based upon the profits of trading during the previous year. Failure to submit accounts may result in financial penalties (see Chapter 7). Although employees have to declare all the income they receive, tax returns are rarely issued to PAYE taxpayers on an annual basis. The Keith Committee recommended that all taxpayers should complete tax returns at least once every three years, but this recommendation has not been implemented (*Cmnd 8822* 1983). It is therefore commonplace for PAYE taxpayers to submit a return only once in five or six years and thus the obligation rests upon the taxpayer to inform the Revenue of any changes in circumstances. Given the infrequency of Revenue requests for information (in the form of tax returns), it is not surprising that tax evasion is more readily perceived as a crime of *omission* rather than of *commission*.

For both trading and non-trading taxpayers it is an offence to make an incorrect statement or submit incorrect accounts (S95(1), Taxes Management Act 1970). But the Taxes Acts recognize two types of offences. First, *minor regulatory offences:* failure to comply in due time, or instances of negligence. Second, *major offences:* substantial failure to comply, or doing something negligent or fraudulent in the course of complying (*Cmnd 8822* 1983: 17.1). But once again the language of tax law may lead to difficulties in defining, for instance, what is meant by 'wilful default':

> Wilful default is understood as 'near fraud' in the sense of deliberate or reckless failure to give proper attention to the requirements of tax law ... intention not to comply.
>
> (*Cmnd 8822* 1983: 17.1)

The term 'evasion' does not itself appear in offences against tax law, although to understate profits, submit incorrect accounts, complete incorrect tax returns or to omit or understate sources of income will all lead to evasion of income tax. Tax offences are defined in relation to the taxpayer's duty to declare all income to the Inland Revenue: 'evasion' therefore 'denotes all those activities which are responsible for a person not paying the tax that the existing law charges on his income' (Leigh 1982: 64). However, there is nothing illegal in avoiding tax through arranging financial affairs so as to pay less tax. Commenting on the case of the Duke of Westminster v Inland Revenue Commissioners (1948), Lord Tomlin acknowledged that

> If he succeeds in ordering [his tax affairs] so as to secure this result, then, however unappreciative the Commissioners of Inland Revenue and his fellow taxpayers may be of his ingenuity, he cannot be compelled to pay increased tax.
>
> (M. Lewis 1977: 25)

Avoidance of tax is, therefore, legal but tax evasion, which minimizes liability by omission, mis-statements or fraud, is illegal.

The blurring of the line separating avoidance and evasion of tax may lead to an ideological and practical 'space' within which tax fiddles can be committed and justified without the full weight of 'criminal' sanction being brought to bear upon the offender. This is accomplished in part because of the ambiguity surrounding the avoidance/evasion distinction (as in the Rossminster case), and in the main because of the form of tax law itself: as Uglow (1984) noted, all the offences which the Revenue can call on in major cases of suspected fraud are offences requiring proof of dishonesty, an element of *mens rea*. As argued earlier, the very complexities of the language and form of tax law serves to mystify and complicate the (already difficult) issue of *intent*.

To summarize, the taxpayer's status as employ*ee* or employ*er* will determine how s/he pays tax: if the former, tax is deducted by employers directly from an employee's weekly wages or monthly salary in accordance with the instructions received (in the form of a code number) from HM Inspector of Taxes. The code number is determined by information taxpayers supply concerning their tax liability on a tax return form. In the case of the latter (sole traders, partnerships or companies), annual accounts are submitted to the Revenue giving details of all income, profits, expenses and losses. The amount of tax calculated to be due is collected directly by the Collector of Taxes under Schedule D. As will be seen below, opportunities to engage in tax fiddles vary between Schedule E (PAYE) and Schedule D taxpayers: they also vary according to the opportunity structures afforded by particular occupations (see Chapter 3).

Supplementary benefits

Supplementary benefit entitlement is calculated through a means test in which the income of eligible claimants is assessed in relation to their requirements, as laid down by Parliament. The decision as to whether an individual is entitled to supplementary benefit is taken by a Benefit Officer in a local DHSS office. The statutory framework within which Benefit Officers make their decisions is provided by the Supplementary Benefit Act 1976, extensively amended by the Social Security Acts of 1980 and 1986 (NACRO 1986; Lynes 1985). In addition, the Secretary of State for Social Services is responsible for the detailed regulations which put the supplementary benefit scheme into operation. Increasingly case law may also augment this legal and administrative framework (Lynes 1985).

Supplementary benefit regulations (in force up to April 1988) mean that 'every person in Great Britain who is aged 16 years or over is entitled to supplementary benefit if his resources are insufficient to meet his requirements'. Except in certain cases, s/he 'must be registered for and available for full-time employment' (Pearl and Gray 1981: 82). Individuals over pension age, those responsible for the care of young children, and sick or disabled people are not required to register for work and may still claim supplementary benefit. But for able-bodied unemployed people the scheme is based upon a work-test as well as a means-test, as they must 'sign on' as available for full-time work in order to claim benefit. (The same principles of safety-net provision, means-testing and work-testing still characterize the post-April 1988 Income Support scheme.)

Another feature which characterizes the supplementary benefits scheme is the presumption of nuclear family relationships when assessing entitlement to benefit. For instance, a lone mother who is 'cohabiting' with a man may not claim in her own right because she is assumed to be financially supported by the man she lives with (Chapter 4 will analyse the gender-specific forms of fraud which are generated by such assumptions). Supplementary benefit entitlement is calculated by adding up the requirements of the 'assessment unit' (whether family or individual) in accordance with fixed 'scale rates' of benefit which are laid down by Parliament. Additions are then made for variables such as rent, rates and special additions for diet and heating where applicable (Lynes 1985). Against this figure of 'total requirements' is set any figure of income which the assessment unit receives, for example in child benefit, part-time earnings, private pensions and National Insurance benefits. Supplementary benefit therefore represents the shortfall between the claimant's statutory financial requirements and his/her income.

The regulations governing the assessment of benefit are both complex and strict. The Social Security Act 1980 sought to reduce many areas of discretion within the operation of the supplementary benefit scheme. But, although officially motivated by the desire to prevent abuse and inconsistency and to save staff time, critics argue that in practical terms the Act led to rigid and excessively technical regulations (Rowell 1982). The 1980 reforms also involved the abolition of the independent administrative body, the Supplementary Benefits Commission (SBC). The responsibility for Social Security provision now rests with the secretary of state, who is directly accountable to Parliament. But commentators differ in their analyses of the motives and the results of the 1980 reforms. The last chairman of the SBC, David Donnison, offered (in 1982) a prophetic view of the changes which were being brought about:

> The reform of supplementary benefits was not conceived simply as a way of bringing a sensitive sector of government under control. But that is how it could be interpreted. Simplification would then become a way of means-testing more and more unemployed people without commensurate increases in staff. The new decision-making system would be a way of transferring powers from the SBC – a body which could at least be exposed to public pressure – to the Chief Supplementary Benefit Officer who is safely insulated from the public. . . . Special case officers may only be used to process the more harrowing cases without too much scandal and protest. And the Social Security Advisory Committee may turn out to be a respectable front office for a service whose function is to divide the poor from the working population and keep them docile.
>
> (Donnison 1982: 182–3)

From this perspective, the 1980, 1986 and 1988 reforms can all be seen as attempts to manage and police the poor more effectively as poverty and unemployment increased. This would involve blunting any effective opposition to tighter regulation of the poor, whether from within the Social

Security system (hence the abolition of the SBC), or from outside the system (hence the dominance of official discourse on 'efficiency' and 'simplification' in popular rhetoric on the Welfare State).

The policing of the poor has long been accomplished, in part, by the very mechanisms of benefit payment: such payments are made by girocheque or order book, at a nominated post office, and with a 'payday' which is predetermined by the department. Although such mechanisms may have been designed to safeguard against abuse, they also function to instil a discipline into the claimant. This is the discipline of the work-force, with a payday and either cash or (giro)cheque. Yet the claiming and payment system inserts the stigma of non-work, for instance through the ignominy of the benefit office and post office queues. These administrative preconditions foster feelings of degradation and mistrust between claimant and departmental staff, and between claimant and worker: the latter categories are, after all, distinguishable within and divided through the post office queue and similar mechanisms which operationalize the welfare sanction. The nexus of mistrust and degradation provides both the conditions under which benefit fraud is committed, and justificatory rationales for its commission (see Chapter 4).

Both administrative and legal frameworks facilitate the relatively easy investigation, apprehension and prosecution of supplementary benefit fraudsters (as compared with tax fraudsters). No proof of intent to defraud is needed: rather, it is sufficient to show that the claimant made a false statement 'knowingly' (Mesher 1983; Uglow 1984; NACRO 1986). Although there are a variety of offences available under social security law and under the general law, it can be argued that.

> The DHSS prefers to use offences under the Supplementary Benefit Act because it is easier to get a conviction on a summary offence before a magistrate than on indictment, say under the Theft Act, before a jury.
> (Stockwell and Clapham Law Centre 1983)

In summary, the law and the administrative framework of the supplementary benefits system facilitate a tight and effective regulation of claimants' lives. Modes of regulation are embodied in the processes of 'claiming' from the state. The forms of regulation are both modified (for instance, to include surveillance) and intensified if a claimant is suspected of fraud. The same may be true if the claimant is merely within a category which is targeted as 'fraud-prone' (see Chapter 6).

Different opportunity structures

The previous sections have argued that the histories of taxation and welfare produced different perceptions of taxpayer and benefit claimant, underpinned by contradictory ideologies of individualism and social justice. These contradictions are also evident in the differential responses to taxpayer and supplementary benefit claimant in terms of the administrative and legal rules used to regulate them. This section will argue that both departmental rules and material opportunities lead to differential access to illegal channels of financial gain for tax and benefit fraudsters (techniques of fraud will be discussed in Chapters 3 and 4).

As already argued, the letter and the spirit of the law offer both scope and justification for the commission of tax fraud. The Revenue's 'sparing' attitude towards tax evaders (discussed in Chapter 5) coupled with administrative procedures stressing the taxpayer's duty to declare any change in circumstances, allow the taxpayer much leeway: for instance, leeway within which (successfully) to commit and justify fraud, escape detection, exploit legal loopholes, avoid penalties or to, almost certainly, avoid prosecution (see Chapter 7). But as taxpayers themselves are subject to different rules, so the opportunities to manipulate administrative rules will differ. For example, PAYE taxpayers have less opportunity than their self-employed counterparts to evade tax. Employees have their taxes deducted at source, whereas the Schedule D taxpayer, in submitting accounts to the Revenue, has greater opportunity to falsify information in annual accounts. But for the majority of taxpayers (who pay by PAYE), the main opportunity for evasion consists of 'moonlighting' and concealing other sources of income. Although there is evidence that such forms of evasion are increasing, they remain relatively small in scale when compared with the evasion by the trading (Schedule D) taxpayer (see Chapter 3).

Large companies are therefore not alone in having access to lucrative opportunities for tax evasion. Self-employed people, partnerships and small businesses may similarly defraud taxes by understating profits, over-stating losses and displaying a variety of 'fiddles' ranging from nominally employing wives on inflated salaries to exaggerating expenses against income (Mars 1982; IRSF 1983). In addition to administrative opportunity, self-employed people and small businesses have greater opportunities successfully to justify their actions in terms of their adherence to the entrepreneurial values of competition and wealth accumulation. Their justifications are thus punctuated with references to incentives, repressive taxation and the desire, above all, to be profitable (see Chapter 3). Such vocabularies are often expropriated by other categories of taxpayers (non-self-employed) who invoke similar justifications for fiddling their taxes. The degree to which such vocabularies of motive are adopted and accepted as justifications for tax fraud contrasts sharply with the rejection of justifications offered for benefit fraud. In both practical and ideological terms the opportunity structure for tax evasion is considerably more open and popularly acceptable than for benefit fraud.

As far as supplementary benefit fraud is concerned, the brief outline of legal and administrative rules above indicates that supplementary benefit claimants are not given the 'benefit of the doubt' in relations with DHSS staff in general, and this is particularly so where an overpayment of benefit has occurred. For instance, the form on which entitlement to benefit is based is not filled in by the claimant (unless a postal claim), but by a local DHSS office clerk who reads back the claimant's statement of income and requirements. This form is then signed, as correct, by the claimant. This practice contrasts with taxpayers completing a tax return form in the privacy of their own home, infrequently and free from official gaze and scrutiny. The presence of a face-to-face contact while making a legally binding statement may reduce opportunity for benefit fraud whereas the anonymity and distance involved in preparing tax forms may increase both opportunity for omission and fraud and the excuse of 'mistake' (Beltram 1984a).

Although a simple example, this instance serves to demonstrate differential opportunity in practice. The conditions under which the false statement which constitutes 'fraud' is made are thus very different for taxpayers and for supplementary benefit claimants. These conditions reflect differences in power and credibility: supplementary benefit claimants do not have the knowledge and power even to record their own histories and circumstances. Taxpayers are given the knowledge and opportunity to make such statements, and are believed when they make them. If later proven false, they often cite innocent error or confusion in justification. These excuses are far more likely to refer to the experience of benefit claimants, yet are usually rejected.

For the supplementary benefit claimant, the principal opportunity for fraud is by working while claiming (Mars 1982; personal communication, 1985). But it should not be overlooked that work opportunities are most open to individuals with marketable skills and this favours those who are relatively successful in the formal economy (IRSF 1983; TUC 1983). It could therefore be argued that the opportunity structure provided by the black economy favours taxpayers (who are thus already in work) to a greater extent than benefit claimants. Moreover, work confers opportunities to learn particular fiddles in association with colleagues (Sutherland 1960; Ditton 1977) and higher status occupations thus generate opportunities for higher status fiddles (Mars 1982; Braithwaite 1984). Supplementary benefit claimants who work while claiming are usually located in marginalized, casualized and low-paid jobs. Their opportunities to fiddle are likely to be determined by material factors, such as unemployment and poverty. The material conditions of taxpayers thus offer a more favourable opportunity structure for fiddles in several ways:

1 *Scope and range:* administrative and legal preconditions enable most taxpayers to fiddle with some degree of impunity (although greater scope is offered to Schedule D taxpayers).
2 *Scale:* taxpayers are likely to be working in more highly paid jobs than

benefit claimants who work on the side as an easily disposable labour reserve. Moreover, taxpayers who submit accounts are dealing with far greater sums (and hence greater possible frauds) than are possible in working while claiming benefit. But, most importantly, benefit claimants' fiddles are limited in scale to the amounts of benefit they receive. Such limits invariably mean that the scale of tax evasion is far greater.

3 *Skills:* taxpayers are likely to have more marketable work-skills than the unemployed benefit claimant. At the same time, the taxpayer is likely to have social skills and knowledge which facilitate fiddling and also help the tax fraudster to manipulate rules, find loopholes and avoid punishment and criminalization (see Chapter 7).

Summary

Supplementary benefit fraud and tax fraud are economic crimes which are committed under particular historical, administrative, legal and material conditions. In order to provide a basis for an explanation of differential response to tax and benefit fraud, this chapter has outlined these differential preconditions, and several important themes have emerged.

The histories of taxation and welfare have given rise to contradictory ideological and political effects (see Table 2). On the one hand the taxpayer

Table 2 Contradictions in the ideological and material circumstances in which tax and supplementary benefit frauds are committed

IDEOLOGICAL DISCOURSES		
Tax as intolerable inquisition as disincentive to effort	v	Means to ensure 'fair shares' (Myth of) redistribution of income and wealth
Welfare as incentive to idleness State and dependency, too costly	v	Safety-net provision for needy
OPPORTUNITY STRUCTURES		
Scope, skills and opportunity for successful tax frauds	v	Limited opportunities for successful benefit frauds
LEGAL CONDITIONS		
Mens rea to be proved for tax fraud	v	Strict liability for supplementary benefit fraud
ECONOMIC CONDITIONS AND DISCOURSES		
Emphasis on: Market regulation Freedom to get (economic) Entrepreneurialism, wealth creation	v	State regulation Freedom to be (individual) Less eligibility, work-tests

can be seen as suffering the 'intolerable inquisition' of state taxation, yet on the other hand is valorized as a provider of 'fair shares' for the poor. These two representations are not mutually exclusive: although the former view may be associated with nineteenth- and early-twentieth-century social policy and the latter view with post-war reconstruction, the discussion above has demonstrated that the history of taxation is riven with such contradictions. The 'new' view of taxation as progressive and redistributive did not simply replace the 'old' one: rather, both are invoked in differing ideological and material conditions. Broadly the new view is invoked to justify levying progressive taxation in order to finance, amongst other things, welfare provision. The old view remains as a powerful reassertion both of the British resistance to taxation, and of the doubts held by many well-off commentators that such tendencies were 'communist' in orientation.

Although apparently contradictory, both views can be seen to underlie contemporary discourses on taxation. For instance, the current Thatcher government has to rely upon the 'new' view in order to seek successfully the compliance of most taxpayers. Good and compliant citizens are thus essential if the state is to gain the taxation revenue it needs to function at all. But this government is at the same time committed to (New Right) ideological principles which seek to minimize state intervention and maximize market regulation in the economic and social spheres. According to such principles the taxpayer is over-burdened and his/her enterprise is stifled as a result of 'excessive' personal taxes. The current incorporation of both views in dominant political discourse thus gives rise to a significant ideological contradiction in relation to tax: paying taxes is a civic duty, but is (in economic terms) counter-productive. It is this contradiction which enables tax fraudsters to justify their actions successfully, both to themselves and to others (see Chapters 3 and 5). These contradictions have, in practice, given rise to the ambiguities and complexities which characterize the law and administration of personal taxation.

The history of state welfare provision is inextricably linked with issues of taxation and work-incentives. For instance, the 1834 Poor Law was conceived as a response to criticisms that poor relief was an excessive burden to ratepayers and was encouraging idleness and dependency amongst the poor. The legacy of the Poor Law is an important feature of the analysis of this book because contemporary discourses about supplementary benefit claimants are deeply imbued with notions of the 'undeserving' poor. For example, Patrick Minford currently advocates a system under which the 'safety net' of welfare provision would be available only to alleviate 'avoidable need': under such a system.

> those elderly who saved conscientiously for their old age will be rewarded: they will be better off than those who merely put aside the minimum. That is both just and good for the economy. Under this system, those who have

illegitimate children will suffer; illegitimacy is therefore discouraged. Families which choose to have many children will have less income per head than those who have fewer... the system discourages avoidable need, which is of course a good thing. The inevitable penalty is the suffering incurred when people fail to avoid such need.

(Minford 1987: 81)

This is clearly an articulation of nineteenth-century arguments that poverty was culpable (or 'avoidable'), the result of individual failing, and so could be deterred. Deterrence could be effected through the principle of less eligibility, put into operation by work-tests and the 'suffering' resulting either from inadequate levels of benefit, or from no benefits at all. Such arguments are as important in analysing responses to the poor in the 1980s as they were in the 1830s.

Beneath these historical contradictions, which inform the law and administration of tax and welfare, lie different conceptions of the role of the state in modern societies. For instance, this chapter has indicated the importance of war, both as a justification for progressive social policies in terms of 'fair shares', and for the collection of personal taxes to finance social policy. But the twin justifications which 'war' offered failed to reconcile the problem of whether the modern capitalist state in which the war was waged (whether war against poverty or against external enemies) was a state geared to the needs of capital accumulation or to the goal of securing consent and legitimation, implicitly through policies geared to social justice (George and Wilding 1984). These contradictory perspectives on the modern state lie at the heart of differential responses to taxpayers and to benefit claimants: the taxpayer is seen to pursue capital accumulation, whereas the benefit claimant is seen as the recipient of state welfare provision.

But legitimation is not guaranteed simply through the existence of such provision in itself. As argued above, the Welfare State rested not so much on 'consensus' as on 'grudging acquiescence' (Deakin 1987). In the last decade this already fragile base has been further eroded: critiques from the left (of poor delivery of services) and from the right (of cossetting welfare and the 'scrounger') have effectively undermined the legitimation function of the Welfare State. At the same time the New Right politics of privatization and de-regulation have gained dominance and so, for the time being at least, the function of accumulation appears to dominate social policy. Yet the state cannot be sustained without popular consent: debates centred on the National Health Service, the 'Poll Tax' and the 1988 Social Security Reforms are evidence of political struggles involved in the winning of such consent.

Struggles over taxation and welfare, both historical and contemporary, therefore reflect fundamental struggles over the nature and role of the state. One element in this struggle is the deconstruction of the problem of differential political, judicial and popular responses to tax and supplementary benefit fraud.

Part II
The Fraudsters

Introduction

A detailed examination of fraudsters' techniques is necessary in order to gain an understanding of precisely what is involved in the commission of tax and supplementary benefit fraud. However, when describing these techniques, fraudsters invariably locate their offences within a specific material context, and thereby implicitly offer justifications for their conduct. Although it is difficult to isolate fraudsters' descriptions of their actions from the rationales which they offer for those actions, some analytic separation is necessary for 'the problem' of tax and benefit fraud to be fully examined. Such an examination reveals similarities both in the types of activities engaged in by some tax and benefit fraudsters, and in their motivational rhetorics. Yet similar (illegal) acts and self-justifications may be perceived entirely differently according to whether those illegal acts have been committed by 'givers' or 'takers' from the state.

3

Tax Fraudsters

The opportunity to evade tax is to some extent determined by an individual's employment status and consequent mode of paying personal tax. Pay-As-You-Earn (PAYE) taxpayers have their tax deducted prior to receiving wages or salary and this inevitably places limits upon their opportunities to fiddle. By contrast self-employed (Schedule D) taxpayers are required to complete annual accounts in which profits are declared and a claim is made for the allowances and expenses which can be offset against those profits. In this way the appropriate figure of tax liability for that year is calculated. Clearly there is far greater scope for tax evasion as a Schedule D taxpayer than for the majority of PAYE taxpayers whose tax is deducted at source. As will be seen below, Schedule D taxpayers may fail to declare profits fully, may overclaim allowances or expenses or do jobs 'on the side' in the black economy if they have the appropriate skills.

The extent of such irregularities in the accounts of some trading taxpayers is revealed when suspicious cases are selected for in-depth investigation: in 1984/5 only 2.8 per cent of traders' accounts were examined in depth, but understated profits were found in 91 per cent of those examined. In half of these cases financial penalties and/or interest were charged, implying the existence of either 'wilful default' or negligence (Board of Inland Revenue 1986a). It could therefore be argued, on the basis of this examination of accounts, that many trading taxpayers could be evading tax. But it would be wrong to push the PAYE/Schedule D distinction too far in *alone* explaining the extent and distribution of tax fraud. There is a good deal of overlap between the techniques of these fraudsters when one considers their activities in the black economy in general.

The black economy is a term used to describe 'all activities which are concealed from the revenue collecting authorities with the specific intention of evading tax' (*Cmnd 8822* 1983: 550). From the Inland Revenue's standpoint the black economy consists primarily of 'ghosts' and 'moon-lighters'. Ghosts are people who are working but remain unknown to the Revenue: moonlighters are known to the Revenue in one area of economic activity, but also engage in other (unknown) business in addition (*Network* July 1985). Identifying such people is a difficult task involving a variety of investigative techniques (discussed in Chapter 5). But it is worth noting that moonlighters may include both PAYE taxpayers who, for instance, do evening work in bars, and the self-employed builder who, for instance, builds an extension in his 'free time' at evenings and week-ends. The black economy therefore includes a wide variety of activities, skills and forms of enterprise, all of which are hidden for the purposes of tax and VAT.

Techniques

It is not easy to impose a structured analytical framework upon such diverse and varied activities as serving behind a bar, installing central heating, driving taxis and architects 'doing a foreigner' by drawing up plans (for a small fee and tax free), for their acquaintances. What follows will therefore look at techniques of fiddling tax within the boundaries of an individual's skill or occupational category, broadly summarized as follows:

1 The building trade
2 The 'one man band' and small commercial traders
3 Auction and street market traders
4 The hotel and catering trade
5 Highly paid employees, directors and the professionals

The building trade

The building trade became a key focus of concern in the 1970s with much publicity, and subsequently investigative effort, centred upon its systems of payment, in particular the evasion of tax by sub-contractors known as 'the lump'. In an effort to combat what appeared to be widespread abuse, tax deduction certificates, called 714's, were issued to sub-contractors who were registered with the Inland Revenue (under S29-31 of the Finance Act 1971). As a result, nowadays if a sub-contractor does not produce a 714 certificate then a main contractor must deduct tax at the basic rate (25 per cent for the year 1988/9) from his payment, and pass the tax on to the Inland Revenue. If the sub-contractor does have a 714, he can be paid in full and the transaction is recorded on an official voucher. Despite attempts to combat continued abuse (for instance by requiring a photograph of the holder to appear on the certificate), there remains a 'black market' both in these 714 'credit cards' and the accompanying vouchers (*Network* July 1986). According to the Revenue, 'The tax known to have been evaded on such cases completed during the year ended 30th September 1985 amounted to £35 million' (*Network* July 1985: 5). But despite the massive amounts involved, most sub-contractor investigations 'are focused on the "mean streets" of labourers' doss houses, or squalid hostels' (ibid.).

Once registered as a self-employed, 'bona-fide' sub-contractor, many individuals none the less go on to engage in seemingly lesser fiddles within the black economy. One such self-employed builder I interviewed was Bill. He clearly distinguished those jobs which did and those which did not 'go through the books'. Jobs which did go through the books included VAT (where applicable) in all the estimates he gave, and information concerning these jobs was passed on to his accountant for inclusion in the end-of-year accounts. Jobs which did not go through the books were usually done (during the evenings or at week-ends) for friends or as 'a favour' and did not include VAT and were not reported to the accountant. Payment for this type of job was invariably in cash, thus avoiding the payment of cheques into his bank account and the resulting attention of the accountant and tax inspector.

Bill also stressed that his skills often enabled him to complete small jobs with very little outlay, in terms of materials, and without the bureaucratic 'red tape' of recording procedures. For example,

> Pointing up a wall or lowering a chimney only needs a bag of cement, a trowel, a ladder and a hammer.
>
> (Bill)

But even when red tape (in the form of building regulations or planning permission) was involved, Bill was prepared to do the job 'on the side' so long as the customer realized it would take longer and involve evening and week-end work. In this way such jobs were seen to serve the interests of the customer who paid less, and the builder, who had a little 'insurance' against problems (such as bad weather or moneys owing), which constantly arose from his 'through the books' work.

These 'jobs on the side' did not form the lion's share of Bill's income but, he argued, they ensure his financial survival by providing ready cash and a fairly constant stream of small jobs (often with little financial outlay) in an uncertain trade. Bill did not consider such 'foreigners' (jobs on the side) as in any way comparable to the activities of 'cowboys', whom he derided as both lacking in skill and accountability. The stereotypical cowboy fiddle was well portrayed in Alan Bleasdale's play, *Boys from the Blackstuff*. The cheap offers to tarmac a drive (using the ubiquitous lorry load 'left over' from a legitimate job) involve fiddling the main contractor in addition to the taxman. The difference between this sort of fiddle and those engaged in by Bill is essentially one of accountability. Bill's reputation as a good builder depends as much upon his week-end jobs as those officially accomplished 'through the books' in the official working week. The 'cowboys' who work primarily in the black economy are frequently in a particular area only fleetingly, have no reputation to maintain and are not therefore accountable to the consumer; they are virtually impossible to track down in the event of any complaint. Opportunities to fiddle are greatly increased by one-off transient transactions akin to a 'passing trade' (Mars 1982: 138).

The building trade offers an excellent entree into what has been referred to variously as the hidden, underground, informal, shadow or black economy (Henry 1978; Gershuny and Pahl 1980; S. Smith 1986). The marketability of the skills involved and, frequently, the absence of additional outlay for the fraudster (particularly if customers buy their own materials for the job) enhance the advantages of the 'cash' economy. Henry argues that the hidden economy forms an 'everyday feature of ordinary people's lives' and, moreover, it is 'the on-the-side, illegal activity of "honest" people who have conventional jobs and would never admit to being dishonest' (Henry 1978: 12). But participants in the black economy whom I have interviewed are acutely aware of the illegality and dishonesty of such activity, yet rationalize them by utilizing a complex set of justifications.

The 'one man band' and small commercial traders

The activities of many sole traders in the black economy in many ways mirror those of the builder. For example, electricians, plumbers and carpenters who are registered as self-employed have similarly marketable skills which can literally be 'cashed in on' outside normal working hours. Often though, such traders see their participation in the black economy in social rather than economic terms. One self-employed plumber, Paul, told me that such jobs were done 'as a favour' for acquaintances. A purely economic rationale is far more evident in the case of individuals who possess these skills and are *employees*. For instance, workers in the formerly 'public service' sectors of electricity and gas provision (pre-privatization), regarded 'jobs on the side' as a useful way of supplementing their earnings. As they were hardly in a position to 'advertise' their availability for such work, jobs were obtained through a grapevine of relatives and 'friends of friends'. A similar situation can be seen in respect of other specialist employees (for instance, car mechanics).

The techniques of evasion in areas of work discussed so far are similar: work is performed on a cash basis and is not declared for tax purposes. Small commercial traders, though, may engage in other fiddles which ultimately serve to reduce their tax liability by dubious and illegal means: for example by regularly pilfering goods or materials from the firm for private use. Such traders often consider that such goods belong to them (even if a partnership is involved) and feel no compunction about writing them off as losses to the firm. These losses may be considerable and in effect a firm's taxable profits are thereby reduced. Although not perceived as theft nor as evasion of tax and VAT, clearly these 'crimes' have been committed. But, as Mars notes, 'theft is a "heavy" word' and the lighter, relatively neutral term 'fiddle' is probably closer to the fiddler's view of his own activities. Furthermore;

> A businessman... might describe his expense allowance as a 'perk'. Viewed from the outside, it will, however, look like a 'fiddle'. And viewed from... – for example, the Inland Revenue – it will more like tax evasion.
>
> (Mars 1982: 166–7)

These differences in terminology are crucial as they implicitly involve self-justifications for the 'fiddler' (or fraudster) concerned.

Another factor affecting the opportunity (and possibly the desire) to fiddle tax is the scale of the business in question. One small-scale carpet retailer told me that he felt it was easier to fiddle when he was a 'one man band' operating from home. Once he had purchased retail premises, the high profile his business acquired led him to be more cautious. He argued that it would be stupid to understate profits when anyone could *see* that the shop was nearly always full of customers. To this extent he believed that visibility was a factor deterring tax fiddles of this kind. He added that if turnover was good there was 'no point' in fiddling anyway, clearly seeing tax evasion as motivated by financial hardship rather than greed. Although this is a debatable point, his belief that 'hidden' areas of trade and business are more fertile ground for potential fiddling does seem to be borne out: for instance, a small building contractor like Bill could moonlight with *relative* impunity, but a larger contractor's busy business premises or signs displayed upon his construction work would belie assertions that business was bad. This is not to say that all commercial traders are as content to pay their taxes as the carpet retailer quoted above, but merely indicates that differential opportunities for fiddling depend not only upon the nature of the occupation but also on its scale and visibility.

It could be argued that the nature of tax fiddles simply changes (as a result of the scale of the enterprise) from the crude to the sophisticated. Relatively straightforward moonlighting (doing jobs 'on the side') is replaced in larger firms by regularized milking of the firm's resources by its directors, or by systematic under-declaration of taxable profits (see pp. 51–3).

Auction and street market traders

This discussion has already focused on moonlighters, but another means of evading tax altogether is by ghosting. Ghosts, as the name implies, are shadowy individuals who are difficult to trace and are consequently invisible to the Revenue. Many day-to-day traders fit into this category: for example, those individuals who set up market stalls on a one-off basis or who irregularly offer to fill the stalls of absent official traders. Although it may appear that the evasion of tax involved in such cases is small, vast sums may be at stake. A senior Inland Revenue official told me of one street trader whose earnings over seven years had totalled £150,000 and whose tax bill (after a Revenue investigation) was correspondingly substantial.

The techniques involved in this form of fiddle centre on constantly moving, preserving anonymity, trading in cash with goods (enabling a quick turnover) and maintaining 'invisibility' with regard to the Inland Revenue. These same techniques are applied to fiddles in the sphere of auctions. An individual may buy up household goods for auction in one area and then sell them at a profit in another. Similarly household goods and furniture obtained through 'house clearances' may be sold at a profit. If the person concerned can pay in cash, they can remain anonymous or alternatively, when buying at auction, they may use a false name.

More recently car auctions have provided a similar opportunity for ghost dealers to emerge. As invisibility is essential, such traders seek to avoid advertising cars or goods for sale in the classified columns of the local press in which, officially, they must include the word 'Trade' when placing adverts. Another trading situation proving lucrative for ghosts is the car boot sale, which fund-raisers often find an increasingly favoured alternative to auctions and jumble sales. For ghosts, the opportunity to buy in goods for resale at a profit, and to sell others, is attractive, cheap and offers the benefits of ease of mobility, cash trade and anonymity. As noted above, in relation to 'cowboy' builders, the existence of transient, cash-based commercial relationships particularly facilitate tax evasion.

The hotel and catering trade

A recent survey by tax offices in one region found that hotel and catering staff in some larger well-known establishments received up to £7,500 a year in tips. The review yielded some £650,000 in tax and the lowest average agreed tips per full-time worker was £750 per annum.

(Lindsay Cook, *Guardian* 11.5.85)

Non-declaration of tips is the simplest and most common form of tax fiddle in the hotel and catering industry. By failing to declare tips, an employee is effectively receiving income without tax being deducted and is therefore, guilty of evasion. However, this type of fiddling is rarely perceived by the recipients as being a criminal act as in other fiddle-prone trades, the gains made are considered to be 'perks' or a means of making up for low 'official' wages (Mars 1982: 152). In effect, fiddling taxes may serve both to facilitate and encourage low-paying employers in an area of the economy which is highly vulnerable, casualized and relatively un-unionized; an area where, according to Mars, two-thirds of employees tend to be underpaid (ibid.).

Another form of fiddling which is prevalent in the hotel and catering industry is moonlighting. Employees working full or part-time elsewhere may top-up their official wages with tax-free earnings from working in bars, hotels, cafes and clubs. As one mechanic noted, moonlighting in the hotel trade has its advantages;

> I'd get a tenner a night, and as many drinks as I wanted. By four in the morning I'd be paralytic and have some ready cash.
>
> (Rawnsley 1985)

Employers are not obliged to deduct tax unless an employee earns an amount in excess of the current single person's tax threshold (£2,605 per annum in 1988/9). However, they *are* required to satisfy themselves that the employee does *not* have employment (or income from) elsewhere. If a part-time employee admits to having another job, a form P46 must be sent to the local tax office who will then note his/her tax records at the main employment and deduct PAYE tax as appropriate. The employer's guide to PAYE clearly indicates that,

> The employer should consult the tax office whenever he is in any doubt as to whether or not PAYE should apply to a particular employee or group of employees.
>
> (Inland Revenue 1983: 9)

If employers ignore this requirement, or simply do not 'ask any questions' regarding possible jobs elsewhere, they may be effectively colluding with moonlighting employees. Furthermore, some unscrupulous employers (often eager to capitalize on low wage rates and casualized labour) may suggest that an employee use a fictitious name so that, when entered on an end-of-year return of all employees, it is not traceable by the Revenue.

Employers may therefore abrogate their responsibility to consult fully with tax offices about employees with other jobs, and thereby fail to deduct PAYE where *total* earnings for *both* employments exceed the tax threshold. This can also result from categorizing an employment 'casual'. Casual employees do not have tax deducted unless their earnings exceed the tax threshold, and only a note of their name and address needs to be kept by the employer. As we have seen, these details may be falsified too. The employee, if moonlighting, will gain by this arrangement because tax is being evaded. The employer gains in two ways: first, he need not incur the administrative costs of operating PAYE and second, he has the advantage of having a cheap, disposable and vulnerable work-force. These fiddles are frequently evident in the hotel and catering industry which is characterized by unsocial hours, part-time and casual working and low wage levels. It must be remembered, however, that other market areas (notably contract cleaners) may operate similar fiddles.

The licensed trades are notable for 'triadic' fiddles, usually involving short-changing customers, over-charging or giving short measures (Mars 1982); frequently the victim is, therefore, the customer. Some pubs may evade tax by, for instance, serving snacks or buffet meals as a 'sideline' without declaring the resulting profits for tax or VAT. However, scope for tax evasion is limited to some extent by the direct comparability of one business with another (or one pub with another), either in terms of proximity or scale. A tax inspector may therefore gauge whether profits are being *grossly* under-estimated in relation to other similar licensed premises. Arguably, the notion of an acceptable fiddle is at work here both on the part of the evaders and the tax inspectors: as long as the 'crime' is not too large, too obvious or too 'cheeky', then it attracts little serious attention. A key technique in this type of fraud appears to be that of assessing the safe scope for fiddling tax; an equivalent technique for the moonlighter, as for the tip-receiving staff, is simply to collude happily with the employer, keep a low profile and take care not to get caught.

Highly paid employees, directors and the professionals

According to a confidential TUC report on tax evasion and avoidance, 'Higher income earners are generally better placed to take advantage of tax allowances, and therefore have more scope to avoid the payment of tax' (TUC 1983). To assess this view, it is necessary to examine the 'allowances' and expenses which may be paid to these employees, and the means by which they are declared to the Revenue.

Employers are obliged to complete a form P.11D annually. This form gives details of 'all expenses, benefits and facilities' provided to highly paid employees, directors and their families. These expenses, benefits and facilities currently include the following: cars available for private use, car fuel provided for private use, entertainment allowances, general expenses allowances, travelling and subsistence, subscriptions (to professional and learned societies, London and provincial clubs and leisure and sporting clubs), private medical and dental treatment (or cost of insurance against such treatment), educational assistance provided, goods and services provided free or below market value, work carried out at the employee's/director's home, personal or domestic staff, vouchers and credit cards, accommodation, cars, property or assets given or transferred to the employee/director, telephone provision or 'any benefits or facilities of whatsoever nature not returned under any previous heading'! (Inland Revenue form P.11D, 1985). In short, any asset or benefit-in-kind provided to an employee or director is taxable. Although penalties may be imposed on employers who delay completing these forms, or who make 'incorrect returns', considerable scope does exist for evasion as ultimately the

Revenue trusts employers to declare fully all benefits paid out, and similarly trusts employees to declare fully all the benefits they receive.

Collusion between employer and employee can serve to conceal untaxed payments in a variety of forms. These may be considered 'perks' by the firms and employees concerned, but are in fact taxable sources of income. Many highly paid employees make a habit of collecting restaurant receipts from their family and friends in order to obtain entertainment allowances from the firm. In addition to fiddling their employer (in one instance by using a receipt for a Saturday evening meal for ten friends as a 'business expense'), by claiming such entertainment allowances, these employees often fiddle their personal tax by not declaring these allowances on their tax returns.

As indicated in the TUC report on the black economy (1983), there is indeed enormous scope for highly paid employees to fiddle their tax. This is a direct result of the higher social status their work is accorded and the consequently higher rewards and allowances that *may* be provided to them by their employers. Employers who wish to retain and to 'motivate' their executive staff may well do so at the expense of the Inland Revenue. As Chapter 5 will argue, the Revenue, in times of severe staffing cut-backs, has insufficient staff to examine forms P.11D in any depth at all. As a result many abuses go unchecked, in every sense.

In addition to the expenses and allowance fiddles already discussed, certain professions appear to be prone to specific fiddles which derive from the opportunity structures within the profession itself. For instance, a senior Revenue official told me of a fiddle engaged in by doctors who prepared the certificates necessary to enable cremations to take place. Doctors received a set fee for their signature on these certificates, and frequently failed to declare these fees for tax. Known in the trade as 'ash cash' these payments are one example of the medical profession's contribution to the black economy.

Other professions are equally fiddle-prone. Academics do not always declare fees for guest lectures, examination marking and occasional publications. However, the Revenue has begun to restrict such opportunities through regulations taxing such payments at source (as is the case for PAYE generally). One architect I spoke to also engaged in professional moonlighting: he regularly drew up plans for extensions for friends, acquaintances and relatives. All payments for his services were in cash and were not declared for tax. Similarly Rawnsley refers to 'local authority architects doing what they call "homers" for private clients whom they've met during the passage of planning application.' (Rawnsley 1985). In this respect professionals, whether self-employed or not, may engage in moonlighting and 'jobs on the side' in exactly the same way as builders, plumbers, car mechanics, hairdressers, gardeners, electricians, caterers and bar staff.

Alternatively the profession itself may offer insider knowledge which provides the basis for a fiddle. One such example concerns fiddles associated with deeds of covenant. This may at first appear only to involve avoidance of tax, but in a routinized and organized form may constitute evasion. The Board's Investigation Office, in recent years, turned its attention to deed of covenant fraud amongst solicitors and accountants. This evasion technique exploited the regulations which enabled individuals to arrange deeds of covenant, for a son, daughter, grandchild or close friend, through which they make an annual payment, typically to a student entering higher education. As students are, typically, not liable to pay tax, the Revenue pays back to the student the tax which the covenanter is assumed to have deducted before paying over the sum. So, for instance, if £1,000 pa was covenanted in 1987, the Revenue paid £270 (the basic rate of tax for that year being 27 per cent) to the student, who was assumed to have received £730 from his/her benefactor. In reality the deed of covenant offered a legitimate tax dodge for many parents of college students, who could supplement parental contributions to student grants with cash from the taxman. However, the system was open to abuse, as a Revenue investigator admitted:

> Until recently this [deed of covenant fraud] has been largely disregarded but the scale of abuse, either through non-payment of the sums covenanted or through reciprocal arrangements in which families agree to covenant for each other's children and share the gain, has meant that it can no longer be ignored.
>
> (*Network* January 1986)

As the result of an investigation into one such fraud, a senior partner in a large firm of accountants was successfully prosecuted (ibid.) But clearly with Revenue staff already over-stretched, much of this type of fraud remained uninvestigated and undetected. Perhaps this accounts for the reforms, announced in the 1988 Budget, which will effectively stop such fiddles by ending tax relief on all but charitable deeds of covenant.

Journalism is also an area of work with its own specific opportunity structure for fiddling expenses and tax. A journalist (working for a regional evening newspaper) explained to me that fiddles often centre on the freedom of many journalists (particularly those working for the national press) to 'chase a story'. The chase could involve much travel: the journalist may find out the rail fare to a town 100 miles away, claim to have stayed overnight and so claim subsistence, add a few pounds for 'entertainment' of the person being interviewed and tot up a sizeable expenses claim. In reality the journalist may never speak to the person involved (that is the story peters out), or may have already obtained sufficient information over the telephone. But once more, there is a consensus regarding what level of fiddling is acceptable, and a good deal of silent collusion on the part of employers, as one journalist confirmed:

It is well known in journalism that 'a good story deserves good expenses', and when I say it's well known, I mean well known by management as well as by staff.

(Mars 1982: 47)

So long as fiddles remain in mutually acceptable bounds and part of a well-kept secret then they are 'safe' for all concerned. But the risks of exposure and detection increase if the perpetrators become too greedy or too cheeky. For instance, in 1979 the Revenue was unable to ignore moonlighting and ghosting Fleet Street workers being paid under the names of 'Mickey Mouse' and 'Donald Duck'. Yet, significantly, an 'amnesty' was offered by the Revenue to the fraudsters (*Daily Telegraph* 5.3.79): this was ostensibly to put an end to such fiddles, but showed a recognition on the part of the Revenue that they were unable to tackle the problem without seeking the *compliance* of the 'taxpayer'.

Highly paid employees, directors and professionals have similar opportunities as other occupational groups to fiddle tax through moonlighting. But *in addition* they have further scope for tax evasion through fiddling allowances and benefits-in-kind, sometimes with either the active connivance or quiet tolerance of their employers or, if self-employed, their accountants.

Summary of tax fraud techniques

A variety of techniques has been described whereby individuals can evade paying the full amount of tax chargeable on their income. One factor which is crucial in determining the means of evasion is the mode of payment of that individual's tax: if tax is deducted through PAYE then obviously the most appropriate techniques involve, for instance, moonlighting. If self-employed, techniques involving the under-statement of profits and over-statement of allowances are additionally appropriate.

In recent years the PAYE taxpayer's opportunities to fiddle have been greatly restricted by changes in the administration of the Inland Revenue, changes which are collectively known as 'the Unification of PAYE'. This term denotes a variety of procedural and legislative changes designed to simplify the assessment and collection of PAYE by gradually removing 'allowances' which used to be off-set against a person's tax liability. This assessment was accomplished by a complex formula, eventually resulting in the computation of the appropriate tax 'code' number. This code was put into operation by employers who used it to calculate the correct amount of tax to be deducted from the person's wage/salary, in accordance with the tax code. But, as unification of PAYE has proceeded, many of the allowances which formed part of the calculation of a tax code have been abolished: for instance child allowances, life assurance relief and building society relief have all been abolished over the last decade.

As a result, PAYE has been simplified by changes such as the direct payment of child benefit, life assurance premiums which incorporate tax relief and the MIRAS scheme (Mortgage Interest Relief at Source). Similarly in 1985 the 'Composite Rate Taxation Scheme' enabled banks and building societies to tax at source all interest they paid out (with the exception of certain low-interest accounts). Evasion of tax by individuals' concealing the bank interest was effectively eliminated by this latest unification measure. Therefore several key variables involved in calculating an individual's tax liability have been eliminated and the personal taxation system considerably simplified. But equally this simplification has removed the PAYE taxpayer's opportunities to fiddle through, for instance, false claims to child allowance and failing to declare bank interest. As one senior tax official noted,

> If you look at Revenue prosecutions historically, the biggest proportion were for false claims to allowances. That was taken over for two reasons: firstly child allowances were abolished and secondly there were the lump prosecutions.
>
> (OVS 1985)

This comment signifies that although one door was closing for tax evasion, another was being opened. The abolition of child allowances clearly eliminated a prevalent form of fraud, but the expansion in the construction industry facilitated the sub-contractor (lump) fiddles which were so prevalent in the 1970s.

It can therefore be argued, following the analysis above, that the techniques used to defraud the Revenue are related to two sets of variables: first, the opportunity structures presented by certain occupations, or by changing conditions in the wider economy. Second, the opportunity structures as delimited by the (changing) administrative procedures used by the Revenue to collect PAYE and Schedule D tax.

At the same time tax fiddles are associated with particular occupational groups, whose techniques can be broadly summarized as constituting:

1 *Moonlighting*: concealed additional earnings.
2 *Ghosting*: failure to pay any tax at all, being invisible to the Revenue.
3 *Sub-Contractor Fraud and fiddles associated with the construction industry*: the lump and 714 Certificate frauds.
4 *Fiddling Expenses, Allowances and Benefits-in-Kind*: an employee's failure to declare payments received from his/her firm/employer.
5 *Fiddling the Accounts*: a self-employed person/trader under-stating his/her profits and /or over-claiming allowances and expenses.

The first three categories of tax fiddle – moonlighting, ghosting and construction industry fraud – constitute a large proportion of what is termed 'the black economy'. By contrast expenses and accounts fiddles form part of an alternative opportunity structure, often associated with highly paid and self-employed people. But no single category is mutually exclusive: for instance, professionals such as doctors and architects can engage in moonlighting, self-employed builders may moonlight and under-estimate profits too!

Tax evasion is by its very nature a secret activity and involves the fraudster in constant efforts to outwit the Revenue. Fraudsters thus become both reactive (reacting to procedural changes instituted by the Revenue) and proactive (seeking out new opportunities within the economy). The typology offered above is therefore a summary of the current techniques of evasion, but is by no means immutable. None the less, the hidden agenda behind the operation of these techniques is a complex set of self-justifications by which fraudsters seek to define themselves in a way which distances them from 'real criminals'. These justificatory rationales will now be analysed.

Justifications

The old saying that 'only two things are inevitable in life – death and taxation' exemplifies a traditional British hatred of personal tax. This view is largely the product of a political and economic culture which stresses the primacy of individualism, and a belief in the market as sole regulating force within the economy. British reluctance to pay centrally collected, state-determined taxes has distinctive political and ideological roots (see Chapter 2). Many of the justifications offered by tax evaders are thus built upon a bedrock of assumptions laid down centuries ago, yet still deeply held within the British culture. At the same time, pragmatic reasons are given for fiddling tax which, together with a variety of personalized moral justifications, enable fraudsters to constitute themselves as rational, morally 'right' and essentially non-criminal, despite the illegality of the act committed.

Justifications are often offered in a conglomerate of cultural, pragmatic and ideological rationales. In order to unravel the constituents of these justifications it is first necessary to examine the common themes which emerged when analysing the comments made by the tax evaders themselves. Certain arguments were identified ás present (in one guise or another) in the justifications offered by all of the tax fraudsters studied in the course of this research. These themes will therefore provide the basis for analysis in this part of the chapter:

1 'An intolerable inquisition' – taxation as anathema to British culture.
2 Taxation as a stifling of incentives.
3 'Everyone does it' – tax evasion as ubiquitous.

'An intolerable inquisition'

This justification for tax evasion centres upon the allegedly intrusive nature of personal taxation and the negative effects which tax is said to have upon the honest, thrifty taxpayer. It is a view which is associated with commentators from, amongst other organizations, the Adam Smith Institute (ASI) and the Institute of Economic Affairs (IEA). The IEA argue that both avoidance and evasion of tax are inevitable, given what they perceive as penal high rates of taxation (IEA 1979). Justifications for evasion are also evident in one IEA contributor's comment that the Inland Revenue displays 'impertinence' in some of its tax collection methods: for instance, in deducting tax at source (Seldon 1979a). Such commentators are implicitly arguing that 'unjustifiable' taxation merits justifiable crime in the form of tax evasion. But the argument is presented in a form which emphasizes the allegedly 'totalitarian' and draconian nature of the Inland Revenue, and which therefore deflects attention from the criminal nature of tax evasion. It is amusing that when one such IEA commentator does acknowledge the 'criminal' element he is referring to Al Capone being jailed for tax evasion (Myddleton 1979)!

The 'intolerable inquisition' school of though stresses that Revenue rules are oppressive in character, and so the nature of the rules actually fosters rule-breaking. Furthermore, this school suggests that attention should instead be drawn to the unacceptably severe rules whose infraction constitutes evasion, rather than to the evading taxpayers themselves (Seldon 1979b). (However, it is significant that these arguments are not applied to all those who violate official regulations: the intrusive and unacceptable features of DHSS rules are not successfully invoked as adequate rationales excusing benefit fraud.)

On a grander scale, some commentators come close to seeing Revenue attempts to counter evasion as pointless, menacing and un-British. For instance, in an article entitled 'The futility of taxation by menaces', former secretary of the Inland Revenue Staff Federation, Lord Houghton, dismissed appeals for more Revenue staff to combat evasion as 'yearning for the impossible'. Although in the current political and ideological climate this may appear a sound observation, Lord Houghton was rather arguing that

> The big stick will not resolve the dilemmas and discontents of people trying to find some grounds for confidence in the future for themselves and their children.
>
> (Houghton 1979)

This former Labour party minister had earlier spoken of essentially 'honest' British taxpayers seeking a better future for their children: on this occasion the argument was used to oppose increases in the powers of tax inspectors:

Are not the fiddles, the lump, the fringe benefits, the moonlighting, the articles and subterfuges of avoidance and evasion signs of the breakdown of the otherwise honest taxpayer caused by the weight of direct taxation upon extra effort and successful enterprise?

(Houghton, *The Times* 16.8.76)

Assertions such as these are little more than a re-hash of reactionary ideological arguments emanating from an individualist perspective on both economics and social policy (see Chapters 1 and 2). Such arguments presuppose a positive relationship between wealth and enterprise and see taxation as a threat to both. Equally, the ideology of liberalism advocates minimal state intervention, as the individual is the primary source of economic and social responsibility, and so represents the tax-collecting activities of the state as both morally dubious and economically counter-productive.

These arguments and the deep contradictions to which they give rise in a capitalist 'Welfare' State remain powerful and persuasive at the level of public ideology. For example, the notion of the intolerable burden of taxation is a popular one: a study found that 62 per cent of those interviewed considered the level of income tax was 'much too high' (Dean *et al.* 1980). This impression, that the British are over-taxed, may be responsible for many citizens thinking that 'most people would hide a small amount of their income if they thought they could get away with it' (Dean 1981: 47).

What is important here is that there is a popular belief that British citizens are over-taxed, and that this popular belief (however ill-founded) surfaces as a justification for evading tax. Certainly all the small businessmen I interviewed considered themselves to be over-taxed, and this factor was often linked with other 'intrusive' aspects of state regulation. For instance Bill, a self-employed builder, linked what he perceived as heavy taxation with the 'red tape' involved in keeping tax and VAT records. He therefore justified his tax evasion as a logical response of a hard-pressed, hard-working, heavily-taxed citizen to the intolerable inquisition of state bureaucracy. Yet at the same time he argued that 'if I do a job for you on the side, I'm doing you a favour by giving you a cheap estimate'. And so although the formal logic used by Bill (and others) to justify tax evasion centres upon the burdensome complexities of state regulation, the effective rationales are self-interest and reciprocity. Thus the black economy is justified because both trader and customer gain financially at the expense of the state. But social scientists studying the formal and informal economies may conflate these formal and effective rationales:

Legal changes also push production from the formal to the informal economy. VAT means that money payments in cash become illegal and unrecorded. Steep rates of personal taxation, obligations to pay high national insurance contributions and employment protection legislation: all these encourage both casual work 'for cash' and do-it-yourself.

(Gershuny and Pahl 1980: 7)

These authors are in danger of arguing that, for example, the birth of VAT automatically led to an explosion in fiddling. This view is excessively deterministic, as it would imply that the state alone and directly creates evasion by creating rules: in this respect Gershuny and Pahl are arguing along the same lines as the IEA. As argued above, there is a far more complex relationship between administrative regulations and techniques of tax evasion. Any analysis needs to focus not only on state regulation and bureaucratic processes, but also on wider economic conditions and on the specific opportunity structures for fiddling. The introduction of VAT is certainly an important variable, but it is not the only one needed to explain the extent and form of the black economy.

Another problem arises from the authors' contention that steep rates of taxation, high national insurance contributions and employment protection legislation have encouraged casual work. These observations relate to high income-earners and employers, and it is the perspective of these groups which is favoured by such rationales for tax evasion. Thus the introduction of employment protection legislation in itself did not effect a shift towards casual labour: workers did not decide to become 'casual' as a result of legislation! Rather, it is the response of employers to such legislation which is of significance. It seems that the rationales of employers and of the (relatively) rich are the ones which dominate public discourses on the justifications for tax fraud. It is therefore not surprising that these justifications, while dominant in legitimizing tax evasion, are not successfully invoked to justify benefit frauds committed by the poor when they work in the black economy.

The National Federation of the Self-Employed and Small Businesses is another organization which, like the IEA, espouses the 'intolerable inquisition' view of taxation and adopts the perspective of employers. Using the imagery of the 'hapless trader' who is 'relentlessly pursued' by the Revenue it represents the self-employed as overburdened with the duties of tax collection and administration imposed upon them by the state (*Guardian* 12.4.85). The Institute of Directors also promoted this view when announcing the results of a survey in August 1986, which indicated that the Thatcher government's policy of de-regulation had failed to remove the heaviest burdens oppressing businessmen – two of these 'burdens' were noted as the operation of PAYE and VAT! At the same time they represent the taxman as 'over-zealous' and accuse the Revenue of 'bullying' small businessmen 'into paying vast sums of money which are not lawfully due' (*Guardian* 27.12.85) Once again the charge of illegality shifts attention from the likely evaders of tax on to the archetypal folk-devil, the taxman. Although assertions of Revenue bully-tactics and illegal purges may seem highly dubious (and I believe they are), such views are not readily dismissed. For example a recent series of *Guardian* articles (written by an accountant and based on a handful of tax investigations) contended that

> There is a new and unhealthy spirit of aggression within the department. Some of the people who make complaints of this sort to me are afraid to speak out publicly because they feel they are always vulnerable to reprisals from the department.
>
> (Joe Horner, *Guardian* 21.11.87)

The notion of 'reprisals' is typically associated with, for instance, terrorist organizations and has an inflammatory effect when discussing the activities of the Inland Revenue! Such notions also grossly exaggerate the power of individual tax inspectors, but at the same time they do make for good newspaper stories. The new 'spirit of aggression' perhaps signifies the gradual impact of compliance initiatives in local tax districts and simultaneous lessening of the Revenue staff's sympathy with those who evade tax. But the language amplifies and distorts these newly perceptible shifts. It constructs the image of taxman as an aggressive post-1984 'Big Brother' and thus reinforces the intolerable inquisition view of taxation.

The small businessmen, directors, farmers and highly paid employees whom I interviewed all set the issue of tax evasion within the context of what they perceived as burdensome state demands, whether in the form of VAT returns, P.11D expenses returns or business accounts. For directors and highly paid employees, the Revenue's tightening up of regulations concerning the taxing of 'car fuel benefits' (Finance Act 1982) had engendered much hostility. What had been regarded as a valuable 'perk' was being clawed back in tax and those individuals with company cars felt they were being *over-taxed* rather than being taxed legitimately on a benefit provided by their firm. A logical consequence of this belief is to see fiddles in relation to expenses and benefits-in-kind as merely attempts to maintain the 'perks' that go with the job. This view was articulated by highly paid sales representatives and a director who, during conversations with me, seemed to subscribe to the sporting theory of tax evasion: at an informal level they appeared to be engaged in a battle to 'beat the taxman'.

Where lower-paid employees are concerned, many justifications offered for tax fiddles also emanate from the traditional British hatred of taxation. But in these instances the justification which is uppermost involves a combination of being *under-paid* while over-taxed at the same time. Tax fiddles are therefore justified as a means of supplementing low wages, and thus become part of the job (Mars 1982; Henry 1978; Ditton 1977). This is particularly relevant in the case of the hotel and catering trade and other low-paid service-sector employment. But tax fiddles in the form of moonlighting are popular amongst a variety of individuals in many occupations which they themselves define as under-paid. For instance, one junior school teacher (Tony) from the Midlands could afford family holidays only by supplementing his earnings through giving private tuition and selling houseplants (*Guardian* 27.12.85). He justified his moonlighting by referring to being low paid and commented, 'Illegal it may be, immoral it isn't'. Tony referred to the building up of a sense of 'community' through the exchange of favours in the black economy, a rationale which is used elsewhere (Gershuny and Pahl 1980). Bill also referred to the favours done for his customers when he saved them money by doing jobs 'on the side'. Nevertheless, the use of justifications involving 'favours', community goodwill or 'morality' merely serves to deflect attention from the essential illegality of tax evasion as well as its negative social and economic consequences.

A further defence offered for tax fraud centres upon the crucial role of the entrepreneur in national wealth creation. It is argued that the regulation of would-be entrepreneurs by the state serves to stifle the potential for creating wealth, and moreover may lead to the channelling of creative capacities into the arena of the black economy. For instance one commentator advocated an end to government controls relating to business premises (which were seen as impeding the natural workings of the market) as this would enable people to

> start businesses in their own garages and encourage enterprising wives to do dressmaking legitimately in their front parlours. It is in such humble ways that many businesses start. As is well said: 'Inside every moonlighter there is a small businessman trying to get out'.
>
> (Vinson 1980: 67)

But it has always been argued above that bona-fide traders are themselves prone to moonlighting. This disproves the assertion that moonlighting is the prerogative only of those who are, as a result of government red tape, prevented from becoming legitimately self-employed. Also worthy of note is the blatant sexism underpinning the image of 'wives' busily 'dressmaking' in front parlours. Not only are their activities and status sexualized, but also they are firmly located within a middle-class frame of reference. Other IEA commentators also demonstrate overwhelmingly support for the interests of the entrepreneurial middle class, but clearly distinguish between this group and the 'new class of administrators, bureaucrats and quango members' who are anathema to the ideals of the liberal minimalist state in which the entrepreneurial spirit thrives (Burton 1985: 75). Burton sees society divided into the taxpaying and tax-consuming 'castes', entrepreneur businessmen belonging to the former caste, and the 'new class' belonging to the latter (as all public sector employees are seen as a drain on national resources). His argument inevitably concludes in the justification of tax avoidance, evasion and the black economy as 'a form of "backdoor" tax revolt against tax-consumers' (ibid.). The underlying theme remains that of the 'intolerable inquisition' which personal taxation is seen to impose in a capitalist state, particularly in a 'Welfare State' in which taxpayers are seen to subsidize unwillingly yet more unproductive members of society – tax-consumers – in the form of elderly, sick, handicapped and unemployed people and one-parent families.

A logical consequence of arguments which stress the intolerable burden which taxation and state regulation imposes is to see tax evasion as at worst non-criminal and at best quasi-legal (Leigh 1982). It is relegated to the level of 'victimless crimes ... if they can be regarded as crimes at all' in the same vein as 'taking your clothes off on remote beaches' (Bracewell-Milnes 1979: 112). But such tolerance does not extend to those who fiddle state welfare benefits!

The 'intolerable inquisition' school of thought frequently sees the administration and collection of taxes not only as burdensome for the taxpayer, but also as an unwieldly system in itself. The cumbersome nature of the British taxation is therefore seen as partly reponsible for tax evasion on two grounds. First, because it unwittingly creates opportunity structures for fiddling on the part of certain occupational groups (for instance highly paid employees and small traders) who manipulate allegedly 'draconian' or ineffectual Revenue rules. This view is allied to the 'sporting' perspective, mentioned above, which aims to discover loopholes in the tax system or to 'beat the taxman' by stealth. Second, the tax system is seen as encouraging evasion because governments unduly overburden the Revenue, ever-extending its scope and scale of operation, thus leading to inefficiency because staff and resources are spread too thinly.

One interesting variation on this second approach was evident in the assertion of one Revenue official who argued that the net of taxation was being cast too widely. He belied that if the tax thresholds were raised in order to bring taxation back to its original role – to tax the wealthy – then 'you could begin to make sense of it' (OVS 1985). Also, he argued, some of the poorer members of society would have the financial imperative to engage in the black economy removed. This may seem an optimistic scenario (and, in the light of the 1988 Budget, a highly improbable one) yet it reflects a pragmatic view. Alternatively, this official privately believed, 'we may have to find a tax system which comes to terms with the black economy'. Nevertheless, he argued that the complex and over-stretched nature of the Inland Revenue system is not in itself a justification for the evasion of tax, but rather is an enabling factor. In this respect he differs from Revenue critics who cite the very existence of the alleged 'inquisition' (in the form of 'oppressive' state taxation) as sufficient justification for fiddling tax. Instead he offers the alternative perspective of a system of personal taxation which taxes rich and (relatively) poor alike, and in so doing has become so unwieldly that cracks appear. These cracks in the system are evident both in the tax loopholes which unwittingly emerge, ripe for exploitation by those 'in the know', and in the prevailing moral vacuum surrounding the issue of tax evasion.

An example which illustrates such 'cracks' concerns the issue of income tax returns, which provide the information (and form the legal basis) on which an individual's tax is assessed. In recent years the frequency with which tax returns are issued has been drastically curtailed in an effort to bring about cuts in Revenue manpower. This has resulted in many taxpayers not receiving tax returns to complete for some five years or more. Such circumstances offer greater opportunities for evasion and, crucially, strengthen the belief that one is not likely to get caught. As one official noted,

> If you never get a return, do six weeks' work for an extra £100 a week and nobody asks you anything, it's asking a lot to expect you to go and knock on the door of your tax inspector and say 'can you give me a bill?'

Therefore the knowledge that the 'taxman' is unlikely to request declarations of income on a frequent or regular basis leaves the initiative with the taxpayer. Evasion can thus be represented as a crime of omission rather than commission by the perpetrator. Justifications in terms of 'They never asked me' are offered, thus denying the taxpayer's culpability and instead focusing on the Revenue's role as inquisitor, and the sporting challenge which this role offers to tax evaders. Effectively the legal and moral issues surrounding tax evasion are dodged in such rationales which assume that tax regulations are bureaucratic, intrusive, exist to be circumvented, and 'good luck' to those who can get away with paying less tax than should be officially charged on their income. But it is worth noting that the sporting approach does not apply equally to those who defraud the DHSS (for whom legal and moral considerations are uppermost in public discourse). The justifications offered by benefit fraudsters themselves often mirror those of the tax evader and yet their actions are perceived and treated very differently by regulatory agencies, and represented as qualitatively different acts in the public rhetoric.

Taxation and the stifling of incentives

In a television interview in November 1985 Mrs Thatcher stated that the black economy was 'big, flourishing, thriving'. She went on to link this with the notion of incentives, an essential ingredient of successful 'enterprise culture' economics:

> What this means to me is this: that where people find a direct relationship between the money they get in their hands and the work they do, they not only do that work but they go out to find it and seek it. The enterprise is still there.
>
> (ITV *Weekend World* 17.11.85)

The fact that this 'direct relationship' between work and cash-in-the-hand was likely to be achieved through evasion of income tax was not regarded as significant. The belief that 'the enterprise is still there' marked a triumphant assertion of the spirit of the 'go-getting society' which Thatcher sees as her aim. The costs at which such aims are realized, in terms of widening gulf between go-getters and 'failures', and the losses in tax and VAT, are not part of her economic calculations. Simplistic notions of what constitutes financial incentives, and how individuals react to them, underlie New Right discourses. For instance, the supply-side economics of the Reagan administration rested on assumptions which are evident in Thatcherism too:

> The basic case here was that the rich were not working and investing because they were receiving too little money and that the poor were not working because they were getting too much. The magic word was incentive – incentives for both the rich and the poor.
>
> (Galbraith in *New Statesman* 25.11.83)

Social policy deriving from such theories has emphasized tax cuts for the rich and increasing stringency in welfare benefits for the poor. But there is no evidence that the concept of 'incentives' upon which such policies rest is a valid one. Higher rates of taxation may in reality force the majority of income-earners to work harder in order to maintain their living standards: high rates of tax may well act as a spur to effort rather than as a disincentive (Break 1957). The alleged disincentive effect of high rates of taxation is therefore difficult to prove. Recent Treasury-sponsored research concluded that the 'income-effect', felt by higher income-earners when their 'high' taxes are reduced, may well produce feelings of financial satisfaction which cancel out the alleged 'incentives' effect of tax cuts (*Guardian* 24.2.88).

Nevertheless, the rhetoric of the incentives school of thought remains both popular and persuasive in spite of the internal weaknesses of its argument. The simplicity of this theory appears to some commentators to elevate its tenets to a 'natural' law of sorts. For instance, a team from the Institute of Fiscal Studies, researching the effects of tax reform on incentives, asserted that

> What matters most in any tax system is the 'marginal rate' – how much tax you pay on each additional pound of income – since it is this which governs the reward to extra effort.... The lower the marginal rate the greater the incentive.
>
> (*Guardian* 1.10.86)

Many justifications offered by tax fiddlers for their actions draw heavily upon the incentives argument. All of the small businessmen I interviewed believed that they were over-taxed, and amongst higher-paid employees the perceived erosion of their 'perks' by the taxman had contributed to the mythology of penally high taxation and the stifling of incentives. Taken together such beliefs offer individuals excuses for their tax fiddles through a reassertion of 'enterprise', albeit illegally, through working in the black economy or through the routine fiddling of personal tax.

A logical corollary of the incentives theory held that higher wages must be paid to those whose marginal rates of tax were high in order to maintain their incentives to effort and so retain highly paid (and, arguably, highly important) employees. But this view was dismissed by the Inland Revenue Staff Federation's (IRSF) General Secretary, Tony Christopher, who considers it a 'facile' approach. He argued (in 1985) that there was no evidence to suggest that since top rates of tax had been reduced to 60 per cent there had been a corresponding reduction either in the salaries of higher-rate taxpayers or in their untaxed benefits. If the incentives argument were accepted and if individuals responded logically, precisely and predictably to changes in rates of taxation, then successive reductions in tax would inevitably lead to a reduction in remuneration necessary to maintain incentives. But clearly the tax cuts (for richer employees) instituted by successive Thatcher governments have not given rise to a rational downward re-adjustment of upper wage levels; rather, the reverse has been the case (Byrne 1987; Rentoul 1988). As Christopher argues, the incentives issue is invoked selectively in order to reassert certain political and economic values rather than to explain and adequately predict the workings of an alleged precisely co-ordinated system of wages and tax rates.

To summarize, the notion of incentives is a problematic one. Individuals cannot be reduced to the simplistic level of economically programmed units who respond accurately and surely to given stimuli in terms of their earned income and tax due. Thus Break (1957) argued that rationality may involve responding to higher taxes by working harder, and Christopher indicates that the full implications of the incentives argument are contradictory where downward variations in tax are concerned. However, for supplementary benefit claimants, 'incentives' do take on a negative interpretation when claimants are expected to suffer downward variations in their benefit levels in order to maintain the incentive to work (*Poverty* 1988a).

Another consequence of accepting a New Right or supply-side logic on incentives is to see the black economy as a thriving sector of the economy and, moreover, a sector which potentially holds the key to an economic recovery in that it is based upon 'go-getting' entrepreneurship. But it is difficult to see the logic of such arguments which, on the one hand, present the black economy positively as evidence of 'enterprise', yet on the other hand regard benefit claimants who fiddle as 'scroungers' whose enterprising efforts to maximize their financial rewards should be roundly condemned. As Rawnsley (1985) argues, the realities of the black economy conflict with political demands to crackdown on social security scroungers and this leads to a 'benign neglect of those who have "got on their bikes" and joined the underground army'.

One telling criticism of this simplistic view of incentives and taxation is that the explosion of national wealth creation and universal prosperity promised as a consequence of tax cuts and the restoration of effort-incentives has, in the mid-to late 1980s, simply not materialized. Loney (1986) quotes a leading American economist, Lekachman, who poses this question:

> Why, it might legitimately be asked, haven't these amply rewarded managers and investors already unleashed the investment boom needed to renew economic growth and make America great again?
>
> (Loney 1986: 21)

In the case of the British economy a similar question can be raised as tax cuts have, arguably, only increased the personal incomes and wealth of the rich themselves (Low Pay Unit/CPAG 1988). Furthermore, if policy-makers place a high priority on economic expansion, then it is difficult to stop short of welcoming the expansion of the black economy which (according to Thatcher) constitutes an area of 'enterprise'. In so doing, some advocates of 'incentives' may condone tax evasion and the consequently skewed distribution of financial rewards in our society which it creates: this distribution is not determined by social policy so much as by the vagaries of the market, through the supposed operation of 'effort' incentives and commensurate (but not 'just') rewards.

Critics argue that the black economy is 'neither the answer to the financial problems caused by unemployment nor an incentive to the creation of wealth through individual enterprise' (TUC 1983). The TUC support this view with Inland Revenue data which demonstrate the detrimental effects of the black economy on honest traders and taxpayers: their prices may be undercut by unfair competition and the honest taxpayer may thus effectively subsidize the dishonest earnings of the fiddlers (TUC 1983: 3). But such legal and moral issues are frequently obscured by straightforwardly 'market' solutions to problems of economic growth. For instance, the assertion that 'people prefer the lowest price for given quantities or qualities of goods' and references to the 'modern economics of public choice' deny the importance of social justice and focus instead on the inevitability of tax evasion which allegedly emanates from consumer choice and the inner logic of the free market economy (Seldon 1979b: 15).

The incentives debate is of central importance when analysing responses to tax fraud. First, it informs public discourse on the nature of our tax system, which as a result is frequently perceived as stifling incentives through penal rates of taxation. Second, it therefore provides individuals with ready justifications for illegal tax evasion, which can be translated into the logical response of long-suffering taxpayers who are, after all, only trying to create wealth for the nation and exercise the modern economics of public choice – the choice to earn and not to pay tax!

'Everyone does it'

Guesstimates of the size of the black economy seem to support the notion that tax evasion is indeed ubiquitous. It appears that although not exactly 'everyone' is resorting to tax evasion, a sizeable proportion of taxpayers are. According to Inland Revenue data the black economy may constitute 7.5 per cent of GDP (*Cmnd 8822* 1983: 551). Furthermore, it was estimated that one in four persons may have undeclared income of £500 pa (Levi 1982). The willingness of individuals to evade tax was demonstrated by Deane *et al.* (1980) whose survey on attitudes towards income tax found that almost 40 per cent of respondents were morally 'neutral' where small-scale tax evasion was concerned; 62 per cent of the sample believed the level of income tax was much too high, and a quarter thought that all or most taxpayers have opportunities for small 'safe' evasions. More telling still, 66 per cent felt that 'all or most taxpayers would exploit such opportunities if they had the chance'. In this way tax evasion is seen as relatively safe, 'neither good nor bad', justifiable in terms of the high level of taxation and a logical course of action for the average taxpayer (ibid: 39). The message behind this and similar research is simply that 'tax evasion is a common activity in the UK, and is widely regarded as morally acceptable' (ibid: 57).

However there is a lack of consistency in arguments which suggest that because tax is too high individuals will inevitably seek to evade it, and because everyone is therefore fiddling tax then such actions cannot be thought reprehensible because, after all, millions of taxpayers cannot be 'wrong'. The alleged popular approval of evasion is therefore underpinned by other excuses. Justifications which involve the plea that 'everyone is doing it' depend in turn upon other rationales offered for tax fiddles, namely the intrusive, burdensome and excessive demands of the Inland Revenue and the stifling of incentives described above. For instance, tax ghost 'Jim' is quoted by Rawnsley (1985) as being 'pissed off' with many aspects of British society – 'appalling pay and boring work', periodic unemployment and the knowledge that 'everyone else is on the dodge anyway'. He added that the entire economy would collapse without the moonlighters and ghosts who undercut the prices of 'legit' firms and so save the punters' money. Similarly Bill had argued that building jobs which did not 'go through the books' were doing the customer a favour, yet working life without the black economy was inconceivable to him: the justification that 'everyone was on the fiddle' was implicit in the nature of his daily work. An alternative perspective was, however, offered by the director of a large building firm whom I spoke to: he argued that the 'cowboys' and fiddlers were undermining the whole building industry because 'legit' firms were being squeezed hard in their efforts to compete with unrealistic work estimates which did not account for tax and VAT. In the long term, he argued, unemployment and shoddy workmanship would result.

Nevertheless the rationale that 'everybody is on the fiddle' (when coupled with other justifications described above) is a crucial means by which individuals can render their own illegal acts explicable and excusable to themselves and to others. With a shrug of the shoulders, most tax fiddlers I spoke to justified their actions in this simple and seemingly unambiguous manner. But considerable ambiguity is evident if their assertions are examined in more detail.

First, this justification rests upon the belief that a certain level of tax evasion is both understandable and tolerable. However, it remains unclear exactly how this 'acceptable' level is determined. In practice the acceptable fiddle seems to be delimited by normative thresholds which mark the tolerable scale and frequency of evasion, but what level of tax fraud can be seen as both acceptable to others and justifiable to the fiddler? It can be argued that perceptions of the relative seriousness of tax evasion shifts according to the amount defrauded. For instance, both Deane *et al.* (1980) and M. Walker (1978) note that while small-scale tax evasion may be condoned, evasion involving 'larger' amounts may not be. As Dean implies, this shift in what is considered acceptable probably has far more to do with 'moral attitudes' than with any rational-economic calculations concerning increased risks of discovery and the subsequent penalties that may be imposed by the Revenue (Jowell and Witherspoon 1985). The essential problem remains one of how boundaries are set upon the nature and scale of tax evasion which 'everyone' is felt to be justified in committing.

Second, it seems probable that a 'moral' element operates in setting boundaries on acceptable fiddles. According to A. Lewis (1982) this moral element may derive from group pressure, just as the impetus to evade tax in the first place may come from workmates. Lewis argues that individuals agree to 'play the game' (particularly if the rest of their workmates are doing so) but take care not to 'go too far':

> It seems probable that there is a subculture of tax evasion governed partly by normative considerations
>
> (A. Lewis 1982: 184)

And so pressures, both to evade tax and to justify it, may differ according to the opportunity structures offered by particular occupations. Tax evasion is not a homogeneous phenomenon. But the justification that 'everyone is doing it' simplifies the complex reality of evasion and overlooks significant differences that exist in the scope and scale of the opportunities individuals have to fiddle. It may well be the case that this excuse merely legitimizes tax fraud as ubiquitous in order to conceal the considerable gains made by certain occupational categories – highly paid employees and self-employed people being the most noteworthy – at the expense of the honest taxpayer.

Another important thread running through such justifications as these is the belief that it is 'natural' to want to pay as little tax as possible and so to evade tax wherever practical. This is most clearly articulated in the work of the IEA who lament that, in relation to avoidance and evasion of tax, 'the trouble is that it is impossible to change human nature' (Seldon 1979b: 40). In discussing the Revenue's anti-evasion efforts Lord Houghton similarly argued that 'it is simply no good yearning for the impossible' (Houghton 1979). Clearly tax fiddles are once again being represented as an immutable part of human nature. But it would seem that such commentators ignore the cultural, political and economic conditions under which people's 'human nature' is created. The values and ideals of modern capitalism (focusing on wealth accumulation and 'free enterprise') which are utilized in justifications for tax evasion are by no means 'natural'. They are ideologically constructed through a variety of interlocking social institutions (see Chapter 1). But it is significant that the same rationalizations, in terms of 'human nature', fail to dominate in discourses surrounding welfare benefit fraud. While it is asserted that it is *natural* for taxpayers to maximize their financial gains, illegally, from the state through tax fraud, this justification is not invoked to explain supplementary benefit fraud, which is rather represented as motivated by greed and idle dependency (Golding and Middleton 1982).

None the less, it is the very simplicity of these excuses for tax evasion, drawing upon notions of 'human nature', which contributes to their potency. In this way, to argue that *everyone* fiddles their taxes is to do no more than to state the obvious and in so doing to rebuke critics, as if to say 'I fiddle my tax, so does everyone else. So, what?' Justifications stressing the ubiquity of tax evasion and its roots in common-sense logic therefore serve to displace 'the problem' of tax evasion (if indeed one is seen to exist), upon the allegedly few honest taxpayers and the agencies of regulation. Responsibility for the commission of an illegal act, the negative economic and social consequences, as well as the divisive implications for social policy are all bypassed in this most common of all excuses.

Research into work-place and white-collar crime has demonstrated the breadth and depth of tax fiddling (Henry 1978; Mars 1982; Chambliss 1978; Pearce 1976; Leigh 1982; Levi 1982; Levi 1987). Such evidence confirms the fears of the National Federation of Self-Employed and Small Businesses that tax evasion is a 'national disease' and Britain is riddled with it. Even as a critic of evasion it is possible to support unwittingly the view that *everyone* is indeed on the fiddle. But such observations do not inevitably lead to the conclusion that tax evasion should be sanctioned: just because fiddling taxes, in the words of one Revenue official, 'goes back to the Bible' should not ensure automatic legitimation. But the belief that everyone else is fiddling makes it far easier for tax fraudsters to justify their activities to themselves and also to those around them who share a similar common-sense idea that if evasion is the norm, then they are not deviants.

Summary of the justifications for tax fraud

Responses to and justifications for tax evasion must be located within the context of the contradictory principles which underlie our understanding of taxation (and welfare). This chapter has analysed the common themes which emerged from an examination of the justificatory rationales offered for tax fraud. The rationales that taxation is in itself an intolerable inquisition and that tax stifles personal effort are both closely related. They both adopt a liberal conception of a minimalist state, a state geared primarily to the goal of capital accumulation. Within such a context it becomes possible to rationalize tax evasion as no more than an excessive zeal in the pursuit of the accumulation of wealth, which is, in turn, seen as the basis for the prosperity of society as a whole (Bosanquet 1983). Against this ideological background, the Inland Revenue may be perceived as stifling wealth creation and minimizing personal (economic) 'freedom' by imposing personal taxation. Evasion of those taxes thus becomes transformed in such discourses into a form of individual rebellion against the power of the intrusive state. For example, IEA commentators regarded those who avoid and evade taxes as crusaders against 'bad law' and against the allegedly totalitarian spectre of redistributive taxation (Shenfield 1968; Seldon 1979a; Bracewell-Milnes 1979).

The social philosophy of individualism and ideology of the free market thus dominate justifications for tax fraud. At a personal level, rationales may be supplemented by *ex post facto* justifications, such as 'everyone does it'. Although a powerful common-sense rationalization, it is clear that everyone does *not* evade their taxes, otherwise the modern capitalist state would be unable to function. But the contradictory demands of the principles of citizenship (to pay one's taxes) and free market individualism (to generate and accumulate wealth) remain unresolved. As a consequence, tax fraud can be successfully justified only if it remains within certain normative boundaries; these boundaries are often delineated by reference to the 'acceptable fiddle' and notions of what can acceptably constitute shrewd business practice'.

4

Supplementary Benefit Fraudsters

Where supplementary benefit fraud is concerned it is difficult, as in the case of tax fraud, to separate the techniques of the fraudsters from the justifications which they offer for those techniques. In the eyes of many benefit fraudsters their illegal actions are understandable only in terms of the material conditions of disadvantage, poverty and degradation in which they live out their lives. In making ends meet as best they can, some claimants may break DHSS regulations and, implicitly, the law. In order to examine precisely how such frauds are committed, it is necessary first to arrive at an analytical framework which will contribute to an understanding of what precisely is involved in the commission of supplementary benefit fraud. For this purpose, fraud techniques will be examined by categories which reflect the DHSS's own analysis of detected fraud.

Techniques

The statistics in Table 3 represents the numbers and types of detected Social Security frauds considered for prosecution in the year ending February 1985 and demonstrate the relative prevalence of key types of offence. Although such statistics can never give a full picture of the extent of benefit fraud (because obviously not all fraud is detected), they none the less give a useful indication of what the most popular forms of (detected) fraud are. Clearly the most widespread form of fiddling is working while drawing benefit, which constituted almost half of all cases considered for prosecution in 1984/5. The second most prevalent form of fraud, accounting for over 12 per cent of cases considered for prosecution, also relates to earnings, but in these cases it is the income of a dependant (usually the claimant's wife) which is not declared.

Table 3 DHSS fraud: cases considered for prosecution in 1984/5 in England, Scotland and Wales (by type of offence)

Offence	Total offences	Offences as % of total
1 Earnings, claimant	24,513	49
2 Earnings, dependant	6,086	12.2
3 Fictitious desertion and living together cases	3,680	7.4
4 Itinerant fraud	3,347	6.7
5 Total of 'other' static fraud	3,129	6.3
6 Rent and other outgoings	2,691	5.4
7 Composition of household; child or adult not maintained or not legally dependent	1,923	3.9
8 Other resources	1,400	2.8
9 Claimant or dependant in receipt of other benefit	1,265	2.5
10 Undeclared payments from liable relative	963	1.9
11 Forged or altered documents	650	1.3
12 False expenses claim	133	0.26
13 Aid and abet	121	0.24
14 Collusive employer	46	0.1
Total	49,947	100

Source: personal communication, DHSS 1986

The third category is a particularly interesting one as it refers overwhelmingly to the frauds of female claimants who are lone mothers. Fictitious desertion occurs when a woman falsely alleges that her husband (or cohabitee) has deserted her. In this way she may claim supplementary benefit, falsely, in her own right. 'Living together as husband and wife' cases (abbreviated to LTHWs in DHSS jargon) are a hotly disputed form of fraud because, as will be seen below, they assume that a financial relationship exists where a domestic and/or sexual one does. In this way a woman who fails to admit the existence of such a domestic and/or sexual relationship and who continues to claim benefit in her own right may be guilty of fraud. Taken together, cases of fictitious desertion and LTHW amounted to 7.4 per cent of cases considered for prosecution in 1984/5. But such statistics may conceal numbers of women who have been informally deprived of their supplementary benefit by special fraud units, who focused on these forms of fraud but adopted a 'non-prosecution policy' (see Chapter 6).

Fourth in the league table of offences is 'itinerant fraud'. This involves fraud by individuals who claim benefit because they have 'no fixed abode', but may visit different supplementary benefit offices in the same day making (false) claims at each. In recent years there has been an increase in this form of fraud which may be compounded, or even initiated, by unscrupulous landlords of cheap bed-and-breakfast accommodation to whom itinerants are often referred by Social Security offices. (In September 1982 'Operation Major' revealed this type of fraud in Oxford.)

The fifth category of 'other static fraud' encompasses a variety of fiddles ranging from multiple claims to falsely alleging a lost giro or purse on benefit payday. Some of these fiddles together with category 11, forged or altered documents, are subsumed under the conglomerate term 'instrument of payment fraud' where such frauds involve altering, forging or feigning the loss of benefit order books or girocheques. Other categories of fraud refer broadly to two kinds of fiddle: first, to specific omissions from a claimant's declaration of resources (such as payments of maintenance from a liable relative, or an occupational pension); and second, to specific false claims for allowances (whether for dependents, rent or expenses against part-time earnings).

The analysis of fraud techniques which follows will utilize the broad headings of fraud categories already discussed, although some of these have been amalgamated or simplified for ease of presentation:

1 Working and claiming
2 Liable relative fraud: fictitious desertion and living together cases
3 Itinerant fraud
4 Instrument of payment fraud
5 Other fiddles

Working and claiming

As explained in Chapter 2 above, people in full-time work cannot normally receive supplementary benefit (Lynes 1985). Because it is means-tested, payment of supplementary benefit depends upon DHSS officials' calculating, in accordance with regulations laid down by Parliament, what the total financial requirements of a claimant (and dependants) are. Then it is necessary to deduct from this figure of financial 'requirements' any income the claimant (and dependants) receives from any source, whether, for instance from other state benefits, part-time earnings or occupational pension schemes. Consequently any alteration in the income of the 'assessment unit' (the claimant and his/her family) may affect the amount of benefit payable under the Social Security regulations. And so both claimant and partner *can* legitimately work part-time so long as their income is declared and then deducted (after allowing for 'disregards' and expenses such as fares to work, childminding, etc.) from their weekly benefit payments. (It should be noted, however, that when Income Support replaced Supplementary Benefit in April 1988 both the number of hours said to constitute 'full-time work' and expenses allowed against earnings were substantially reduced: see CPAG's *Welfare Rights*, April 1988). The fiddle involved in 'working while claiming' therefore simply involves claimants making a *false declaration* in stating that they do not work at all, or under-declaring the amount earned.

As Table 3 indicates, working while claiming is the most prevalent form of fraud amongst supplementary benefit claimants, and on the surface seems by its very nature to confirm the worst 'scrounger' stereotypes. It is argued that there is indeed plenty of work available to those who genuinely seek it: the numbers of claimants who *do* work allegedly indicates this. Furthermore, the greed of benefit fraudsters is played upon by those emphasizing the extent of this type of fraud. After all, it is argued, they have the advantage of high levels of state benefits and wages to boot (Golding and Middleton 1982)! But what needs to be examined are the specific types of work often involved in such frauds, and the techniques used by claimants trying to (successfully) fiddle by these means.

> Low paid, insecure work and social security fraud fuel each other and feed off each other.
>
> (Harrison 1983: 147)

This statement refers to a description of life in Hackney where, the author argues, inadequate benefit levels and low pay fail to meet the social needs of individuals and families in the area. But this analysis is not only confined to the inner city areas so well described by Harrison. The strong link between casualized, low-paid and part-time work (often in the black economy) and social security fraud is acknowledged as having more than local significance (Harrison 1983; Mars 1982; TUC 1983). Nevertheless, the double-bind which working supplementary benefit claimants suffer must be emphasized. First, as a TUC report noted, those who work in the black economy suffer inferior conditions and rewards:

> 'Black' earnings are generally low as employers are often able to cut the price of labour without fear of repercussions from a vulnerable and uncoordinated labour force. Training and safety requirements tend to be neglected and therefore workers are often unqualified and uninsured.
>
> (TUC 1983: 3)

Second, both the Inland Revenue and the Supplementary Benefit Commission (prior to its abolition in 1980) acknowledged that those who succeed in the black economy were likely to be those groups who succeed in the formal economy (DHSS 1979; Donnison 1982). In other words, benefit claimants without the facilities and contacts of a work environment find themselves pushed further down into dependence upon less than scrupulous employers who are well aware of their plight.

For example, an analysis of local newspaper coverage of supplementary benefit fraud prosecutions in one Midlands town indicates that employers from the service sector (such as contract cleaning firms) rely upon a casual, temporary work-force which is readily available from the ranks of the unemployed. Moreover, those unemployed individuals who seek such casualized and irregular work are unlikely to cease claiming benefit when starting work: the wages are simply too low to live on, and such jobs are characterized by instability. It is therefore apparent that some employers gain a great deal economically by using a willing reserve army of labour, drafted in and disposed of at will, and prepared to work for wages that are patently too low to provide a sole family income. At the same time, these employers provide DHSS investigators with an easy 'catch' of fiddling claimants, yet appear to receive no reprimand or sanction themselves for their collusion in social security fraud. This is despite the assertion made by several fraudsters prosecuted by the DHSS that employers are well aware that they are hiring claimants. According to one fraudster, his employer even suggested that he use a false name in an attempt to avoid detection (see Chapter 6).

There exists a link, then, between the black economy in general terms and the most popular form of supplementary benefit fraud – working while claiming benefit. Clearly those avenues which enable tax fraud, on the face of it, enable this kind of benefit fiddle too. But it must be remembered that, as in many other respects, benefit claimants are marginalized, socially and economically, and for the most part to fail to 'cash in' on the black economy to the same extent as the employed moonlighters, ghosters and tax evaders do. As Donnison argues,

> Since you need skills, confidence and contacts to make a lot of money from concealed jobs, most of this fraud is committed by the working population, not the people on social security payments.
>
> (Donnison 1982: 70-11)

At the same time the double-bind already described serves to render claimants who fiddle more vulnerable than moonlighting employees, because the claimant's economic position is weaker and involves greater dependence on collusive employers and, as will be argued below, greater likelihood of being investigated by regulatory agencies.

Perhaps because of these harsher facts of life for claimants on the fiddle, strategies to minimize the chance of getting caught are uppermost in the minds of many fraudsters. For instance, most claimants I interviewed mentioned that it was certainly preferable to get work which did not involve National Insurance 'cards', which would, they felt, increase their chances of getting caught. For this reason many female claimants resort to home-working, which is notoriously badly paid yet feels 'safe' from the claimants' perspective. Jobs involving sewing skirts and stuffing soft toys therefore keep women claimants in the home, engaging in monotonous yet domestically suitable tasks for very low wages. Marginalization, exclusion and exploitation all reinforce each other, and make comfortable profits for employers, arguably on the backs of both taxpayer and benefit claimants alike through the undercutting of legitimate firms and adequate wage levels.

Other jobs which involve a minimum of record-keeping on the part of employers are equally convenient for working claimants. Seasonal work, whether on farms or the holiday catering trade, offers opportunities for claimants to earn cash, albeit spasmodically, on a fairly anonymous basis. In reality they remain vulnerable because anonymity is illusory: as seasonal work is 'targeted' as a likely area of fraud, employers are often approached by investigators. Nevertheless, this type of work remains popular despite often appalling conditions. For example, in rural areas 'spud-bashing' (harvesting potatoes) and fruit-picking involves back-breaking labour for small reward. It seems a measure of the desperation of benefit claimants that such unrewarding labour is sought at all.

Jobs such as 'spud-bashing' seem to be allocated on the basis of willingness and being 'in the know' as a result of a network of personal contacts. Although seasonal workers such as these now have to fill in more paperwork than previously, giving false names and information may circumvent attempts to keep track of casual employees. Employers (or sub-contracting link-men) provide transport to farms, collecting workers from certain pick-up points. According to fraudsters interviewed, employers rarely 'grass' on workers known to be fiddling Social Security. But the anonymous tip-off is a significant problem for these fiddlers (see Chapter 6): once approached by investigators, employers are obliged to comply and give full accounts of dates worked by claimants and wages paid to them.

In keeping with the theme of casualization and minimum record-keeping, the building and catering trades offer scope for supplementary benefit claimants to work on a part-time or irregular basis. As mentioned above, claimants appear to form a source of menial labour at the lower end of the occupational ladder. They are more likely to work as general site labourers than skilled plasterers, plumbers, brick-layers and carpenters. In the catering and licensed trades they are likely to work as part-time bar staff, waitresses and cleaners. For female claimants these jobs are more readily combined with the demands of bringing up infants and school-age children. A relatively recent development enabling additional commission-based employment for women is the 'party plan' selling scheme. One woman, 'Terry', indicated to Harrison (1983) how such schemes worked:

> I've always got to do casual jobs, with no cards. If I did a regular job with cards, I'd get caught. I started doing demonstrations for a pottery firm – you know, in people's houses.... You had to use your own car and your own petrol. You didn't get any wage, just commission, 12% on what you sold. If you damaged any of the pots, they took it out of your commission.
>
> (Harrison 1983: 152)

It is significant that Terry later worked as a barmaid and home-worker, with little financial success and much physical and emotional strain. One lone mother I interviewed emphasized her fear of getting caught:

> Working is dodgy now, with more tracing through National Insurance cards. There seemed more casual work in the past.

Speaking (in 1986) in an area of high unemployment, she clearly believed that for her, the opportunities to work 'on the side' were limited. This is borne out in evidence which suggests that

> the jobless blackspots of the North are the least fertile ground for the hidden economy. If it is a disease, it is more contagious in the still bouyant South than in the cash-starved North.

> (Rawnsley 1985)

At the same time there is evidence that, in national terms, casualized, part-time and low-paid work is increasing as the current economic recession deepens (Low Pay Unit 1986). In addition, the growing trend towards payment by commission rather than wages or salary has eased the financial and administrative 'burden' on employers, who are no longer responsible for the deduction of tax and National Insurance: persons receiving commission only are usually classed as self-employed rather than as employees. At the same time, commission-based jobs (whether selling pottery, underwear, double-glazing or collecting debt and hire-purchase payments) appear to offer a casualized form of 'self-employment' for claimants looking for work on the side. It seems to be popular because of flexibility in hours worked and minimal official record-keeping. But once more it can be argued that this form of work serves the interests of the firms and agencies involved at the expense, literally, of individuals who would surely rather seek secure, protected, legal, full-time employment.

If it is the case that economic recession creates casualized vulnerable and part-time jobs, then it seems that supplementary benefit claimants who seek to add to their income (illegally) by working on the side will be increasingly forced into these lowest paid, least secure and least desirable jobs available in both the formal and informal economies. This situation serves to exploit and further marginalize benefit claimants who fiddle, and gives rise to the added fear of financial and possibly custodial punishment should they get caught.

It is apparent from the discussion so far that the vast majority of cases of benefit fraud by 'working while claiming' are both unsophisticated and risky, involving less 'technique' on the part of the fraudster than many of the tax frauds discussed above. But one fraudster I interviewed utilized many skills in the commission of working and claiming fiddles which indicate a level of sophistication on a par with tax fraud. Mark was a well-educated young man living in London. Because of the high cost of living there, he found himself unable to earn enough money (on a regular basis) to rent adequate accommodation. However, supplementary benefit payments coupled with earnings enabled him to live decently. He managed to avoid detection by the DHSS by using the complexity of the benefit system and its overworked staff to his own advantage. His technique involved working full time in a variety of jobs: office work, though poorly paid, was acceptable so long as he could leave the office to sign on fortnightly. At the time of the interview (in 1986), he was working as a painter and decorator which, although physically demanding, offered better pay.

Mark explained that although contact with Social Security offices is minimal (particularly since home visiting had all but ceased for new claims) in time 'the DHSS paperwork catches up with you'. If he received a letter requesting him to attend the local Social Security office for interview, he felt it wise to cease claiming, but took care to do so in an 'above board' manner. He explained to DHSS clerk, falsely, that he had written to them 'over a week ago' to let them know he had found work, and went on to query, 'Haven't you had my letter?' Mark used a pleasant approach to DHSS staff in which he sympathized, genuinely, with their intolerable workload which, he said, must explain the 'mislaid' letter telling them of his changed circumstances. No action was ever taken against him, although if he felt that the suspicions of the DHSS or Inland Revenue were aroused (official letters requesting details of former employment or past addresses, for instance) then the easiest solution was to 'disappear'. This meant changing his address on a fairly regular basis, but he found no problem in so doing. Mark's charm and intelligence clearly enabled him to work and claim benefit in a systematic manner without attracting the attentions of DHSS officials. By playing the system, realizing its weaknesses, he has so far evaded detection. Mark's smart appearance and demeanour did not fit the 'scrounger' stereotype, but his actions would certainly be represented by many commentators as evidence of the cunning and greed attributed to that stereotype. Significantly his justifications for fiddling are consistent with those offered by all other claimants I spoke to who were 'working on the side' – they derive from frustration, poverty and hardship rather than from greed.

Liable relative fraud: fictitious desertion and living together cases

The family forms the key assessment unit upon which the DHSS bases its calculations of benefit payable. If husband and wife separate, they become two assessment units, and each can then claim benefit for themselves and any dependent children living with them. Similarly unmarried parents can claim for their own needs and those of their children. But under the Supplementary Benefits Act 1976, a man is legally liable to maintain his wife and children (including illegitimate children) and in the same way a wife is liable to maintain her husband and children (Lynes 1985). For this reason the DHSS recovers as much money as possible from the 'liable relative' in order to minimize the amount paid from public funds. As a result, when a separated wife claims benefit for the first time she may be

> questioned in some detail about the circumstances of her separation. Such inquiries may be necessary to enable the DHSS to decide what action, if any, should be taken to induce the husband to fulfil his obligations.
>
> (Lynes 1985: 212)

Liable relative fraud may take two forms, both of which are enabled by the DHSS emphasis upon the ideal-type nuclear family as the key assessment unit for the purposes of supplementary benefit.

First, *fictitious (or 'collusive') desertion*. This may arise when

> the wife denies knowledge of her husband's whereabouts although he is in fact living with her, or his temporary absence has been arranged to enable her to claim benefit.
>
> (ibid.)

The couple therefore collude in falsely stating that desertion has taken place, so enabling the 'lone' parent to claim benefit in his/her own right thus fraudulently increasing the family income.

As will be seen below, the justifications for this form of fraud are financial. It is frequently the case that collusive desertion occurs in times of financial difficulty for families. It offers the family involved an extra source of income, supplementary benefit, to pay off accumulated debts and so provides a temporary escape from dire money problems. Once again, this form of fraud can be seen to arise from desperation rather than greed.

Second, *cohabitation* (or 'LTHW' cases) can involve more complex issues which arise from the assumptions made by the DHSS concerning such relationships. A couple's reasons for living together are not necessarily economically motivated, yet the DHSS assumes that an economic relationship exists between couples whom they adjudge to be 'living together as husband and wife'. Within the Welfare State, as elsewhere in British society, the relationship between men and women is assumed to be that of breadwinner and dependant respectively (Smart and Smart 1978; Wilson 1977). But the case of Carol (a lone mother who had lived with her divorced boyfriend) casts doubt on this assumption: 'He didn't give me any money so my commitments still stood and I needed my benefit. It was really me keeping him!' Nevertheless, the DHSS may well have assumed a 'husband and wife' relationship, based on subjective assessments of shared expenses, stability of the relationship, 'public appearance' and sexual relations (Esam *et al.* 1985; Lynes 1985). As a result Carol had, technically, committed fraud, although the man she lived with made no financial contribution to Carol or to her children.

Many feminists argue that the living together rule which creates this category of fraud implicitly assumes payment by men for women's sexual and domestic services and so constitutes a form of prostitution (Wilson 1983; Fairbairns 1985). But such rules are perfectly understandable when located within the operation of a Welfare State based upon the principles of Beveridge. These principles need to be examined in order to place in political, economic and social policy context the regulation of women on supplementary benefit in general, and that of female benefit fraudsters in particular.

The Beveridge Report (*Cmd 6404* 1942) rested upon pre-war assumptions concerning the family (Wilson 1980). Distinctions were drawn between married and unmarried women, the former belonging in the home, bearing children and 'ensuring the continuance of the British race and of British ideals in the world' (ibid: 52). Insurance classes reflected distinctions between married and single, men and women: single men and women were treated equally but married men and women were not (Allatt 1981). Beveridge's plans assumed the universality of the patriarchal nuclear family, and so failed to recognize adequately the status of single parenthood. Between 1961 and 1983 the number of single-parent families doubled. By the mid-1980s there were over 1 million single-parent families in Britain, the vast majority being headed by females, over half of whom relied on supplementary benefit (*Annual Abstract of Statistics* 1985; *Social Trends No.16* 1986).

The modern British Welfare State is therefore organized around assumptions of an ideal-type nuclear family that does not correspond to the experience of increasing numbers of women. Moreover, if supplementary benefit is defined as a 'poverty line' (Holman 1978), then increasing numbers of women are living on the poverty line because they cannot play their part in the economic marriage of breadwinner/dependent, assumed to be the norm since Beveridge (Smart and Smart 1978; Wilson 1977). It is hardly surprising, then, that single-parent status is socially regarded as a transient phase for women, because 'sooner or later it is likely, and even hoped, that a mother will solve her problems by marrying again' (Atkins and Hoggett 1984: 98). In so doing she will solve society's problems too, reducing Welfare State expenditure and recreating a 'good family' (see Chapters 1 and 8).

Women on welfare benefits can also be seen to suffer doubly as a result of their gender and working-class situation (Harrison 1983; Beltram 1984). Initially they are often dependent on poorly paid men, thereafter upon the 'safety net' of Welfare State provision. In practice women are, once more, pushed into financial dependence upon men (from whom they have separated) though the 'liable relative' regulations. The (pre-April 1988) higher-earnings disregard available for single parents is in itself acknowledgement of the necessity for them to supplement low-scale rates of supplementary benefit with part-time wages. But lone mothers are likely to suffer the double-bind of being in an already weak position in a 'dual' work-force, while at the same time contradicting notions of the 'good family': in good families, as typified by Beveridge and New Right commentators, mothers do not work, the family is not dependent on the state and is certainly not female-headed (Fitzgerald 1983). In summary

> The harsh earnings rules, low pay and 'liable relative' and cohabitation tests place obstructions in the way of women single parents who wish to work or enter any kind of friendship. They must either make a dramatic change – go to work full-time or set up joint home with a man – or stay as they are. Most women single parents and their children face the choice between poverty and dependence.
>
> (Esam et al. 1985: 65–6)

Against this background of privation and dependency, this category of supplementary benefit fraud could be seen as an alternative path for some women who seek both financial independence (albeit through relatively meagre state benefits) and an emotional/sexual relationship with a man.

For such women the financial gain from cohabitation which is assumed by the DHSS is often illusory. As Carol (quoted earlier) indicated, an emotional and sexual relationship does not necessarily involve a man giving money to a woman: her boyfriend was divorced and paid over a sizeable proportion of his wages in the form of maintenance to his ex-wife and children. The DHSS regulations concerning cohabitation therefore assume not only traditional breadwinner/dependant roles between men and women, but also a traditional 'ideal' form of nuclear family which fails to come to terms with the realities of divorce and single parenthood. As a result it can be argued that poorer women whose family style fails to conform to this ideal may be effectively criminalized when they violate the cohabitation rule.

In analysing the various techniques by which benefit claimants may defraud the state, this category is less straightforward than other forms of fraud because the motivation of financial gain is not always present. Another important distinction involved in this category of fraud centres upon claimants being defined as fraudsters by virtue of their domestic and personal circumstances rather than by their engaging in a purely financial transaction as, for instance, in the case of working while claiming. Although there are undoubtedly women who *do* gain financially from cohabitation with (working) men, this is not *necessarily* the case. In addition, this category of fraud more than any other demonstrates the capacity of the Welfare State to police the private arena of a claimant's life and personal relationships under the veil of the prevention of fraud and abuse. One may well ask, 'How on earth did the State get into all this?' (Donnison 1982: 109). The answer lies in the operation of a family-based household means test for the poor in which the patriarchal nuclear family pattern is first assumed, then, if not in evidence, actively promoted, through the stigma, deterrence and investigation methods used in the policing of female claimants. It is within this context that the commission of fraud by women on welfare must be located.

Itinerant fraud

This category of fraud encompasses a variety of activities, all of which are bound up with claimants' responses to lack of permanent accommodation. The term 'itinerant' implies vagrancy, yet supplementary benefit claimants so termed are rarely wilful vagrants. More often, as Lord Scarman noted, homelessness is accompanied by 'unemployment, marital breakdown, poverty, ill-health or the disabilities of old age' (*Guardian* 6.1.87). In recent years concern about this form of fraud has increased, probably due to the dramatic rise in numbers of claimants living temporarily in bed-and-breakfast accommodation effectively subsidized by the DHSS. However, as the Social Security Advisory Committee noted,

> claimants have turned, for one reason or another and in increasing numbers to board and lodging accommodation not from choice, but because they have no alternative.
>
> (CHAR 1986: 145)

None the less government concern about fraud and abuse by claimants in such accommodation had, by September 1982, culminated in 'Operation Major' in Oxford. The link between this ruthless pursuit of the homeless poor and the desire for maximum publicity for the DHSS's anti-fraud campaign has been well documented (Franey 1983; R. Smith 1985). It may be argued that an emphasis on the homeless 'scrounger' is another example of implicit distinctions being drawn between the allegedly undeserving poor (vagrants, work-shy, unemployed and some single-parent families) and the deserving poor (elderly, sick and handicapped people for instance). The historical roots of such distinctions can be traced back to the Poor law, yet (as argued in Chapter 1) remain influential in the representations of the poor in the 1980s.

Not all commentators agree with amplified assessments of the extent of this form of fraud put forward by media and right-wing political voices. Former DHSS Under-Secretary Geoffrey Beltram told the Public Accounts Committee in 1983 that

> this kind of itinerant fraud is not in fact one of the most serious areas of fraud for us, simply because of the limited number of people involved nationally.
>
> (*HC 102* 1983: para 21)

This is perhaps borne out in Table 3 where itinerant fraud constituted only 6.7 per cent of cases considered for prosecution in 1984/5.

Techniques employed in this category of fraud are, broadly, of two types. First, a homeless claimant may visit more than one Social Security office in the same day (possibly giving false names) and claim the daily NFA (No Fixed Address) rate of benefit at each office. In certain areas, London and Glasgow for instance, the opportunities for this form of fraud have been curtailed by the setting up of 'Special Offices' to which the homeless and those in lodging houses are sent. Procedures for dealing with claims in these offices are very different from those in other DHSS offices: they have no appointment system and are characterized by an emphasis on establishing the claimant's identity and 'Unemployment Review'. These features, acording to former DHSS Under-Secretary Lynda Chalker, are geared towards 'greater control of the fraud and abuse which occurs in a proportion of these cases' (CHAR 1986: 97). But more practical factors, such as an average waiting time of up to five hours, also serve to restrict this type of fiddle (ibid.).

A second type of fraud involves claimants without a permanent home engaging in a collusive fiddle with a landlord of bed-and-breakfast 'hotel' or lodgings. This type of fiddle was the target of Operation Major in Oxford where landlords of DHSS-approved lodging houses falsely confirmed claimants' residence at their property (for a fee), and took a proportion of their benefit payments in order that homeless claimants could, falsely, receive full board and lodging rates of benefit rather than the 'meals only' NFA rate (*New Society*) 27.1.83: 141). The landlords, Cronin and Patel, who made vast sums from exploiting claimants and DHSS alike were, however, not prosecuted for their part in such frauds in Oxford: Cronin appeared as a prosecution witness instead. Despite the fact that a claimant may not gain as much from such frauds as a collusive landlord, this form of fiddle is regarded as an extremely serious one by the DHSS and courts alike, often attracting prosecution under the Theft Act which enables harsher punishments than under the Supplementary Benefits Act 1976 (NACRO 1986).

When identifying the techniques involved in what has been termed 'itinerant fraud' it is essential to locate the actions of these claimants in the context of their extremely vulnerable social and economic position. The homeless have for centuries constituted one of the most powerless and disadvantaged groups in our society. The responses to the so-called 'hippy commune' in the summers of 1985 and 1986 indicates the contemporary hostility of Britain's control culture to groups who reject mainstream material values (Vincent-Jones 1986). At the same time this particular group's status as benefit claimants was the subject of vociferous condemnation, both in Parliament and in the tabloid press. Paradoxically many of Britain's homeless poor do not reject mainstream material values and are, as Scarman noted, the victims of economic and domestic circumstances which have rendered them powerless. These economic and social factors underpin the justifications which homeless claimants offer for their actions.

Instrument of payment fraud

This category of fraud does not appear as a distinct classification in Table 3 as it is subsumed under the heading of 'other static fraud'. 'Instrument of payment fraud' is itself a composite term for a variety of fiddles associated with the theft, alteration or forgery of the claimant's 'instrument of payment'. These are primarily the supplementary benefit order books and giros which are cashed through post offices.

Techniques involved in these forms of fraud vary. For instance, one example involving several such instrument of payment frauds came to light when ten (female) claimants were prosecuted. The local press detailed how the women had swapped orders in different order books, reported the books missing or stolen and subsequently received replacements from the DHSS, which they also cashed. 'Crude alterations' were made to the books as, according to an investigator, 'they [the women] became too confident of getting away with the fraud' (Shropshire Star 16.4.86). Clearly these frauds were relatively unsophisticated and demonstrated the fraudsters' ignorance of DHSS procedures and anti-fraud safeguards. Many alterations to giros are easily recognized: as one senior DHSS official told the Public Accounts Committee, 'we have defences built into the Giro cheques against alteration'. A fraudster's initial confidence that s/he has 'got away with it' may be misplaced because although post office counter staff may cash giros with convincing but false signatures, all allegedly lost and stolen giros and orders are thoroughly traced back after encashment (HC 102 1983). A fraudster may therefore be initially unaware that the offence has been detected.

It is important to remember that DHSS staff themselves have to make judgements about the 'genuineness' of claimants who allege that their giro has not yet arrived, has been lost or stolen. Suspicions are bound to be aroused if such assertions are made by the same claimant on more than one occasion. Therefore those who attempt instrument of payment fraud are more liable to get caught (particularly if engaging in several frauds) unless their fiddles are highly organized. It is perhaps a measure of the desperation of these claimants that they even attempt relatively crass frauds of this kind. As will be argued below, these forms of fraud should be seen in the material context of poverty, despair and degradation in which they take place.

Other fiddles

Table 3 indicates that there are additional forms of benefit fraud which, although statistically not as important as those already discussed, need to be analysed in terms of the fraudsters' techniques. They all involve different means of 'knowingly making a false statement in order to obtain benefit', which is the essence of the illegal act involved in the commission of supplementary benefit fraud (NACRO 1986). As already discussed, working 'on the side', cohabitation, fictitious desertion, itinerant and instrument of payment frauds all involve making false statements when claiming benefit, or when benefit entitlement is reviewed, or when cashing payments at a post office. But false statements relating to other aspects of a claim can also give rise to fraud. Such false statements refer to the income and outgoings of the claimant, or the 'assessment unit': for instance the concealment of *income* from occupational pensions, employer's sick pay, grants, redundancy or maintenance payments, Family Income Supplement and Child Benefit constitutes an offence for the same reasons as working on the side. The same applies to concealing savings.

False statements can also refer to a claimant's *outgoings* which are equally essential for an accurate assessment of supplementary benefit. For instance, falsely inflated figures of rent payable (and possibly forged rent book) can lead to an over-claiming of benefit. Similarly to claim for children or adults who are not in fact being maintained within the assessment unit is also fraudulent.

Another technique which does not readily fit into earlier categories of fraud is that of multiple claiming. This form of fraud seemed increasingly evident when home visits were reduced and, from 1982, postal claims became the standard method of collecting information about claimants' circumstances. However, the effects of deepening economic recession, mass unemployment and a consequent upsurge in the numbers of supplementary benefit claimants in the 1980s should not be overlooked as influential factors. The switch to postal claiming alone may be insufficient to explain the growth of frauds involving multiple claims. This fraud involves a claimant (or several claimants) applying for supplementary benefit from a series of false addresses and/or in a number of false names. The techniques involved were described in press coverage of one such fraud: the case of a Wolverhampton couple, prosecuted in 1985

> They had a network of 19 false names and 10 accommodation addresses in Wolverhampton, Kidderminster, Leicester and Coventry.... And they made regular trips to sign on at benefit offices and collect Giro cheques at the various addresses.
>
> (*Express and Star* 15.2.85)

In this case the figure of benefit defrauded was relatively large – £50,000 according to press reports – and the techniques involved were complex, involving a high degree of organization.

Finally, fraudsters may falsify details relating to their domestic circumstances in order to claim benefit. Geoffrey Beltram gives examples of this form of fraud, associated with multi-occupied accommodation in which claimants falsely 'pose as householders' (Beltram 1984a: 99). Beltram notes the link which is often made between this form of fraud and ethnic minorities, but is sensitive both to the problems experienced by black people, and to those of the DHSS staff who serve them: according to his study some DHSS officers did make racist comments and some (at best) appeared to lack sympathetic understanding. Others found difficulty in dealing with claimants whose circumstances (for instance in relation to cohabitation and multi-occupation) did not conform to the typical 'family' catered for in the DHSS regulations. At the same time, Beltram indicates that there are individuals within *all* communities who commit fraud. However, he underestimates the extent to which racism exaggerates the alleged 'problem' of fraud and abuse, and so ultimately influences the extent and character of the policing of black claimants. In this way already negative popular views on the issue of 'scrounging' and race are exaggerated and distorted still further (Golding and Middleton 1982).

Summary of supplementary benefit fraud techniques

Individuals who defraud the DHSS utilize a variety of techniques in order to gain illegal financial advantage from the state. Some techniques are identical to those involved in defrauding the Inland Revenue: for instance, moonlighting, ghosting and the falsification of statements of income and outgoings are the precise techniques used by tax fraudsters. But significantly the same actions may be both justified and perceived in differing ways. For instance, a businessman falsifying accounts may see his actions as a logical response to repressive state agencies (the Revenue Departments) and at the same time a reassertion of the inherent values of a capitalist society – entrepreneurial spirit and the creation of personal wealth. Benefit fraudsters are more likely to cite poverty and the inadequacy of supplementary benefit levels as the prime motive for their actions. Both tax and benefit frauds are motivated by economic imperatives, but the interpretation of these motives by regulatory agencies and in the public rhetoric is entirely different (see Chapters 7 and 8).

The opportunity structure available to benefit fraudsters is relatively restricted in comparison with the opportunities available to the tax evader. For the benefit fraudster opportunities to fiddle centre upon low-paid casualized work, manipulation of information on personal circumstances, and 'risky' activities such as fiddling giros and order books and multiple claiming. Furthermore, the financial gain available is far less, being based on the low and finite limits of the supplementary benefit scale rates. By contrast most forms of tax fraud offer greater gains for less risk, both in terms of getting caught and in terms of severity of punishment meted out.

When describing their techniques of fraud, almost all the fraudsters I interviewed invoked vocabularies of poverty, need, stigma and despair in justifying their actions. It was, for most of them, impossible to separate the *means* of benefit fraud from the allegedly legitimate *ends* which they felt it served. By contrast, tax fraudsters' accounts of their techniques reflect a more 'sporting' view of fraud, whereby the complexities of the taxation system are utilized in order to outwit the taxman. No matter how cunning the benefit fraud, claimants are not perceived as engaged in a battle of wits with the DHSS, or as victims of a complex system of social security benefits. The reasons for differential responses to tax and benefit fraud are not located in qualitative differences in the commission of the criminal acts described in this chapter. Rather, they are located in the social, economic and ideological context in which these acts take place.

Justifications

When talking to supplementary benefit claimants the harsh realities of life on the poverty line became apparent. All supplementary benefit fraudsters I interviewed referred to the inadequacy of the scale rates of benefit payments when they spoke of their reasons for fiddling. Clearly it is essential, when examining their self-justifications, to take account of the broader socio-economic context in which fraud takes place.

The common themes which emerged when questioning claimants about reasons for fiddling all relate to the material conditions under which they live. Their rationales incorporate the effects of being a 'claimant' on the individual's self-image, the effects of strained interactions with DHSS staff, and negative societal reaction to them as welfare 'scroungers' in addition to their purely economic motives. The themes which emerged will therefore be analysed under the following headings:

1 'Fiddling for necessities': the inadequacy of supplementary benefit levels.
2 The nexus of mistrust and degradation: claimant/staff relations, the interactions of DHSS offices, and claimants' perceptions of their 'scrounger' status.
3 Swings and roundabouts: fiddling as a response to the vagaries of the benefit system.
4 'Everyone does it': the belief that we are 'all' on the fiddle.

'Fiddling for necessities'

> It's simply lack of money. You don't have enough to live on. You fiddle for necessities and don't look for any luxuries.
>
> (Carol, lone mother of three)

Carol described her life on supplementary benefit as 'hell'. She first claimed benefit at the age of 19 when she had separated from her first husband and returned to her parents' home with her baby daughter. Years later, when her second marriage broke down, she had to claim once more, this time as a mother of three children with her own rented home. But she had great difficulty managing on what she regarded as inadequate supplementary benefit payments from the DHSS:

> The kids never had any new things: it was always rummage and second-

hand....I couldn't shop weekly, I just shopped to replace essential things.... At Christmas I took old toys down from the loft, did them up and re-wrapped them.... I couldn't cope with Christmas, birthdays and new clothes.

(Carol)

Her experience is one shared by many families dependent upon supplementary benefit; in one CPAG study, the following comments were typical

The real problem is making ends meet.... Having to live from day to day. You can never plan anything.... A constant struggle.... It's just not enough to live on.

(Burghes 1980: 13)

More recent research has confirmed that many of those forced to live on supplementary benefit are not held in the 'safety net' *above* the poverty line, but rather are living *in* conditions of poverty, this being especially so in the case of families with dependent children (Beltram 1984a; George and Wilding 1984; *Poverty* 1988b). This is certainly the case if poverty is defined in the manner advocated by the Supplementary Benefits Commission (in 1978) under its last chairman David Donnison. Their definition is worth quoting in full because of its relevance to the experiences of the families described above:

To keep out of poverty, people must have an income which enables them to participate in the life of the community. They must be able, for example, to keep themselves reasonably well fed, and well enough dressed to maintain their self-respect and to attend interviews for jobs with confidence. Their homes must be reasonably warm; their children should not be shamed by the quality of their clothing; the family must be able to visit relatives, and give them something on their birthdays and at Christmas time; they must be able to read newspapers, and retain their membership of trades unions and churches. And they must be able to live in a way which ensures, so far as possible, that public officials, doctors, teachers, landlords and others treat them with the courtesy due to every member of the community.

(Donnison 1982: 8)

In terms of this definition, which sees poverty as a relative concept, related to the lives and expectations of others in the community, all of the supplementary benefit claimants I have interviewed are certainly living in poverty.

The justification of poverty was invoked by Barry, a 26-year-old unemployed father of four who had been able to obtain only casual work since he left school at the age of 16. Barry and his wife spoke to me of not being able to afford new shoes for their three elder children (all under 7 years old). When, two years earlier, the DHSS had refused them a grant for nappies for their newly born baby, Barry took a week's casual work 'spud-bashing' on a local farm and continued to claim supplementary benefit. A neighbour 'grassed' on him and he was prosecuted by the DHSS (see Chapter 7). Yet Barry still feels that benefit fraud is justified so long as the cash defrauded is used 'to buy food, clothes and shoes for the kids' as, he argues, was the case for him. But he condemned 'fiddles for beer money'. He clearly felt that it was justifiable to fiddle for need but not for 'greed'.

Normative considerations therefore seem to operate for many benefit claimants who delineate justifiable 'fiddling for necessities' in contrast to the unacceptable fiddling of those whom it is felt do not *need* the cash. Another example of such considerations was provided by responses to an unemployed carpenter who was 'on the social' and working on the side. He was regarded as 'greedy' because, according to workmates, he was suffering no financial hardship and 'he could have got a job if he'd wanted to'. In another instance an odd-job man who was claiming benefit was 'shopped' by a relative, not only because he had allegedly over-charged her for a small repair job, but also because his standard of living was still high despite his 'unemployment', and so even his family considered him to be 'greedy'! But for the vast majority of claimants supplementary benefit proves insufficient income to provide the 'necessities' in terms of clothing, a good varied diet, warmth and household amenities. Under such circumstances fiddling for those necessities becomes a logical and pragmatic response.

Other research involving analysis of the material conditions of supplementary benefit claimants (and their own perceptions of those conditions) arrives at similar conclusions regarding the material and psychological deprivation they suffer (Marsden 1982; Campbell 1984; Harrison 1983). But, it is true to say that not all benefit claimants believe themselves to be living in the depths of poverty: 'one or two still had some residue of past affluence, others help from relatives, to ward off hardship' (Beltram 1984b: 140).

Nevertheless, the effects of living at this level of income for any length of time are dire, and mass unemployment has pushed more individuals and families into poverty. For instance, Manchester City Council in 1986 calculated that unemployment, the main reason for the growth of poverty in the city, had more than doubled since 1978. The unemployment rate then stood at 10.6 per cent, but by 1985 had reached 23.6 per cent. Over a similar period the percentage of the city's population dependent upon supplementary benefit had increased from 18 per cent in 1979 to 31 per cent in 1984 (ibid.). In this structural context of economic decline it becomes difficult to argue that poverty is the result of individual idleness, mismanagement and personal failing. Yet the consequences for individuals and families on supplementary benefit are inescapable. It is particularly significant that a former high-ranking DHSS official should admit that

It seemed clear that families with dependent children could not reasonably be expected to maintain an acceptable standard of life on incomes at, or close to, the ordinary basic S.B. level for any considerable length of time, unless they also had help from other sources. . . . Indeed, without extra support they would generally continue to be hard pressed when, after a year on S.B., they qualified for the higher long-term rate, a boon so far denied to the unemployed.

(Beltram 1984a: 84)

Furthermore, it has been argued that levels of supplementary benefit are in fact declining in relation to the average wage, and that the numbers of children in poverty has tripled since 1975 (Walker and Walker 1987). The majority of these new poor are the children of unemployed people (Piachaud 1987).

The justification for benefit fraud as fiddling for necessities therefore takes on added meaning when the realities of life on supplementary benefit are contemplated. Such realities are not appreciated by the right-wing critics and politicians who represent life on welfare benefits as cossetting and encouraging idleness. Two Conservative MPs, Matthew Parris and Piers Merchant, could not rise to the challenge of living comfortably on supplementary benefit for seven days, let alone the daunting prospect of 'dole' as a relatively permanent way of life. Three claimants recently prosecuted for supplementary fraud put the situation to me graphically in their comments upon the proceedings in a Magistrates' Court (see Chapter 7). One of them complained,

They don't live in the same world as us. They don't know what our life is like.

Another agreed and added,

They're on another planet, mate.

In their disadvantaged situation (often with rent arrears, fuel debts and crippling 'club' payments) they responded by working 'on the side'. The response was seen as logical and the risks involved were accepted:

There are more getting caught, but you pay your money and take your choice, I suppose.

Justifications which stress poverty and necessity are not therefore merely 'excuses' for benefit fraud. The material conditions (described here) indicate that poverty *causes* such fraud. But one problem arising from this observation is 'why is it that all supplementary benefit claimants do not engage in fraud?' Possible reasons derive from the diversity of people's individual responses to their material conditions, and the meanings which they attach to them. For instance, Beltram noted that not all pensioners believed themselves to be poor – but some were cushioned from the worst effects of reliance on state benefits by savings or family support. In addition, some families' needs are greater than others: as noted above, those who suffer most from long periods on 'safety net' levels of benefit are the long-term unemployed, particularly those who have children. Finally, as Box

(1987) notes, responses to unemployment (and deprivation) depend on what this experience *means* to those suffering it, what is perceived as its likely *duration*, and what is believed to have *caused* it. Hence, not all individuals in the same circumstances will resort to law-breaking. But that is not to say that the motives of those who *do* are merely 'excuses'. On the basis of my interviews with benefit claimants (whether fiddling or not) most fraud is attributed to economic necessity which arises from harsh material conditions, which are worsening, particularly in the former industrial heartlands.

Such conditions are well documented by Gofton and Gofton (1984) in their description of life in Consett, known locally as 'Giro City'. The authors detail how a culture of worklessness evolved, centred upon the DHSS economy. Empty shops, amusement arcades, and 'cheap shops' (selling cut-price goods) co-exist with back-street motor repairers, builders and painters. The unemployed find ways of 'making out' as moonlighting 'dole-wallahs' who also serve to buttress the employers of the formal economy by providing cheap and disposable labour. Although they are breaking the law, the authors argue that 'it's difficult to feel any moral indignation about it. "What do you *want* me to do?" they say. "In this world you've got to look after *yourself"*' (ibid: 282).

It could, nevertheless, be argued that care must be taken not to accept uncritically those rationales for fraud which cite economic imperatives, not least because this is also a justification frequently given by tax fraudsters for evasion. But in the light of evidence presented here, the privation suffered by supplementary benefit claimants is demonstrable; the same cannot be said of the alleged financial hardships of 'long-suffering' taxpayers.

The nexus of mistrust and degradation

Justifications for benefit fraud may also be rooted in feelings of degradation and worthlessness created through the process of claiming and receiving supplementary benefit. Reserch has demonstrated the extent of such feelings amongst claimants (Cooper 1985; Beltram 1984a; Campbell 1984) and the effective 'rationing' of welfare benefits is well documented (Foster 1983; MacGregor 1981; Deacon and Bradshaw 1983). Rationing devices can include delays, lost files, failure to inform claimants of their full rights and the forbidding character of the benefit system itself. Whether by device or by mischance, such factors contribute to a framework within which claimants may feel 'guilty', even if they have committed no offence other than the sin of being poor.

One claimant (a lone mother being questioned about 'boyfriends' and how often they called) felt as if she was 'guilty until proven innocent'. When she initially claimed benefit on separating from her husband she had been angered and disgusted at her treatment by a visiting officer:

They wanted all the mucky details... who I slept with, when and where and how many times. I'm surprised they didn't ask what position too.... They didn't want to *help* me.

She felt she was being treated like a 'scrounger'. In these circumstances, she explained, her attitude toward committing fraud changed:

I thought 'so what? They think I'm fiddling so I may as well be!'

Some time later when the opportunity to fiddle arose she took it, and her fiance unofficially moved into her home while she continued to claim benefit. However, she *had* enquired, on more than one occasion, about the cohabitation rule, but had been treated with great suspicion:

They told me that if I was even thinking about it to send my book in. I tried the CAB, but I had no information at all.

In this case an official's mistrust, coupled with the claimant's belief that 'they treat you like an imbecile', contributed to a situation in which the claimant felt that fraud was justifiable.

It would be difficult to argue that the stigma suffered by claimants and the mistrust shown to them by DHSS staff is alone sufficient to explain why some claimants turn to fraud. But, coupled with inadequate benefit levels, these factors may offer a contributory justification.

Ironically it is probably the concern to prevent fraud and abuse which leads DHSS staff effectively to label certain of their claimants potential fraudsters and so possibly to contribute towards a self-fulfilling prophecy. This has long been the case:

Officers seemed more anxious that they should not be taken in by a hard luck story than that they should fail to meet genuine need.

(Sinfield 1970: 233)

More recently, Cooper (1985) noted the comments of the manager of an urban DHSS office who had been dealing with claimants since the days of the National Assistance Board (NAB):

I run a tight ship here, and I know how to do that because I've been in the business since the NAB days. In those days we didn't give anything out unless it was really needed and unless it was an honest, deserving claim. Now it's easy for claimants; too easy.... I can tell you that it takes a lot of pride out of the job, when you know that nine out of ten of your customers are fiddling you. What's more, welfare rights egg them on so you begin to feel you're anyone's mug. In this office we've a reputation for being a bit shrewd, a bit harder; that's deliberate. I tell all my staff to be on their watch and get all the information they can on people. There's just too much abuse.

(Cooper 1985: 13)

These comments are interesting for a variety of reasons: first, the manager appears to personalize the issue of fraud which he sees as making 'mugs' of staff, taking away their 'pride' in the job and making 'fools' of them. This presents the staff–claimant relationship as adversarial. The effect of this personalization is therefore to perceive interactions with claimants as a battle of wits, bearing in mind that the claimant is highly likely to be a cunning fraudster (as nine out of ten are, according to this manager). Such comments appear to justify the belief of several claimants I interviewed, that they were labelled 'scroungers' by the very fact that they were claiming supplementary benefit. Such beliefs are also supported when advocates of 'effort' refer to the receipt of social benefits as a 'moral hazard' in itself (Parker 1982; see Chapter 1).

Second, the DHSS office manager clearly distinguishes between 'deserving' and 'undeserving' (hence suspicious) claims. Further observations noted by Cooper seem to indicate that staff are more likely to regard as 'deserving' those claimants who are from a middle-class background (whether unemployed or not), sick people (unless suffering from 'back trouble'), disabled and elderly people. Therefore many single-parent families and unemployed people may be unofficially categorized as potential 'scroungers' by the staff who deal with their claims. But it is important to recognize that these categorizations are not merely the product of the individual prejudices of DHSS staff: as already argued, the legacy of the 1834 Poor Law still informs images of the 'deserving' and 'undeserving' poor. As a result discourses about the morality and pathology of welfare recipients are 'naturalized' in the public rhetoric (Golding and Middleton 1982). Although generalizations about staff–claimant relations would be difficult to make (because, as Cooper indicates, there are sympathetic, caring and efficient staff too) it appears reasonable to assert that if claimants encounter staff who regard them as fiddlers, they may well lose self-esteem and become increasingly frustrated. Such frustration leads to loss of confidence in the supplementary benefit system which may provide a rationale for fiddling. For instance, many claimants I spoke to had been annoyed at what could be termed informal rationing or 'mucking about' (Foster 1983). They referred to the refusal of Exceptional Needs Payments (ENPs) seemingly unfairly or without explanation, delayed giros, lack of explanation of entitlement and intrusive interviews. All contribute to a feeling of degradation, mistrust and mutual hostility between claimants and DHSS staff, which may make the commission of fraud more likely (see also discussion of benefit office conditions and adverse effects on take-up of benefits in Chapter 6).

Third, the manager in question seems to regard it not only as a virtue to be 'hard' and intrusive towards the 'customer', but also as a necessity in view of the role of welfare agencies in 'egging them on' to claim. The payment of benefit is thus presented here not as a *right* but as a privilege, conferred on the 'customers' by DHSS staff, once officials have been convinced of the honesty (and desert) of the claim. As knowledge confers power within this complex social security system, such knowledge is jealously guarded and thus the activities of welfare rights advisers are resented. The rhetoric of the effort school of thought is evidently informing such attitudes towards welfare: for example, it is assumed that 'undeserving' claims can be deterred through the 'tests' informally administered by officials who make the claiming process as difficult as possible. Furthermore, the misgivings about claimants gaining *all* the benefits to which they are entitled could be seen to represent the fear that the principles of 'less eligibility' may be eroded and that the poor may thus 'enjoy their servitude' and dependency (Boyson 1978: 110).

This 'hard' attitude is transmitted in staff–claimant interactions; claimants frequently used phrases like 'you'd think it was their own money' when describing to me the attitudes of some benefit staff. In the light of Cooper's observations this would seem a common sentiment amongst claimants. This clearly signifies that feelings of mistrust and degradation are important elements in analysing the way in which many claimants perceive the supplementary benefit system. Although DHSS staff are by no means uniformly hostile, Cooper's evidence suggests that the legacy of the harsh 'NAB days' dies hard. This legacy, like that of the Poor Law, gives rise to ideological contradictions which enable supplementary benefit claimants in the 1980s to be represented as idle, feckless and culpable (Boyson 1971; Golding and Middleton 1982).

As a result, many claimants may feel that they are stigmatized and degraded by the staff who administer welfare, and by 'society' in general, as evidenced in popular imagery of the 'scrounger'. At the same time, the realities of mistrust and the scrounger mythology serve to shift official and popular discourses away from issues of poor take-up of benefits, poor service to claimants and, crucially, inadequate (and decreasing) levels of benefits. In this way the 'problem' of supplementary benefit fraud is being ideologically constructed, and alternative discourses suppressed. As Beltram (1985) notes, the DHSS's policy and practice of policing supplementary benefit has important effects: for instance,

> honest people who are deterred from claiming by publicity about scroungers, or fear of being asked distressing questions, or past experience of official incivility.
>
> (Beltram 1985: 27)

It is within this framework, I would argue, that fraud can be seen partly as a product of a staff–claimant nexus of distrust on the one side and, on the other, a feeling of degradation claimants feel as a result of being perceived as 'undeserving' scroungers.

Swings and roundabouts

The complex nature of the supplementary benefit system itself may also contribute to the commission of fraud. Fraud may arise as much from omission as commission, and in many cases claimants fail to inform the DHSS of relevant changes in their circumstances for fear that a reassessment of their entitlement would delay their benefit payments. This was so in the case of Anne, who received maintenance payments from her husband very rarely indeed. On the few occasions that she did receive money from him, she did not always inform the DHSS because of the administrative disruption this would cause: when she did inform them, her entitlement was reassessed but as a result her benefit payments were often delayed, leaving her temporarily without money. Anne justified not telling the DHSS about occasional maintenance payments in terms of 'swings and roundabouts': she felt that any advantage gained through this fiddle had previously been earned through the disadvantages she suffered while on irregular payments.

A similar situation may arise in relation to part-time earnings. Brian was unemployed and had a part-time job, for one evening per week, and so he declared any earnings when he signed on. As a result he was told to sign weekly as his earnings might vary. Although he explained that he earned identical amounts each week, he was required to produce a verification weekly. His supplementary benefit was delayed and he often ran short of money. By the time his part-time job ended, his attitude towards the benefits system had changed: he indicated that in future he would probably not be so scrupulously honest in declaring any part-time earnings.

The justification of 'swings and roundabouts' offered by claimants is an important contributory rationale, bearing in mind the primary cause of supplementary benefit fraud – poverty. It enables claimants to legitimize their illegal gains from the state in terms of the perceived failings of the operation of the Welfare State itself. Effectively, such justifications shift the responsibility for fraud from the fraudster to the operation of the 'system', and certainly helps claimants who are on the fiddle to rationalize their actions. If they have suffered bureaucratic delay, if the whole benefit system was seen as collapsing under the strain of mass unemployment and staff cut-backs, if their levels of benefit are seen as inadequate, payments as at times unreliable and quality of service poor, then clearly fiddling will appear to be a legitimate response to a capricious system.

The interplay of a variety of such justifications is well demonstrated by Harrison, who locates factors such as mutual mistrust and the vagaries of the benefit system within the context of deepening recession as Britain entered the 1980s:

> The British social security system, never generous, became Scrooge-like, and acted as an incentive and a provocation to abuse. There was the widening gap between the basic rates of benefit and basic needs ... and the even broader chasm between the rates and the level of expectations generated by the media. There was the often arbitrary denial of entitlement: if the system did not play fair with its dependants, it could hardly expect them to play fair in return. And

there was the suspicion and scepticism about claims: if people were treated as potential scroungers even when they were honest, then they might as well be scroungers for real.

(Harrison 1983: 148)

'Everyone does it'

The belief that everyone is on the fiddle can also serve to reduce any anxiety that benefit fraudsters suffer when attempting to justify their actions. At the same time it makes fraud appear 'natural' and thus presents the fraudster's activities as less deviant. The belief that benefit fraud is widespread is a very popular one and was expressed by the majority of fraudsters I spoke to. For instance, in response to the question 'How many of your fellow claimants do you feel are fiddling?', some of the answers were

Many of them... for their children.

(Barry)

Everyone I know on Sup. Ben. is fiddling.

(Carol)

A lot!

(Caroline)

In response to a question on the apparently increasing number of DHSS prosecutions being mounted locally, one convicted fraudster commented wryly, 'There's just more getting caught.'

It is widely acknowledged that it is impossible to estimate the scale of supplementary benefit fraud with any confidence (Harrison 1983; NACRO 1986; CPAG 1982: *HC 102* 1983). It can reasonably be argued that it is not insignificant in scope, but hardly merits the political over-reaction which has occurred since the 1970s (Harrison 1983; Donnison 1982; Levi 1987). Unfortunately when claimants use the rationale that 'everyone' is fiddling, they unwittingly play into the hands of those right-wing critics of the Welfare State who seek to maintain the imagery of the idle, feckless scrounger (see Chapter 1). This form of justification therefore presents a paradox: if 'everyone' is on the fiddle then the harsh regulatory techniques sometimes used by the DHSS to police claimants may gain acceptability. Furthermore, the 'scrounger' imagery (so prevalent in public representations of benefit fraud) gains credibility too. Yet this imagery occludes the fact that the vast majority of claims are perfectly honest (Donnison 1982).

I would argue that this form of justification operates in the same way as it does for the tax evader who asserts that 'everyone is on the fiddle'. It serves to appease fraudsters' consciences by making it seem that their actions are the norm. However, when the tax fraudster invokes the vocabulary that 'everyone does it', their frauds are often successfully justified: the money which they defraud is perceived as their own hard-earned cash which they merely 'prefer to keep', and their fiddles attract public acquiescence. But when claimants allege that 'everyone' fiddles, they merely reinforce the imagery of claimants as 'scroungers' who are seen to take money *from* the state. Therefore differential societal responses to this rationale are, rather, attributable to basic differences in the perceived relationships between taxpayer and the state, and supplementary benefit claimant and the state.

Summary of the justifications offered for supplementary benefit fraud

The justifications which supplementary benefits fraudsters offer for their actions need to be located in both material and ideological contexts. The material realities of life on 'safety-net' levels of welfare provision enable claimants to assert that they fiddle for financial survival. As discussed above, there is much empirical evidence which supports these assertions (for instance, Walker and Walker 1987; CPAG 1987). At the same time, material preconditions and ideological factors combine to create conditions of mistrust and degradation which may encourage the commission of fraud. For instance, the strained interactions between DHSS staff and claimants can be largely attributed to staff attitudes which are underpinned both by (historical) conceptions of the deserving and undeserving poor, and by contemporary 'scrounger' stereotypes. In turn, the scrounger mythology, when coupled with the material realities of social security bureaucracy, can give rise to the justification that fiddling supplementary benefit is a logical response first, because certain (undeserving) categories of claimants are perceived as scroungers anyway, and second, because the benefits system is inefficient and unfair.

The contradictions between the social philosophies of individualism and collectivism are important in explaining the genesis of such justifications. For example, ideologies of individualism stress individual culpability for poverty and thus promote the notion of the feckless, idle and thus 'undeserving' poor. But the Welfare State's provision for the 'deserving' poor – elderly, sick and handicapped people – depends upon a collectivist approach, funded (ostensibly) by personal taxation. Hence the principles of individualism and collectivism are differentially invoked both historically and according to claimant categories.

Such contradictions enable alternative discourses about welfare and scrounging which are differentially invoked by fraudsters, departmental staff and in official and public rhetoric. For instance, official discourse centres on 'fraud and abuse' within the Social Security system, rather than the alternative issues of inadequate benefit levels and poor service-delivery to claimants. Thus for departmental staff the agenda for dealing with claimants is set in adversarial terms, dominated by the concern to prevent abuse. By contrast, the fraudsters' self-justifications emphasize the issues of poverty, inequality, powerlessness and degradation as the primary motives for committing fraud.

Summary of Part II

Chapter 3 examined the principal techniques which individuals use to evade personal taxes. Such techniques were found to be influenced by the opportunity structures presented by certain occupations, and by the limitations which could be placed on these opportunities by changes in Inland Revenue procedures. Tax fraudsters were thus analysed as both proactive (seeking out new opportunity structures) and reactive (reacting to procedural changes made by the Revenue). But the commission of tax fraud is accompanied by a complex set of self-justifications which enable the fraudsters to rationalize their actions as rational, moral and non-criminal.

Rationality is ensured if tax fraud is seen to be located in the context of a capitalist state, geared to entrepreneurial wealth creation (see Table 4). The ideologies of individualism and the free market are therefore invoked in vocabularies which present fiddling taxes as the 'natural' product of wealth-creating, crusading, clever and moral people. Morality is ensured either if one accepts that economic growth (even through the black economy) benefits *all* members of society, or if one accepts that the taxes evaded are the individual's *own* money which s/he merely prefers to keep. The notion that tax evasion is 'non-criminal' is constructed within the material and ideological context of an unequal society. Discourses which emphasize the functional aspects of differential reward (buttressed by incentives) create the ideological space within which the law-breaking activities of the most 'valuable' citizens (the taxpayers) may be effectively de-criminalized (see Chapters 5 and 7).

Chapter 4 examined the techniques most commonly used to defraud supplementary benefit. To some extent these techniques were related to particular claimant groups: for instance, liable relative fraud is almost

Table 4 Justifications for tax and supplementary benefit fraud and their economic and ideological roots

SUPPLEMENTARY BENEFIT FRAUDSTERS	
Justifications	*Economic and ideological conditions enabling the justifications*
1 Fiddling for necessities	Poverty, inequality
2 Nexus of mistrust and degradation	'Social justice' ideology
3 Swings and roundabouts	Democratic interventionist state
4 'Everyone does it'	Focus on 'scrounger' stereotypes, stigma
TAX FRAUDSTERS	
Justifications	*Economic and ideological conditions enabling the justifications*
1 Tax as 'intolerable inquisition'	'Free market' ideology
2 Taxation stifles incentives	Liberal minimalist state
3 'Everyone does it'	Focus on individualism, wealth creation, effort

exclusively committed by women as it is a form of fraud generated by assumptions about the universal desirability of the patriarchal nuclear family. But the principal form of supplementary benefit fraud is working while claiming: these frauds are thus largely determined by occupational opportunity structures (as indeed much tax fraud is). However, from the analysis above, it is clear that such opportunities are relatively limited for benefit claimants, who are by definition unsuccessful in the formal economy. These limits, coupled with employers' desires for a cheap, disposable work-force, kept claimants working in the most marginalized, casualized and non-unionized sectors of the economy.

Benefit fraudsters implicitly invoke social justice ideologies when they justify their actions as a rational response to their economic deprivation and personal sense of degradation. In such discourses the state's function of 'accumulation' (invoked by tax fraudsters) is challenged, and an alternative goal of 'legitimation' through social justice is posed (see Table 4). But (as suggested in Chapters 1 and 2) such discourses fail to dominate official and public rhetoric because of the inherent tensions which have (historically) rendered official and public commitment to the Welfare State 'grudging', and yet have at the same time presented taxation as an intolerable inquisition.

Therefore historical and contemporary struggles over the extent of state regulation (whether by personal taxation or welfare provision), inform the vocabularies which fraudsters use to justify tax and benefit fraud, and also influence the extent to which such rationales attract official, judicial and popular assent.

Part III
Investigation

Introduction

The Inland Revenue and DHSS are both government departments with an enforcement role. As will be argued below, both are concerned to enforce rules (relating to the collection of revenue, or to the payment of benefits) which are ultimately laid down by Parliament. In Chapters 5 and 6 the official aims of these enforcing departments will be discussed, together with the investigatory practices that are designed to meet those aims. Official discourses concerning both tax 'compliance' and the policing of welfare benefits will be analysed in order to demonstrate contradictions between *official* policy goals and their effective practical outcomes. The practical outcomes of departmental policies will be assessed through analysis both of the regulatory techniques used by Revenue and DHSS staff, and of the differing assumptions (concerning the taxpayer and claimant respectively) which underpin the nature and operation of such techniques.

The 'gap' between the theory and practice of enforcement policies enables the paradox of differential response to those who defraud the DHSS and those who defraud the Revenue.

5

Tax Investigations

Enforcement policy

> You have important rights and entitlements as a taxpayer. You are entitled to expect that... the staff of the Inland Revenue and Customs and Excise will help you in every reasonable way to obtain your rights and to understand and meet your obligations under the tax laws.
>
> (Board of Inland Revenue 1986b)

The *Taxpayers' Charter* quoted here marked an attempt by the Revenue to establish its aims as an enforcing department and, crucially, to establish the rights of taxpayers to 'Information, courtesy and consideration... fairness, privacy and confidentiality... rights of independent appeal and review' while 'minimising compliance costs' (Board of Inland Revenue 1986b).

The primary function of the Revenue according to officials I have interviewed is 'the care and management of the Taxes Acts', which involves collecting 'the tax which parliament says is due'. Recently this primary objective has been accompanied by attempts to make good the damage done to relations with taxpayers by a massive backlog of work (which stood at 2.7 million unworked papers at the end of 1985). This backlog had arisen largely as a result of staffing cut-backs which involved the loss of almost 16,000 jobs in eight years (Board of Inland Revenue 1986a). The Charter signalled an attempt to restore public confidence and, although derided in some quarters, it does state the rights and duties of taxpayer and Revenue in a clear and open manner. (As will be discussed below, no similar document exists for supplementary benefit claimants.) In summary, the Revenue's main function is to administer the Taxes Acts efficiently and equitably, with the aim of securing the taxpayer's *compliance* to them.

The word 'compliance' is itself of significance: it reflects Revenue attitudes towards activities which the DHSS would simply term 'fraud and abuse': the language used to refer to taxation is altogether more obliging, equivocal and morally neutral than the vocabulary of welfare benefits. A crucial factor in obtaining the taxpayer's compliance is an unspoken agreement that financial reparation, not official punishment, is sought by the Revenue when an 'omission' from returns of income is discovered. In practice this involves the under-classification of many offences in order to 'spare the taxpayers' feelings' (*Cmnd 8822* 1983: 423). As the Revenue told the Keith Committee in 1983, 'We do not allege an offence more serious than is necessary to secure a reasonable settlement by agreement' (ibid: 422). Such settlements may involve the payment of interest on tax found to be due (up to six previous years may normally be investigated, though this time limit may be extended in cases of wilful default or fraud) and also added financial penalties where appropriate (see Chapter 7). The tendency to under-classify offences is justified on the grounds that lesser offences require a 'lower burden of proof', yet a subjective element is also evident in the Revenue's assertion that 'it is generally sufficient to establish wilful default and not to have to accuse the taxpayer of fraud' (ibid: 422).

As the Keith Committee noted, this policy of sparing the taxpayers' feelings may have objectionable consequences:

> On the one hand ... a taxpayer who vigorously protests innocent error and whose defence is rejected finds himself at once in a penalty category that in practice accommodates both the inadvertent and deliberate defaulter.... On the other hand, some offenders who have deliberately understated their income are likely to be treated in practice as no more than negligent.
>
> (ibid: 423)

Despite such problems in applying rules fairly, compliance and agreement form essential features of Revenue investigation policy. In practice the outcome of such a policy may be a structure of financial penalty which, in mitigation, stresses the degree of the taxpayer's *compliance* rather than issues of deliberate *intent* to default or defraud the Inland Revenue. This anomaly reflects the essentially pragmatic nature of a policy which is directed first and foremost to the collection of tax rather than to equity or to retributive justice. Retribution is, however, frequently demanded when benefit claimants fail to comply with DHSS regulations, despite the fact that they pay back money owing to the public purse just as the tax fiddler does (see Chapter 7). Pragmatism therefore cannot be considered as the sole (or even the primary) explanation for the relatively lenient treatment of the tax fraudster. The practicalities of collecting unpaid tax therefore dominate the *official* rhetoric of investigation policy, though the urbane treatment of tax fraud is not simply a product of these practicalities: rather it is enabled by more complex contradictions emanating from differing relations between taxpayer and the state, and benefit claimant and the state.

Beneath the official rhetoric of Revenue investigation policy lie the contradictory ideals of collectivism (realized by citizens' willing contributions to the state in the form of taxes), and individualism (realized in the entrepreneurial spirit, wealth creation and private accumulation of property). On the one hand it can be argued that the Inland Revenue performs the function of collecting *the state's* revenue from complying citizens, and on the other hand (as is implicit in much of the Revenue's regulatory practice), it can be argued that tax revenue is the *citizen's* to give, by agreement. The relatively lenient treatment of tax fraudsters therefore has a great deal to do with which perspective is adopted and, as a result, *whose* money is seen to be defrauded.

The ideology of individualism and cultural emphasis upon individual material accumulation serves to present the tax fraudster as a victim of repressive taxation, someone who merely 'prefers to keep' a larger slice of *their* marginal earnings than the coercive taxman permits (Myddleton 1979: 47). According to critics of the Revenue,

> Successive governments, obsessed with naive notions of social justice, have taxed to the point where the relation between effort and income has all but disappeared: where the industry of the people is obstructed in the maximum degree.
>
> (I. Pearce 1977: 105)

Furthermore, others argue that 'There are *no* ethics in taxation. There is no moral law in taxation' (Houghton 1977: 60). Morality and civic duty are seen to play no part in influencing the individual to (willingly) pay personal taxes.

Alternatively the ideals of social justice and the mutual obligations of civic duty can be seen as essential (and functional) components of modern Welfare Capitalism: for instance Titmuss argued that 'the Gift Relationship' when applied to social policy promoted social solidarity, whereas market principles in social policy encouraged self-centredness (Titmuss 1970). Thus both the 'civic duty' and 'coercive' models of taxation form important elements in the debates (both historical and contemporary) concerning the relations between the individual and the state in an industrial society. It would be facile simply to locate the 'civic duty' view in the historical context of the 'Butskellite consensus' and the 'coercive' view in the context of the New Right (Mishra 1984). As argued in Chapter 1, concepts and beliefs that appeared to have been superseded are never simply replaced by alternatives: instead, they often either inform or take on new meaning within subsequent discourses. So it has been with the contradictions deriving from liberal and democratic conceptions of the state. Evident throughout twentieth-century British social policy, these contradictions are nowhere more evident than in the case of debates surrounding taxation and welfare policy.

As far as taxation is concerned, the liberal view sees the Revenue's enforcement role as intrusive and stifling enterprise (Seldon 1979a). The democratic view sees taxation enabling collective provision for a social minimum for all citizens, and therefore sees investigatory procedures as essential in preserving the efficiency and integrity of the personal taxation system and, ultimately, social justice (IRSF 1982). When analysing the aims of the Inland Revenue as an enforcing department it is therefore necessary to consider both the *official* rhetoric through which departmental policy is articulated, and the *hidden* assumptions which inform and mould departmental practice. The Revenue's official aims are to ensure both compliance to the Taxes Acts and the rights of the individual taxpayer. Latent aims are to collect tax owed to the Revenue by the most agreeable means available; this involves seeking a bargain with taxpayers which will minimize the following:

1 *Administrative hassle* – hence under-classification of offences, for instance;
2 *Taxpayer's resistance* – 'sparing the taxpayer's feelings'.

I would argue that underpinning an ostensibly pragmatic approach to regulation of tax fraud is the 'coercive' view of personal taxation and ultimately (and most effectively) the ideology of liberalism. When tax fiddles occur, issues of crime, lack of civic duty or fiddling the state's revenue are not the operant ones: the 'individual's elemental right of property' dominates official and unofficial discourses (Denning in *Daily Telegraph* 17.7.79). Given this emphasis on the individual's right to accumulate personal wealth, it is not surprising that the aim of seeking the taxpayer's *compliance* dominates Revenue investigation policy and practice.

Regulation

Before analysing the regulatory techniques used by the Revenue, it is necessary first to outline the organizational structure in which investigations take place. Revenue investigation work is carried out through two major channels, reflecting the type and scale of the fraud itself. First, frauds not regarded as 'serious' are dealt with by staff based in *local offices*. Second, 'serious' frauds and those related to specific occupational groups are dealt with by staff working in *specialist units* under the Board's 'Technical Division 2'.

Local office investigations

The majority of Revenue investigations take place at local office level where tax inspectors are engaged in the routine examination of accounts, and in the vetting of other cases referred to them when, for instance, suspicion has arisen as a result of other officers examining tax returns. Local investigations are primarily geared to obtaining financial settlement, but 'serious' cases may be referred to Enquiry Branch where prosecution can be considered (see 1 below).

Since 1984 additional staff have been deployed in local offices on compliance work but, in a time of overall staffing cut-backs, commitment to this area of work remains questionable: although 850 additional compliance officers were scheduled to be deployed between 1984 and 1988, by March 1987 only 380 of these extra investigators were in post, due to a 'shortage of trained staff' (Board of Inland Revenue 1987: 34).

Specialist investigations

There are six specialist units engaged in investigation work, although only four are relevant here (as this analysis concentrates upon the fiddles of the individual taxpayer and small trader rather than upon larger-scale international tax frauds or tax avoidance schemes).

1 *Enquiry Branch* deals with cases of serious fraud in business accounts and cases where 'the honesty or competence of professional tax advisers is suspect' (ibid: 36). According to the Keith Committee about three-fifths of referrals to Enquiry Branch come from local tax district offices who suspect that a 'serious' fraud has been committed. Investigation guidelines (discussed by the Public Accounts Committee) indicate that an understatement of income of £50,000 or more is 'serious' (*HC 123* 1985).
2 *The Board's Investigation Office* (BIO) deals with a variety of suspected offences where trading accounts are *not* involved. Most BIO officers not only are engaged in cases of suspected frauds connected with the construction industry (contractor and sub-contractor frauds), but also deal with false claims to allowances and expenses, and offences connected with repayment claims. They also investigate any suspected irregularities by Inland Revenue staff. Overall, 'they are regarded as the Board's police' in the sense that 'the offences they deal with are regarded as more in the nature of conventional crimes, and are thus more likely to be prosecuted' (ibid: 9.10.3). (The link between what is regarded as 'conventional crime' and the type of offences most likely to attract Revenue prosecution will be explored in Chapter 7.)
3 *Special Offices* are concerned with problems of avoidance, evasion and non-compliance which are outside the field of other investigation units. In addition they deal with complex cases which are beyond the resources of the local district offices.
4 *PAYE Audit units* regulate the operation of PAYE by employers (inspecting employers' records and documents) and also check the operation of the special tax deduction scheme for the construction industry.

An indication of the overall effectiveness of Revenue Investigation work can be gained from analysis of the yield, in cash terms, of the various investigation units. For instance, total yields from counter-evasion and counter-avoidance work have more than doubled since 1983 and amounted to £741 million in 1987: this figure included £402 million yielded from tax office investigations in 1987 (as compared with £174 million in 1983) (Board of Inland Revenue 1987). Revenue figures of the 'cost-yield ratios' of investigation staff also demonstrate increasing effectiveness: for instance an investigator based at a Special Office can yield around 31 times his/her salary in taxes recouped. Although lower cost-yield ratios apply to tax office staff (13 times salary), local offices none the less carry out a greater number of Revenue investigations and so account for the vast majority of tax yield in cash terms. However, as argued earlier, there are doubts concerning the political commitment to current Revenue investigation efforts. For example, the IRSF has recently expressed concern that compliance officers may be taken from their assigned work and placed on 'general office duties' to clear arrears of work, built up as a result of staff cuts (*Assessment* December 1987). If tax district offices remain understaffed and this trend continues, figures of investigation yields may in the long term be adversely affected, and hence the future funding of compliance work, ostensibly based on cost-effectiveness, could be jeopardized.

Techniques of regulation

The organization of investigation units, described above, inevitably gives rise to some specialization in regulatory techniques. However there are some methods which are common to many areas of Revenue investigation work. What follows will seek both to identify the major techniques commonly used in most Revenue investigations, and to outline the particular techniques of specialist officers. In so doing the analysis will concentrate upon the regulation of the individual taxpayer, small trader or businessman: this will enable meaningful comparisons with the regulation of supplementary benefit claimants. The main emphasis will therefore be on local office investigations (both routine enquiries and compliance initiatives) as these most often affect the individual taxpayer.

Routine investigation and compliance work

Making connections
This phrase describes the investigatory work which centres upon using information already to hand, routinely supplied to the Revenue from a variety of sources. For instance, all firms are required to inform the Revenue of fees, expenses and commission paid out to individuals or traders. Financial institutions such as banks and building societies also furnish the Revenue with information, providing details of interest payments made to a sample of their investors. The task of the routine

investigator is simply to trace the tax records of the individual who has been paid fees/commission/expenses, or who has received investment income, and to check that they have fully declared all sources of income.

According to one senior Revenue official interviewed, although much information is already to hand within local offices, resources are insufficient to follow up more than a small selection of cases for investigation. Recent compliance initiatives are an attempt to utilize this available information, but such efforts only scratch the surface in terms of the numbers of investigations which *could* be undertaken, given increased staffing.

Examination of business returns, undertaken by Inspectors of Taxes, may also reveal potential avenues for investigation. For instance, in examining the accounts of medical practices locum fees are recorded: these may then be traced back to check if the recipient has declared them. The payment of 'ash cash' (discussed in Chapter 3) was revealed by examining returns of fees paid out by crematoria. Yet Inspectors of Taxes examine in depth only a small selection of traders' accounts (2.8 per cent of eligible accounts in 1984/5): in addition to discovering irregularities in a high proportion of the traders' accounts challenged (in 91 per cent of such cases in 1984/5), in-depth examination of accounts may also pave the way for a routine investigation of other individuals who may or may not be known to the Revenue. For instance, an Inspector may follow up details, provided in these accounts, of payments made to other traders or sub-contractors and thereafter can check that these third parties have made full declarations of income on their own tax returns.

Employers also have to complete end-of-year returns (P14) giving details of their employees' pay, tax and National Insurance. Also, a supplementary return (P38) must be completed for employees who are paid over £100 in the tax year, but who do not earn enough to pay PAYE tax (Inland Revenue P7 1983). This return in effect provides a list of staff who are employed on a casual basis or at wages less than the taxable minimum. If individuals earn less than taxable levels of income in respect of *one* particular source of employment, they may effectively undertake *several* part-time or casual jobs and still remain 'invisible' to the Revenue, with the exception of their appearance on returns P38. These 'ghosts' can in theory be traced through end-of-year employers' returns, although the chances of this are severely limited because of lack of staff to examine regularly and thoroughly this information, readily supplied to local tax offices. An infamous example of the employment of 'ghost' casual staff was revealed in the case of Fleet Street, where names such as 'Mickey Mouse' appeared on official employer returns (see Chapter 3). The institutionalized nature and sheer audacity of this particular fiddle are perhaps indicative of the Revenue's inability to cope with routine examination of information already to hand: clearly the Fleet Street printers who used the names of Disney characters felt confident that they were not likely to be discovered!

Making connections may also involve tracing the local agents of large firms who (in cases ranging from double glazing to football pools) pay on a commission basis and similarly provide lists of employees. Returns of commission thus provide another source of information, from within the tax office itself, which investigators may follow up. Once again the investigatory techniques involved in the tracing of agents resembles a paper chase: from information given in the firm's end-of-year returns to the tax records of the income-recipient. But the Inland Revenue is currently speeding-up the tracing process, through the computerization of the records of PAYE and Schedule D taxpayers, and in the development of a scheme of National Tracing using computers. In years to come the 'paper chase' may involve no 'paper' at all, and may well facilitate quick and efficient tracing of individuals receiving remuneration from whatever geographical or occupational source. In the mean time, the connections which are made are dependent upon the experience and expertise of the Tax Inspectors and compliance officers in local offices who utilize available information to best effect, given current constraints of resources and manpower.

Another potential investigatory route, using information supplied to the Revenue, involves the examination of expenses paid to directors and highly paid employees. As explained in Chapter 3, firms supply details of expenses paid out, which may be checked against the declarations of the individual employees concerned. Since 1982 regulations governing the taxation of expenses and allowances have been considerably tightened, particularly for the 'company car', a previously taken-for-granted 'perk' for many employees and directors. Also the use of financial penalties for false expenses claims has been extended. However, the Revenue still relies on the co-operation of *employers* to implement these regulations. But tax officers believe that many abuses, involving employers' connivance, remain: for instance, undeclared payments to employees for the types of expenses outlined in Chapter 3 – firm's cars (and private mileage), provision of private health care, entertainment allowances, membership of leisure and sporting clubs, gift vouchers and credit facilities and so on. It is likely that fiddles involving 'incentives' through gift vouchers, expensive holidays and entertainment are particularly evident at Christmas time. Firms may feel that they have to keep 'one step ahead of the taxman' in order to retain and motivate their most 'valuable' employees. Far more time and manpower would be necessary to examine expenses returns in depth and to reveal the nature and extent of such abuses: in the current political and ideological climate, in which success, competitiveness and profit maximization are so highly valued, it is difficult to see resources being directed towards regulating the 'perks' of the most 'successful' earners.

The Revenue's current compliance initiatives which stress cost-effectiveness therefore tend to concentrate on easier targets which offer greater pay-offs, in terms of tax recouped, for less investment, in terms of staff and time: thorough examination of employers' returns of expenses paid is very time-consuming. As already discussed, returns of fees, commission and casual employees are becoming increasingly easy to trace (with computerization and National Tracing) and so may offer the Revenue a means of identifying tax evaders such as moonlighters and, to a lesser extent, ghosts.

Ghosts are unknown to the Revenue and their detection often involves the targeting of the areas of trade in which, according to experience, they are most likely to be found. But a relatively easy technique which involves making connections entails the scrutiny of classified advertisements in the local press and then tracing the advertiser or trader to check if they are known to the Revenue. According to one senior Revenue official such advertisements are 'fair game', particularly for compliance officers who have a certain degree of operational freedom. This freedom has enabled a proactive approach to investigation work which was previously not characteristic of the Inland Revenue. It is to this proactive approach (involving in particular the targeting of likely areas of evasion) that discussion now turns.

Targeting occupations and locations

When analysing the techniques individuals use to fiddle tax, a strong link emerged between certain occupational groups and the availability of opportunities for tax evasion. The building, catering and seasonal trades, for instance, offered specific opportunity structures. Although tax evasion is a covert activity, these areas of particular abuse are identified through the experience and vigilance of tax officials. As a result, there is sufficient knowledge of existing areas of fraud upon which to estimate what the most productive areas for future investigation are likely to be. When the Revenue first set up Black Economy Units (or, in official terms, Schedule D Compliance Units) on an experimental basis in 1981, targeting was clearly evident: in addition to the focus on particular forms of evasion ('moonlighters and ghosts') the experiment concentrated staff 'in areas of the country thought ripe for action . . . such as holiday resorts and big cities' (*Assessment* November 1981).

Compliance units are now a key feature of Revenue investigatory work throughout the country, and the essential characteristics of the original experimental groups remain: the focus on moonlighting and ghosts utilizing methods which involve the targeting of particular trades or locations:

> We'll do a purge . . . concentrating on a single area to take note of all the commercial activity going on. Or we might decide to look specifically at particular trades or occupations.
>
> (Compliance officer, quoted in *Network* July 1985)

Caterers, video shops, street markets, auctions and taxi ranks are common targets. Officers also use their own initiative and local experience to set up investigations. A degree of operational freedom enables compliance officers to follow their own 'hunches', providing that they eventually prove fruitful: for instance, checking council planning applications (usually involving home extensions) for architects' signatures on plans and thereafter checking any non-declarations of fees on the individual's income tax return. Another proactive technique involves attending auctions (whether selling antiques, household goods or cars) and noting down the names of multiple purchasers suspected of being 'ghost' dealers. But whatever the target or the *modus operandi* of the investigation, the Revenue ensure that adequate evidence is gathered before interviewing suspected fraudsters:

> We get leads from a variety of sources. But we can't just go on hearsay. Unless the information is quite specific we need to back it up with our own enquiries. That could mean a visit for observation or a check with other sources. But it's only when we're pretty sure of our facts that we confront people.
>
> (ibid.)

'Leads' and 'information' are more likely to come from other Revenue staff in local offices who have come across irregularities in the course of their routine work than from anonymous tip-offs, which form such an important source of DHSS investigations. 'Other sources' against which compliance officers' information is checked do not normally involve formal links with other departments, except contact with the DHSS should the Revenue need to check an individual's National Insurance number. (Informally, however, there may be some utilization of the DVLC computer in checking car registrations.) Links with the police are *not* a regular feature of Revenue enquiries at local level, but the same cannot be said of DHSS investigations.

It may appear that there is an element of 'cloak and dagger' attached to some aspects of compliance work: for instance the use of surveillance and radio-links by some units. In addition the vocabulary associated with their activities envokes somewhat dramatic images: 'detectives...'. ghostbusters... leads... mission' (ibid.). This perhaps reflects the Inland Revenue's concern to project a more dynamic image of investigation work, and hence to deter fraud and encourage public compliance. But the proactive approach of compliance work is still a relatively new phenomenon in the Revenue, and has yet to assume its own language and mythology. In contrast to the well-known nicknames applied to DHSS investigators (snoopers, super-snoopers, nashies, and more recently, Dolebusters) a specific vocabulary has yet to emerge in relation to Revenue investigators: when one compliance officer was asked if any nickname or distinctive epithet was given to him and his fellow officers by the 'punters', he paused and then replied, 'They just call us "bastards"!'.

According to a senior Revenue official, the staff who are most likely to be chosen for compliance work are younger Tax Officers Higher Grade (TOs HG) who are likely promotion candidates: they are therefore likely to be ambitious, hard-working and well motivated. These characteristics, coupled with the identification of moonlighting and ghosting as the principal area for their investigations are products of the need (in view of departmental cost constraints) to utilize these 'lower'level staff in order to gain maximum financial benefit from investigation work. Therefore the primary rationale of the Revenue in relation to compliance units is to recoup the maximum tax due and to encourage 'compliance' in the most cost-effective manner. Personal 'targets' which officers are supposed to meet do play a part in maintaining this effectiveness: compliance units are under an obligation to pay for themselves. But this does not present any problems, simply because of the scale of tax evasion itself – there is always plenty of abuse which can relatively easily be discovered by the techniques outlined above.

Specialist investigations

The work of certain specialist investigation units will be mentioned only briefly here because their role is too specialized to affect the many individuals, traders and small businessman who form the focus of this study. The specialist units which are most directly relevant here are the Board's Investigation Office (BIO) and Enquiry Branch: this analysis will therefore concentrate primarily on their investigatory techniques.

The BIO are regarded as the Board's police in the sense that the offences that they investigate come closest to what could be termed 'crimes' in the conventional sense. As mentioned above, their primary focus is the construction industry and frauds associated with sub-contractor certificates 714. Many of these frauds involve forgery, falsification, selling and theft of these certificates, hence the link between BIO techniques used to combat these forms of fraud and 'police' methods. Prosecutions brought as a result of BIO investigations usually involve charges for theft, forgery, handling, deception or conspiracy (*Network* January 1986). Techniques of investigation include elements of 'undercover' work such as surveillance of suspects (using cameras and radios), long and irregular hours of work, and contact with other investigative agencies, such as Customs and Excise (ibid.). Suspects are observed (often literally 'on site'), their activities monitored and visual and documentary evidence is collected. Although the cloak-and-dagger image may seem to fit such activities, it must be remembered that most sub-contractor investigations are focused on the seedy 'mean streets' of labourers' doss houses and hostels (ibid: 5).

Cases may be referred to the BIO by the PAYE Audit section and local tax district offices, but most cases arise from within the unit itself following the routine examination of certificates and 714 vouchers forwarded to a Certificate Centre. Although this specialist unit investigates only around

700 sub-contractor frauds per year, the sums of tax involved are huge: the tax known to have been evaded on cases dealt with in the year to 30 September 1985 was £35 million (ibid.).

Other areas of fraud dealt with by BIO include false claims to allowances and expenses, and deed of covenant frauds. In the case of the former, cases regarded with suspicion (because of amendments to invoices, for instance) are referred to the BIO from local offices. Similarly if local officers suspect a 'ring' of deeds of covenant, the BIO may become involved. These frauds are likely to involve solicitors and accountants who claim tax relief on 'manufactured' covenants to each other's dependents (see Chapter 3). Losses in tax can be considerable: hence, perhaps, the abolition of all but charitable deeds of covenant announced in the 1988 Budget.

The BIO, none the less, represent a unit set up to deal with a particular form of tax fraud, related to one key industry – construction. Administrative and legislative changes in the last decade have sought to counter tax evasion in the construction industry through the use of 714 certificates (with photographs of the holder as an added safeguard) and a system of vouchers which the sub-contractor presents to the main contractor. None the less, the entire 714 system is circumvented if main contractors themselves connive to employ 'subbies' who have no 714 (and are not therefore bona-fide sub-contractors). Main contractors may collude in this way in order to pay 'lump' subbies less than bona-fide contractors rates, and so cut costs. One large contractor explained to me that this practice was commonplace and that 'you have to' fiddle in this way 'to keep in business'. Ultimately the only techniques which could be employed to counter such frauds would involve far greater manpower, surveillance and higher profile policing of the construction industry than the BIO are capable of, and than would be considered politically acceptable.

Enquiry Branch specializes in the investigation of business accounts and also any irregularities concerning the work of professional tax advisers. Their regulatory techniques involve lower profile activities than those of many compliance and BIO officers: essentially what is involved is the in-depth examination of trading accounts by highly qualified staff:

> [Enquiry Branch] specialises in the investigation of fraud involving trading profits, work demanding a detailed knowledge of book-keeping and accountancy as well as a full technical knowledge of income tax.
> (Cmnd 8822 1983: 9.10.2)

It is extremely difficult to identify specific techniques used in such a technical area of investigation. In brief, although the examination of business records is a complex process, Enquiry Branch officers seek to identify and pursue suspected irregularities in business accounts: for instance, their initial enquiries may include looking through invoices for 'dummies' or alterations, looking for 'dummy employees' in records of wages paid out, checking directors' expenses accounts and checking the numerical sequence of invoices for missing numbers. Most referrals to Enquiry Branch come from district offices who have reason to believe one of the following: that profits in excess of £50,000 are understated *HC123* 1985), that forgery or collusion with intent to defraud the Revenue has taken place, or that false statements of 'full disclosure' have been made by a taxpayer who has been under investigation (*Cmnd 8822* 1983: 9.11). Cases arising from 'Informers' number only 14 to 15 per year on average.

The difficulties involved when attempting to analyse Enquiry Branch techniques reflect the difficulties which the investigators themselves face in their task: as one witness to the Keith Committee put it,

> the taxpayer builds a taxproof castle; if the Inspector could see inside it he would see the weaknesses in the castle's structure, but the taxpayer does all he can to make sure that the Inspector never sees inside it.
>
> (ibid: 7.3.5)

If accounts do reveal serious irregularities, Enquiry Branch officers interview the suspect 'by appointment in the presence of the taxpayer's advisers' (ibid: 9.13.3). The taxpayer (and advisers) initial a verbatim copy of all questions and answers as the interview proceeds, and receive a copy at the end. These interview techniques and respect accorded to the taxpayer's rights contrast sharply with the treatment of suspected supplementary benefit fraudsters at the DHSS interviews described below.

Summary

Cost-effectiveness and pragmatism are the *apparent* rationales which underlie Revenue investigation policy, but the *effective* rationale is, rather, a desire to seek the *compliance* of the taxpayer (see Table 5, p. 144). Therefore, in effect Revenue policy implicitly acknowledges the primacy of the coercive view of personal taxation and, ultimately, enables empathy for the tax evader. This is evident in the view expressed by a former Enquiry Branch officer who described the Revenue's financial settlement policy as 'The only sensible way to carry on' because 'after all, we have all sinned!' (ITV *World in Action* 7.2.83). It is also evident in the emphasis on financial settlement which characterizes most Revenue investigations, whether conducted in local offices or by specialist units.

The analysis of enforcement policy and practice has shown that official discourses which centre on cost-effectiveness and the pragmatism of tax collection are problematic. For example, cost-effectiveness does not result if (as under current policies) insufficient staff and resources are directed to counter-evasion work, and so vast amounts of tax remain unpaid. At the same time, the counter-evasion initiatives which have been undertaken in recent years have centred upon relatively 'easy' targets which demand the least time and money to investigate. Thus the richer pickings which are available through the investigation of highly paid taxpayers, directors and trading accounts are largely ignored in favour of the type of investigations which are quick (and cheap) to undertake, with fewer lower-level staff. In the longer term cost-effectiveness is not served by such policies. Furthermore, the emphasis on cost-effectiveness may be open to serious criticism on the grounds that *equity* as well as efficiency should be a principle underpinning the work of any enforcing department.

The dominance of 'pragmatism' in the justificatory rhetoric of policy-makers is also more apparent than real: beneath this justification is, once again, the desire to 'spare the taxpayers' feelings'. Although, it could be argued, there are indeed practical difficulties in mounting successful Revenue prosecutions, these practical difficulties cannot alone explain a policy which advocates financial penalty in all but a *very few* of the 'most serious' of fraud cases, while around twenty times as many individuals are likely to be prosecuted for supplementary benefit fraud, despite the DHSS's *non-prosecution* policy (see Chapter 7)! The effective discourse shaping such policy therefore reflects the coercive view of tax – as an intolerable inquisition – and so implictly reflects the ideology of the free market rather than social justice (see Table 5).

Nevertheless, the notion of citizenship may still be invoked (even at a time of New Right ideological dominance) in order to maintain the integrity and legitimacy of the tax system: hence the Thatcher government, though committed to New Right free market economic policies, must implicitly invoke the citizenship view of personal taxation when launching compliance initiatives. Moreover those initiatives are (even for those who see tax as an 'intolerable inquisition') necessary: first, to maintain the legitimacy of the Revenue as an equitable enforcing department and, second, to collect additional revenue which is essential (even for a minimalist) state in a time of economic stringency. It is misleading, therefore, to see 'the state' as immutable or monolithic: its policies are moulded by specific material conditions under which it may be possible to invoke entirely contradictory discourses, particularly concerning the twin issues of taxation and welfare. It is from such contradictions that differential responses to tax and benefit fraud are both produced and justified (see Chapter 8).

6

Supplementary Benefit Investigations

Enforcement policy

The formal criteria which appear to govern DHSS policy are similar to those of the Inland Revenue: the safeguarding of public funds while assuring the rights of the individual. However, as NACRO has indicated, inherent tensions surface when these principles are applied in practice:

> there is an unavoidable tension between the Department's first duty - prompt payment of benefit and relief of need with due consideration for people's dignity and welfare - and the highly important but secondary function of combatting fraud and abuse.
>
> (NACRO 1986: 16)

While policy statements apparently emphasize the importance of efficient payment of benefits for the relief of need, effective DHSS practices involve rigorous testing by the DHSS to establish an individual's 'need', rather than the payment of benefits as of 'right'. The concept of rights may be subverted by policies which concentrate on *prevention* of abuse rather than on the efficient and courteous delivery of an individual's benefit *entitlement*.

The tension between the department's first *duty* and its secondary *function* (identified by NACRO) has been exacerbated in recent years by certain changes in policy. Prior to 1980 it had been recognized that

> the first defence against fraud and abuse is a good standard of investigation and interviewing by officers dealing with ordinary claims on the counter and by home visits ... prompt and humane attention to individual needs.
>
> (DHSS 1979: 10.43)

Since then, though ministerial assurances have asserted that good standards of service to claimants are being maintained, Civil Service trades unions have voiced considerable disquiet over policy shifts which, since 1980, have focused increasingly on the DHSS's enforcement role at the expense of its primary role of ensuring that individuals receive the state benefits to which they are entitled under the law. For instance, reductions in the home-visiting of claimants, administrative changes in the handling of claims, staff cut-backs and new anti-fraud measures were all implemented with the official justification of 'efficiency', but all too have resulted in a deterioration in service to, and relations with, claimants.

These policies are the product of certain material and political preconditions. Political priorities have, in the 1980s, been geared to monitoring and controlling public expenditure. Despite the fact that the civil service is not an industry, outside industrial and commercial advisers (such as Sir Derek Rayner) were brought in to create a more 'efficient' service. Although the profit motive was not directly applicable, the notion of 'financial management' was substituted: from 1982 local DHSS office managers were delegated responsibility for setting objectives and promoting incentives to ensure that their budgets were not exceeded (McKnight 1985). But, as argued by McKnight, a senior official for the Society of Civil and Public Servants (SCPS), the work of the DHSS cannot be measured simply in quantitative terms: 'The quality of work and the level of service to claimants must also be considered' (ibid: 32). Economies in purely cash terms may have detrimental effects, as indicated to the Public Accounts Committee, who were told in December 1986 of a series of 'prizes' paid to local office staff who introduced economies:

> An office prize of £35 was given to the DHSS Hornchurch office for the idea of employing part-time cleaners rather than full-time staff, to save National Insurance contributions and meals allowances even though the public lavatories were not cleaned during the day.
>
> (*Guardian* 2.12.86)

Although only a seemingly minor example, the cumulative effect of such cut-backs may have more far-reaching effects on claimants and office staff who are caught up in a vicious circle of tension caused by staff cuts, high arrears of work and consequently increasing numbers of office callers: as one DHSS officer commented,

> DHSS public waiting rooms have absorbed the anger, frustration and despair of claimants long enough for us to know that any peace in such places is at best fragile. . . . Irregular incidents of people urinating, vomiting or even defecating in the waiting room can also add to the standard discomforts endured during the wait.
>
> (Mandla 1987: 14)

The 'wait' involved in many offices runs to several hours. In the south London (Oval) office, described by Mandla, claimants begin to queue outside the office at 8.00 am and 'at 9.30 am the first 150 are granted access and the remainder are turned away' despite the fact that the DHSS is officially meant to provide six hours of public service every day (ibid.). Inevitably anger and frustration spill over in the form of violence: attacks on DHSS staff are on the increase, largely as the result of the 'squeeze' on claimants brought about by staffing cuts rather than because of any demonstrable change in the nature of the claimants themselves (Coetzee 1983; Mandla 1987). According to one DHSS official I interviewed the increasing number of assaults on staff is bound up with several recent policy changes: he argued that fewer home visits to claimants had led to more mistakes being made by the staff who calculated their benefits. In turn, these mistakes (and the consequent disruption to benefit payments while correction takes place) led to desperation on the part of claimants and to soured, hostile relations with DHSS staff. This argument is supported by the evidence of independent surveys on the quality of service provided to DHSS claimants (Ward 1985a; PSI 1985) by statistics demonstrating increases in the error rates of the DHSS (Beltram 1984a; NAO 1987) and by evidence provided by DHSS staff trade unions: for instance, a SCPS representative stated that an audit in the Swansea area had shown 'that 60% of payments made to people in urgent need were wrongly calculated because staff were under such pressure' (*Guardian* 12.11.86). Another representative graphically illustrated the consequences of staff cuts on claimants and staff alike in an inner London office:

> People queue outside from first thing in the morning. . . . Sometimes they wait up to eight hours, and then their papers might be missing. Management have created a state of siege following violent incidents and there has been a 50% staff turnover in the past year.
>
> (ibid.).

Accounts such as this demonstrate the tension between the DHSS's two functions in practical terms. The primary function of ensuring an individual's rights to benefit while according him or her due respect does seem to have been rendered impossible in the face of policies aimed at cost-cutting. But while staffing at local offices has been squeezed, additional staff have been made available for the department's (secondary) function: the prevention of fraud and abuse. Two examples serve to illustrate the severe problems, for local staff and claimants alike, which such contradictions can create: first, the collapse of the administration of social security payments in Birmingham during 1982–3. Second, the situation in Oxford DHSS offices in 1982.

In Birmingham economic collapse had put enormous stress upon local DHSS offices as 27,702 additional supplementary benefit claims were made in one twelve-month period leading up to the crisis of September 1982 (Coetzee 1983). But this increase in workload had been accompanied by reductions in staffing: in Handsworth, for instance, the number of claimants had increased (over three years) from 18,160 to 20,362 while staff had decreased from 244 to 199 during the same period (ibid: 17). By September 1982 the Erdington office 'looked as if it had been struck by a tornado': storage space for case-papers ran out and files were stored in cardboard boxes or piled up on the floor, 1,500 pieces of post were outstanding and hundreds of callers (either by telephone or in person) were complaining of delayed benefit payments. Coetzee explained the sequence of events which finally led to the strike which closed the office for eight months:

> Two of the three receptionists telephoned in sick. The third went to open the office up and found about 80 people lined up outside. She...burst into tears. Three other staff were drafted in from other parts of the office to run the public counter. In the domino effect this creates...three desks were left unattended.

> (ibid: 22)

Inevitably empty desks meant yet more delay in dealing with outstanding claims, phone calls and post. This domino effect thus contributes to a worsening of relations between staff and claimants in which feelings of anger, mistrust and degradation are rife. But staff and claimants were, and still are, victims of a government policy which has stressed departmental economies at the expense, literally, of service to claimants. In the Birmingham example it is significant that the emergency centres which were set up to administer urgent payments during this dispute were staffed, in part, by officers of the anti-fraud Special Claims Control (SCC) Unit. Political concern to counter fraud and abuse had overriden cost concerns, as this area of work was expanded at a time of acute cuts in overall staffing. At the same time the DHSS's apparent policy aim (of ensuring prompt payment of benefits to those entitled to them by right) was subverted by the latent policy goal of cutting government expenditure, whether by a crude 'welfare rationing' in overworked offices, or by effectively deterring claims to benefit through the department's emphasis on anti-fraud work.

A situation of stress and frustration similar to that described in Birmingham offices came to light in Oxford in the same year, as economic recession and hence increasing numbers of claims coincided with effective reductions in local office staff. The Oxford DHSS office was staffed in accordance with a notional 'live caseload' of 12,742 claimants. By August 1982 the actual caseload had risen to 19,113, 'Yet because of a shift to fraud and investigation work, the number of staff actually dealing with benefits [had been] reduced' (Franey 1983: 72). This imbalance became all the more evident as the anti-fraud swoop 'Operation Major' was mounted in September 1982 (jointly) by the DHSS and the Thames Valley Serious Crimes Squad. It involved operational costs estimated at £180,546, not including the costs of the 175 prosecutions which resulted (ibid: 25). Local DHSS staff union officials repeated the view of local fraud officers that

> Had the office been adequately staffed, both in their own section and in visiting and on interviewing time, then we would have coped with the problem without the need for any exercise or operation.
>
> (BBC *Grapevine* 1983: 7)

Therefore in both Birmingham and Oxford the government's official policy of promoting efficiency, cash limits and cost-cutting had been used to justify staff reductions in routine local office work. At the same time certain political, economic and ideological preconditions promoted the effective contradiction of those policies through the increased expenditure on anti-fraud initiatives. As already argued, the New Right ideology which interprets taxpayers as victims of coercive state regulation views many recipients of state welfare benefits as cossetted by a state which denies them incentives to effort and self-motivation (Boyson 1978: Parker 1982; Levitas 1986). But the practical application of such ideas has given rise to a far greater degree of intrusion by the state into the lives of citizens on welfare than previously: for example, through a series of complex work-tests for unemployed claimants, compulsory training schemes for young people and the randomized policing of lone mothers by SCC Units (see below). Such state control over the lives of the poor contrasts starkly with the state's efforts to de-regulate the lives of the rich – particularly of employers, whether large firms or small businessmen. Once again it may be argued that it is from the operation of politically based contradictions such as these that differential response to tax and benefit derives.

Further contradictions between apparent (official) policy rationales and their effective results in practice are evident when analysing other administrative and procedural changes introduced with the *apparent* aim of reducing costs and promoting departmental efficiency: for instance, reductions in home visiting and the consequent widening of the system of postal claiming. Official rationales were again belied by the practical consequences of these policies. For instance, while reductions in home visiting were ostensibly geared to greater 'cost-effectiveness', DHSS staff argued that the lessening of direct contact with claimants led to more departmental errors and to more abuse. Similarly the postal claim form (initially dubbed 'the purple peril') may have led to incorrect payments of benefit, either as a result of claimants' errors in completing the form itself, or from the increased opportunities for fiddling in a system where postal (not personal) contact is the norm. It can also be argued that postal claiming presents difficulties for some groups of claimants and may either deter them from claiming altogether, or prevent them from obtaining the full benefits to which they are entitled. This may be a particularly pertinent argument in the case of elderly claimants and those from ethnic minorities

(Beltram 1984a); it also raises the issue of possible 'welfare rationing' and invites a negative evaluation of the DHSS's ability to perform its first function – to ensure that individuals receive the full benefits to which they are entitled under the law.

In political circles the under-claiming of benefits can be regarded as tolerable, and even acceptable, for two sets of reasons: because first low take-up is seen to reflect a (laudable) reluctance on the part of citizens to rely upon state benefits. Second, because the social security system could not cope if all citizens *did* claim all the benefits to which they were entitled (Donnison 1982). The Institute of Directors reflects these views:

> Some think these low take-up rates a weakness of the present system; we think them a strength. First, a low take-up saves large amounts of Government spending. Second, it is in substantial measure the result of self-selection amongst potential users of the welfare system . . . some people are reluctant to accept such payments . . . for reasons of self-respect. We see nothing wrong in this sentiment and many would consider it admirable.
>
> (NCASSC 1985: 2)

Government's ambivalence to improving benefit take-up can be regarded by some as a pragmatic response to burgeoning public expenditure on social security and the desire to promote an unwillingness to rely on state welfare. This may ultimately lead to a situation in which 'entitlement' to benefit means little and governments effectively ration welfare benefit payments at their source:

> [The government] never seems sure how many claimants it *wants* to get what they're entitled to. A recent example in the system of single payments for one-off expensive items like cookers and beds. They were going to a tiny minority of the clients eligible. Last year, welfare rights campaigns . . . led to a huge increase in claims. The government's response was to tighten up the regulations.
>
> (Laurance 1987: 23)

In April 1988 these single payments were abolished in favour of *loans* from the finite 'Social Fund'.

As mentioned above, no equivalent to the Taxpayers' Charter exists for supplementary benefit claimants. The regulations governing the payment of welfare benefits are extremely complex, yet the DHSS seems to believe that its responsibility is simply to *pay* benefits and not to advise people to claim them: according to a leaked memorandum, the DHSS attempted to 'postpone or change' a Channel 4 television campaign advertising welfare benefits (planned for February 1987), because it would involve too much extra work for DHSS offices (*Guardian* 28.2.87). As Laurance notes, attempts to encourage claimants to obtain their full rights are met with hostility: the work of the 'benefit shops' and advice centres who advised claimants to request exceptional needs payments was described by Conservative MP's as 'total abuse' and furthermore 'the taxpayer is being ripped off by this gross abuse of the system' (*Hansard* 21.7.86: cols 22 and 24). Vitriolic attacks like this are rarely made upon accountants and tax advisers who seek to maximize financial benefits for their clients. Yet, as Laurance notes,

> Helping people get what they are entitled to is not equivalent to advising the well-off on tax avoidance. It is not a matter of maximising income but of making survival possible.

> (Laurance 1987: 23)

Unfortunately it seems that only lip service is paid to the policy of ensuring claimants' full rights. Although glossy TV adverts and free telephone help-lines heralded the birth of Income Support in April 1988, a bewildering lack of hard information on the 'simplified' new scheme generated confusion and anxiety for claimants and DHSS staff alike (*Welfare Rights* June 1988).

If information itself confers power, then the taxpayer has far more power than the supplementary benefit claimant. This inequality is accentuated where taxpayer and claimant are accused of fiddling, as will be evident when examining DHSS investigatory techniques. Moreover, lack of knowledge on the part of benefit claimants may be seen as essential in order to render an increasingly unworkable system workable. Lack of knowledge (or reluctance) to claim welfare benefits can also be seen as the result of the effectiveness of certain political ideologies: notions of the 'undeserving poor', the cosseting welfare state and the 'scrounger' mythology inevitably have an adverse affect on benefit take-up (Golding and Middleton 1982; Smith 1985).

In 1983/4 supplementary benefit unclaimed was estimated at £570 million (*Welfare Rights* June 1988). The extent to which politicians actively foster such benefit losses to citizens (and gains for the treasury) is debatable. But what is more significant for the purposes of this study is the relative dominance of the issue of fraud and abuse on the public and political agenda, over the 'hidden' issue of the amounts of unclaimed welfare benefits which far exceed all estimates of fraud losses. The material and ideological conditions enabling the effective displacement of the DHSS's primary function of ensuring the individual's rights and welfare (NACRO 1986) have already been outlined in Chapter 1. The DHSS's function can, alternatively, be seen as 'protecting the public purse' through the rigorous testing of means and policing of claimants, and through cutting costs in the administration of the benefit system itself. These *operative* rationales underlying DHSS policy (particularly since the abolition of the Supplementary Benefits Commission in 1980) are also revealed through an analysis of the organization and practice of supplementary benefit fraud investigations.

Regulation

The scale of the enforcement task facing the DHSS is far from clear. Estimates of the extent of supplementary benefit fraud show extreme disparities: for instance, in 1980 a DHSS official estimated such fraud at £15 million pa (CPAG 1982), but an 'economic adviser' to the Public Accounts Committee in 1983 estimated supplementary benefit fraud losses at £500 million pa (*HC 102* 1983). However, a senior DHSS official noted that this figure was not a true 'estimate' but

> just a statement that if 10% of those receiving benefit were not entitled to it, that would cost about £500 million... these are all hypotheses and assumptions.
>
> (ibid: 1780)

Estimates of fraud therefore vary in accordance with certain political conditions and the DHSS policy rationales which result from them. If ideological conditions favour the 'scrounger' mythology and/or the dominance of New Right critiques of the Welfare State, then counter-fraud measures must be justified in terms of the ubiquity of fiddling amongst the idle poor. Under such circumstances estimates of the scale of benefit fraud increase dramatically, and so counter-measures are justified. In this way anti-fraud drives can be seen as effective products of political 'campaigns' based on anti-collectivist ideologies, rather than as reactions to any objective change in the amount of fiddling taking place.

Regulation of supplementary benefit fraud is therefore organized and executed in accordance with political priorities. As already seen, the same is true of the regulation of tax fraud, although the practical consequences of those political priorities are very different. The regulation of benefit fraud is currently dominated by a liberal conception of the role of the state and by an individualist (self-helping, 'on your bike') philosophy; the principles of social justice, collectivism and the concepts of universal 'rights' to benefit are not invoked. By contrast 'rights' figure strongly in the *Taxpayers' Charter* and in the practice of tax investigations. At the same time the philosophy of state de-regulation, individualism (self-helping, wealth-accumulating) and the free-market serves to justify the actions of taxpayers who seek to maximize their income, whether by avoidance or evasion of taxes.

Against the background of these political and ideological rationales must be set the material realities of investigatory practice: first, in terms of departmental organization and second, in terms of regulatory techniques used.

Investigation of supplementary benefit fraud is organized at both regional and local office level and involves three type of officers:

1 *Fraud Officers (FOs)*, who are based at local offices
2 *Special Investigators (SIs)*, who have a greater degree of operational freedom, but still work in conjunction with local FO's.

3 *Special Claims Control Units (SCCUs)*, which from 1980 to 1986 operated from regional offices and selected local offices for anti-fraud drives.

The DHSS has 451 local offices (grouped in seven regions) which deal with the payment of supplementary benefit. Most offices have one or more specialist FOs among the staff: in 1984/5 they totalled 1,512 officers, and SIs numbered 564 in addition (NACRO 1986).

1 *Fraud Officers* are responsible for vetting cases of suspected fraud referred to them by other local office staff. Suspicions can arise in a number of ways: from a 'fraud awareness report' or 'signs of affluence' recorded by visiting officers, most frequently from anonymous tip-offs and letters from the public, or possibly from a 'hunch' on the part of visiting or fraud officers that a claimant is 'suspicious'.

2 *Special Investigators* are responsible for investigating cases (often referred to them by FOs), where further evidence is needed in order to establish if there is a prima facie case of fraud. This may entail working outside normal office hours and travelling beyond the local office area. (To this extent SIs have greater operational freedom than FOs.)

3 *Special Claims Control Units* SCCU's were set up on an experimental basis in one region in the late 1970s and their anti-fraud activities were extended to cover the rest of Britain by 1981. By 1984/5 there were around 112 officers working from regional offices organized in teams of six (ibid: 43). Teams selected certain offices within their region for anti-fraud drives, or 'swoops' according to local office staff. The techniques SCC squads used in order to maximize 'savings' of benefit came under intense criticism (to be discussed in depth below), and when further increases in anti-fraud staff were announced in May 1986 'new' Regional Benefit Fraud Teams were set up to replace SCCUs. But, significantly, the other innovation – 180 staff attached to inner city offices where board-and-lodging claims are common – is unofficially referred to as 'Board and Lodge SCC' despite DHSS assertions that SCC techniques ceased in June 1986 (ibid: 44; OVS 1986).

It is difficult to assess the effectiveness of the DHSS's anti-fraud efforts because of the lack of systematic, comprehensive and reliable annual statistics. Since the abolition of the Supplementary Benefit Commission in 1980 there has been no form of annual report published which enables an assessment of the performance of departmental investigators or an accurate assessment of yields (in terms of actual benefits saved) from investigatory work. The statistics that have been analysed in the course of this research – from parliamentary, departmental and anonymous official sources – indicate more about political and departmental policy priorities than about specific yields in cash terms. As I have already pointed out, there is correlation between the size of estimates of the scale of benefit fraud and the political and ideological preconditions under which department policy is formulated. Similarly there is a 'knock-on' effect caused by spiralling estimates of the scale of fraud, the political energy then directed towards detecting more fraud, and the consequent need to demonstrate the effectiveness of anti-fraud policies by ever-increasing claims of success through investigation 'yields' netted. The end result is an inevitable (and tautologous) justification of the political and policy stance which was taken in the first place!

This circular rationale can be demonstrated in two ways: first, by seeking out and detecting more fraud, the DHSS are seen as 'saving' money otherwise paid out in benefits to the undeserving. Second, inflated figures of benefit savings can thereafter justify *further* fraud drives (and the negative attitudes towards benefit claimants which result) on the grounds that there is more fraud yet to be discovered. So the ideology of the undeserving 'scrounging' poor and the wasteful Welfare State is both justified and regenerated through policies which concentrate on the issue of benefit fraud.

The problems involved in assessing the alleged yields from DHSS investigation work are revealed in the following analysis of various types of investigation work: confidential documents indicated the following differences between the yields (per man-year) of FOs, SIs and SCC officers respectively for the year 1983/4:

FO – £39,000   SI – £103,000   SCC – £128,000

These figures were based upon the use of 'multipliers' which estimate how many weeks a fraudulent claim would have been likely to have persisted, and multiply weekly benefit payments by that number to arrive at a figure of how much benefit has been 'saved' as a result of investigatory efforts. In these yield figures a 52-week multiplier had been used, despite the fact that many claimants may well have re-claimed benefit only a few weeks after the completion of a fraud investigation. To assume that a full year's benefit had been saved is therefore misleading. The use of 52-week multipliers came under a great deal of criticism: a SCPS union official indicated the possible misuse of such figures

> Undoubtedly, far more people are being chased off the books for three or four weeks at a time. . . . The government then multiplies the saving and is kidding itself that it is on target in its fraud drive.
>
> (*The Times* 4.8.80)

But the dissemination of such figures (through government publicity) may, more importantly, 'kid' the public by persuading them of the necessity for such drives and reinforcing the circle of justification discussed above.

The DHSS eventually acknowledged the validity of some of the criticisms made of 52-week multipliers and, in 1984/5, researched the alternatives. The multipliers used thereafter varied according to the type of investigator dealing with the case, and this in turn reflected different categories of fraudster dealt with by FOs, SIs and SCC respectively. The 'yields' per man-year calculated thereafter presented a very different picture, as reduced multipliers were used: and so for the year 1983/4 quoted above, the revised figure yielded by FOs would be £25,000 (down £14,000), the figure for SIs would be £64,000 (down £39,000) and, most significantly, the figure for SCC would be reduced from £128,000 to £54,000. Clearly the use of misleading figures of benefit savings in the early years of the Thatcher government may have given the impression that detected benefit fraud was a more costly problem than, in measurable terms, it was. In addition the impression was given that anti-fraud efforts were more effective than, in measurable terms, they were. In summary, the anti-fraud policy adopted from 1979 was sustained and justified, in theory and in practice, by several misleading assumptions about the organization and efficiency of fraud investigations.

In the case of detected tax evasion, the yields quoted in the Boards' Annual Report represent actual figures of tax calculated as unpaid and found to be recoverable from the taxpayer as the result of investigatory work. This is in stark comparison to the situation in relation to benefit fraud where the *actual* figures of overpayments (due to fraud), recoverable as a result of investigations, are not available. Instead the DHSS has, since 1979, concentrated on demonstrating 'benefit savings' in order to prove the alleged merits of a 'cost-effective' approach to the investigation of fraud. The political principles advocated by this New Right administration were therefore realized in practice through the operational policies of two key enforcing departments – the Inland Revenue and the DHSS. These principles are discernible in an accentuation of the disparities in the political and practical responses towards tax and welfare fraud in recent years. It is to the practice of regulating the latter that this analysis now turns.

Techniques of regulation

There is considerable overlap in the techniques used by the three types of investigators referred to above: for instance, all use some form of targeting and respond to anonymous tip-offs. The analysis which follows will therefore initially deal with the techniques common to most investigators and thereafter will concentrate on how these techniques are both amplified and modified in the case of SCC work and intensive fraud drives.

Targeting: occupations and claimant types

The most common type of supplementary benefit fraud is failure to declare earnings and certain occupations have been identified as particularly likely to attract claimants who seek to fiddle by this means. Jobs involving part-time, casualized, seasonal and low-paid work are particularly open to claimants: their work status is vulnerable because work is itself covert, and they are more likely to settle for inferior pay and work conditions because wages are an (illegal) addition to benefits: they are in no position to bargain.

There is a common-sense knowledge amongst DHSS investigators of employers in their locality who are most prone to recruiting such a disadvantaged work-force: contract cleaning firms have been mentioned as possible employers of claimants, in view of the casualized, low-paid, part-time characteristics of the work. Similarly in agricultural areas farms may well employ claimants for short-term seasonal work: for instance, fruit and vegetable picking or potato harvesting. In seaside areas the catering and holiday trades may provide similar casual work opportunities and throughout the country the construction industry (discussed above in relation to tax evasion) offers opportunities for casual or temporary site labouring work. As a result of this knowledge investigators can target particular employers operating in their area, visit their premises and review lists of part-time and casual employees, later checking them against records of claimants' names. If claimants are found to have received wages they are called to attend for interview by fraud officers and asked to give a signed statement of their circumstances, revealing all income.

The co-operation of employers with investigation staff cannot be guaranteed, but information on employees is usually forthcoming. Co-operation is all the more probable if the employer has colluded with claimants' fiddles: a collusive employer (who has, for instance, suggested that claimants use false names to avoid detection) is hardly likely to refuse DHSS staff access and risk 'rocking the boat' still further. One claimant who did casual work on a farm told me that the farmer did not want to 'grass' on him, but felt there was no alternative because the DHSS 'were on to him anyway'. The techniques involved in routinely targeting key employers (inspecting their employee records and linking this information with claimant records at the local office) are therefore both simple and effective.

A description of life in the Durham coalfields showed an alternative view of the 'targeting' of probable areas of abuse. The author described the way in which dozens of unemployed men were to be seen collecting seacoal along the despoiled Durham beaches. This coal could then be sold for £2 to £3 a bag, providing an important source of income for the families of the men who collected it. According to one such man the 'dolies' or 'nashies' (the latter euphemism for the DHSS investigators being a throwback to the days of the National Assistance Board) lay in wait observing those who collected the coal. The author wryly concluded:

> If the dolies can prove this seacoal is being sold ... they can stop benefits and haul the beachcombers into court. A triumph for the hard-working taxpayer over the shiftless, work-shy scrounger.... If several hundred residents of

Brighton spent 12 hours a day bent double in the surf-garnering what amounts to waste-in order to keep their families in decent rather than indecent poverty, the scandal would not be tolerated.

(Chesshyre in *Observer* 6.9.87)

Clearly it is a matter of political values whether the 'scandal' here is to be defined as the supplementary benefit fraud itself, or the material conditions which generate the necessity for it.

Once certain jobs or locations have been targeted by investigators, then techniques of surveillance and identification may also come into play. In the Durham example, the individuals scavenging for coal would have to be identified and their movements traced in order to prove that a financial gain had been made by selling the coal. Special Investigators have operational scope for following claimants by car and for working out of office hours, but mistakes can arise. For instance, a self-employed builder whom I interviewed was followed to work by DHSS investigators, to a site several miles from his home, having been wrongly identified as a supplementary benefit claimant. Similarly a DHSS official told me of a lengthy surveillance operation on casual forestry workers: after a three-day surveillance of four workers (from a car, at a distance, from dawn to dusk) the suspects eventually turned to confront the investigators. It was then discovered that the identities of the men had been mistaken and that they were not claiming benefit.

Targeting can also be applied to certain categories of claimants, who are regarded as being more prone to fraud than 'deserving' elderly, sick and handicapped people. Historically, lone and deserted mothers have always been considered likely targets for investigation because, as explained in Chapter 4, the supplementary benefit payment system assumes an ideal-type nuclear family as the principal 'assessment unit', and as a result lone mothers are regarded as 'between men' rather than as alternative heads of families. Consequently DHSS investigators (and routine visiting officers in the past) were instructed to look for visible signs of a male presence (such as clothing, shoes) at the homes of lone mothers who were claiming benefit. If a man was thought to be living there (as 'husband') then, according to the DHSS, he should assume the role of head of the household and financially support the women and children within it. The effective rationales behind such administrative practice are the assumptions that:

1 Lone mothers are potential fraudsters because of their lack of marital status and lack of economic dependence upon a male.
2 That the status of lone motherhood is transient until the woman finds another man to support herself and her children.
3 That a man's emotional and sexual relationship with a female supplementary benefit claimant should be accompanied by an economic relationship.

(Cook 1987)

It is significant, then, that a mother who fails to take proceedings against a 'liable relative', or whose liable relative has disappeared, may be considered as a possible case for a fraud investigation (OWS 1985). Targeting in such instances is a reflection of broader ideological principles concerning the perceived value of the ideal-type nuclear family, the dominance of the housewife-mother role as the ideal one for women, (providing, of course, that the Welfare State is not subsidizing such a role!), and the evils of dependence on state benefits.

The extent to which this form of targeting is gender-specific is revealed in the following description of the treatment by a visiting officer of a 'cohabiting' male claimant, a post-graduate student living in Oxford:

> The visiting officer found him living in a room which was almost entirely filled by a double bed. The garments and cosmetics scattered about made it clear that the room was shared – by a girl working as a secretary, he explained. But they were not living as husband and wife. They were only together for this term: after that – who knows? The DHSS did not cut off his benefit, deciding that this was not what most people meant by a husband and wife relationship. Not in Oxford anyway. 'And besides', said the visiting officer, 'how do you argue with a man who's studying to be a doctor of philosophy?'
>
> (Donnison 1982: 108)

Not only was the claimant in this case male, but also he was confident, articulate and middle class. The women who are most likely to find themselves suspected of cohabiting are, by contrast, poor and probably lacking in confidence: female claimants are therefore prone to suffer doubly as a result of their gender and marital status (or lack of it), and their working-class position.

Unemployed people form another claimant category likely to be targeted for fraud investigation, especially when the individual has a 'marketable skill' or a history of self-employment (OWS 1983). Once again, this is a consequence of investigators' common-sense knowledge of the opportunity structures available for fiddling by 'working on the side'. In local offices Unemployment Review Officers (UROs) had, in the past, a twin role to perform in regulating unemployed people: ensuring that unemployed claimants were helped to seek work or training actively, and the prevention of fraud and abuse by these claimants. This may be regarded as a mixture of 'counselling and policing', although most recently the former function has been largely displaced by the latter: growing numbers of unemployed claimants and shrinking employment and training opportunities have meant that only a tiny number of claimants go 'off the books' as the result of UROs' counselling role. The vast majority of URO 'successes' in these terms are claimants whose benefit is stopped because they fail to attend for interviews (NACRO 1986). UROs may refer to fraud officers those cases where working and claiming is suspected and thereafter FOs assemble and review the facts of the case.

Informal targeting arises from broader ideological notions about the deserving and undeserving poor. Historically, able-bodied unemployed people have been regarded as least deserving of state support (Fraser 1973). Again, the ideology of individualism espoused by New Right politics has contributed to negative stereotyping of able-bodied poor people who are, in the 1980s more than ever, regarded as unmotivated, uncompetitive failures in a society imbued with entrepreneurial values. But this general ideological position interrelates with other more specific elements to form other additional targets: namely lone mothers, itinerants and certain ethnic minorities. The ideological principles which underpin the negative 'target' status of such claimants are realized in the attitudes of DHSS staff. Although staff attitudes to an extent mirror those of the wider society (Beltram 1984), the perceptions of claimants held by benefit staff are crucial elements which construct the material reality of the stigmatization of certain claimant groups through staff–claimant interactions.

A recent PSI study concluded that 'personal judgements [by benefit staff] could have an important bearing on staff–claimant relationships, and could significantly affect some benefit decisions' (Cooper 1985: 67). Racial prejudice forms part of personal judgement which, according to Cooper, could influence 'decisions which were liable to variable treatment' (ibid: 68). Decisions on the investigation or referral of cases of suspected fraud would come under this heading of 'decisions liable to variable treatment', and therefore the possibility of racism influencing the targeting of cases for investigation cannot be ruled out.

Negative attitudes towards lone mothers may similarly influence investigatory practice and the qualitative treatment of female claimants. This is demonstrated in the following responses of two interviewing officers (Mike and Margaret) to a variety of supplementary benefit claimants. To an unmarried mother of West Indian origin, 'Mike was cold and brusque', yet appeared 'decent and pleasant' to a male invalid in his 50s (Cooper 1985: 52–3). His comments following interviews with a young Pakistani and with a deserted wife were neither objective nor polite:

> Bloody odd! . . . We get quite a few Pakis like that wandering in like lost sheep.

> Magic isn't it! Old man walks out, we take over looking after the family. Sometimes I think we've got it all wrong. We ought to send her old man the bill.

> (Mike)

Margaret's attitude to a lone mother was similarly negative and clearly influenced her decision-making:

> I can't understand why people like her think they've a right to rely on the taxpayer for everything. . . . I think people should have it brought home to

them that they have got to stand up for themselves.... Lassies like that I haven't got a lot of sympathy for.

(Margaret)

She also demonstrated a distrust of a young man with a chronic back condition: the office had 'information' that he was living with a woman (also receiving benefit) in the same street. This 'information' may well have been the result of an anonymous call or neighbourhood gossip, but he was none the less labelled as

> One we have to watch very closely – always taking liberties. . . . There's quite a few around who can't work because of 'back trouble', if you know what I mean.

(Margaret)

The 1980 reforms of the Social Security system involved some narrowing of the scope for personal judgements by benefit staff and a shift away from the exercise of staff discretion. Nevertheless, personal judgements still influence the quality and tone of the service to claimants. It can also affect decisions concerning which types of claimants are 'taking liberties' and which should be viewed as potential fraudsters.

Increasingly punitive attitudes towards certain claimant groups (particularly unemployed people, itinerants, ethnic minorities and lone mothers) are to be expected within a political climate which extols the values of economic success and the morality of the 'normal' nuclear family (Levitas 1986; David 1986; Fitzgerald 1983). In relation to the political celebration of 'family values', the consequences for those who deviate from these values (particularly if they are poor) are castigation, and blame for most of society's evils. According to Dr Rhodes Boyson, speaking at the 1986 Conservative party conference, single parents had created 'probably the most evil product of our time', manifesting itself in wild youth, football hooliganism and inner city revolt. As already argued (in Chapter 1) single-parent families are often represented as deviant by 'choice' and not 'misfortune'. As such, moral indignation accompanies the imagery of dependence and 'scrounging'. In this way lone mothers are often regarded as undeserving of state 'subsidy'.

Both formal departmental policy and informal social attitudes are therefore influenced by ideologies which valorize the family and advocate a 'go-getting society' based on individual competition and wealth. Lone mothers and other claimants who are unable to (or fail to) aspire to these values are therefore particularly stigmatized. They may also find themselves targeted as potential fraudsters.

Anonymous tip-offs

Anonymous allegations are acknowledged by the DHSS to form an important source of many supplementary benefit investigations (*The Times*

14.6.85). As a former SBC chairman noted, letters complaining about too many handouts, layabouts and scroungers 'rarely came on headed notepaper from leafy suburbs. Most of them are written by ordinary voters and taxpayers' (Donnison 1982: 48). In one Midlands town the number of anonymous calls received by the local DHSS office was said to have risen from around 80 calls in a month early in 1985 to 300 calls in November of the same year (OVS 1986). Following up such allegations constitutes a significant part of DHSS routine investigatory work.

Two claimants I interviewed were prosecuted for supplementary benefit fraud following investigations arising from anonymous tip-offs. The first was Caroline who was 20 years old when, in 1978, she worked part-time at a pub while claiming benefit. She sought this work more 'for the company' than for the money (her earnings were around £8 per week) and to alleviate the boredom of unemployment. After a few weeks the landlord 'made a pass' at her, which she rejected. Caroline soon stopped work at the pub. Shortly afterwards she was called for interview (which proceeded under caution) at the local office and realized that her employer had informed the DHSS (anonymously) about her earnings, which amounted to approximately £58. Caroline was subsequently prosecuted and received a custodial sentence (discussed in Chapter 7). Clearly tip-offs such as this are both straightforward and fairly quick to investigate, and present easy pickings for the fraud staff involved.

Barry was a 23-year-old father of four when he engaged in casual work on a local farm 'to buy the kids shoes', and new nappies and clothes for his 3-month-old baby (having been refused an exceptional needs payment for these items). The DHSS received an anonymous letter and wrote to the employer to confirm that Barry had worked there. Investigators subsequently visited Barry at his home, where he admitted making a false representation, and was later prosecuted (see Chapter 7). He believed that a workmate had probably 'grassed' on him, but seemed philosophical about it: he was aware of many other cases where even family and close friends had informed on claimants who were working and drawing benefit. But Barry accepted this as an inevitable risk involved in fiddling the DHSS.

Caroline's view was less philosophical. She had been informed on by an initially collusive employer who, she felt, betrayed her unfairly because she had rejected his sexual advances. Many anonymous tip-offs are indeed motivated by anger, jealousy or the desire for revenge. For instance a carpenter, who fiddled 'the social' by working on the side, had fitted a replacement window in the home of his aunt, who felt that she had been over-charged by him. She subsequently wrote an anonymous letter to the local DHSS office informing on her nephew.

Following up anonymous allegations may appear a distasteful investigatory technique, yet tip-offs remain a fruitful source of information for investigators. The DHSS has encountered criticism for encouraging the practice of 'snitching' on friends and neighbours by offering payment for information leading to a successful investigation (*Guardian* 23.9.85). The wife of an unemployed shipyard worker from Sunderland explained that her husband had been reported by a neighbour who had seen him leave the house at the same time each morning and suspected him of working: benefit payments to the family were stopped as the result of the 'super snitcher' (ibid; ITV *World in Action* 23.9.85). DHSS representatives did not deny allegations that 'if you do get a successful snitch, you get £25 out of the kitty, under the counter.'

The practice of payment for information leading to a successful investigation is also used by the Inland Revenue, although Enquiry Branch informers average only 14 or 15 per year, and local tax district offices rarely receive anonymous tip-offs relating to tax evasion. None the less, the Revenue do have discretion to pay rewards up to £50 to 'any person who informs them of any offence against any Act relating to inland revenue' (*Cmnd 8822* 1983: 199). Only seven rewards were paid in the five years to July 1982 (ibid.). It can be argued that the far greater numbers of individuals informing on alleged benefit fraudsters are a reflection of factors other than simply the frequency of the offences committed: if this latter were the case then tax fraud 'snitchers' would be legion. The explanation for wide differences in the numbers of anonymous allegations received by the two departments are rather related to contradictory ideological principles underpinning public perceptions of tax and welfare.

It has been argued that there is a common-sense view that it is far more reprehensible to take money illegally *from* the state than illegally to fail to pay money due in taxes *to* the state (Chapter 1). This view is rooted in the principles of liberalism which effectively contradict official discourse (which apparently centres on the collective provision of welfare and the 'rights' of benefit claimants). Given these effective contradictions, it is hardly surprising that very few individuals (are encouraged to) inform on tax fraudsters, whereas those who inform on benefit fraudsters are promoted (in official discourse) as public-spirited guardians of the public purse. Ingenuity and thrift legitimize and promote tax fiddles which are dismissed, with a wink and a nudge, because it is seen as 'natural' to want to beat the taxman and maximize one's own financial gains.

Fraud drives and 'knocker squads'

The techniques collectively analysed here under the heading of 'fraud drives' encompass a variety of investigatory methods (some already discussed) and utilize all levels of fraud staff, local and regional. The common themes which underlie fraud drives are

1 *The specific targeting* of a claimant group, location or occupation for intensive investigation. (Within this target area/group there may be an element of

randomized investigation of some claimants *on suspicion* of fraud but without evidence that a fraud has taken place).

2 *A proactive approach* in which investigators are seen to be taking the initiative in countering fraud (as opposed to the reactive approach of much routine fraud work evident in, for instance, following up information and tip-offs received at the local office).

3 *High profile publicity* of the results of the 'drive'. (Fraud drives are geared as much to the notion of 'deterrence' as to immediate cost-effectiveness.

In 1981 a DHSS trade union representative cast doubt upon the motives and methods of fraud drives which were mounted against claimants adjuged to be in 'at risk groups':

> This of course is totally objectionable in every way, as seeking to categorise claimants in this fashion can lead not to more success in detecting fraud but to even more alienation between claimants and staff who serve them...the slavish adherence to the political intent of fraud drives will increase the present gulf between claimant and staff and lead to even more friction in public caller areas... these fraud drives are... politically dishonest, save hardly any money in real terms and do nothing to improve the relationship between claimant and staff.
>
> (OWS 1981)

Significantly this official noted that there was very little difference between the *modus operandi* of fraud drives and the methods used by SCCUs (discussed below). For this reason the former were sometimes referred to as 'knocker squads' because of the possibility of random calls on claimants whose only 'crime' may have been their past work record (a marketable skill or history of self-employment) or their marital status (lone mothers). The specific methods of SCC will be discussed below, but it is important to recognize the importance of the departmental emphasis on the 'fraud drive' approach, particularly in relation to broader political objectives.

During the 1979 election campaign allegations had been made about widespread social security fraud and in February 1980 'Reg Prentice did his best to gain some political mileage out of the issue by launching a big campaign' (Donnison 1982: 209). This campaign did not focus on the collusive employers who enable the commission of the majority of benefit frauds – working while drawing benefit. Rather, the characteristics of these fraud drives were determined by political factors;

> the politically necessary job of showing that the government were 'doing something' about fraud, without upsetting the ordinary voters who, as customers, workers or employers, often participated in fraudulent transactions
>
> (ibid: 210)

In 1980 Patrick Jenkin had warned the Conservative party conference, 'Watch out! It's time the fiddling has to stop.' (Presumably he was directing his remarks against Social Security claimants and not referring to the business practices of his conference audience.) Combatting benefit fraud and abuse therefore became a means of rallying the faithful–whether the 'honest' taxpayer or the party faithful–and effectively a means of galvanizing comfortable public opinion against welfare recipients through the 'scrounger' stereotype.

The amount of publicity generated by departmental fraud drives confirms the ideological function that they are designed to perform: for instance recent drives against Heathrow Airport staff (cab drivers, hotel and catering staff in particular) were publicized by the Department of Employment because ministers had decided 'the campaign should be given a much higher profile' (*Guardian* 16.9.87). On the day of the announcement of the drive on these 'dole cheats', every national television news broadcast carried the Heathrow story, which in the Midlands was followed up with publicity of a similar drive against workers at the National Exhibition Centre (NEC) in Birmingham (ITV *Central News* 16.9.87). This belied the BBC correspondent's assertion on the national bulletins that these fraud drives were being concentrated in the Thames Valley and areas of lowest unemployment in the South of England.

The Heathrow and NEC fraud drives were mounted by the Department of Employment's Regional Fraud teams against individuals who were claiming unemployment benefit and working, although some of those investigated would be in receipt of supplementary benefit in addition. Regional Fraud Teams, formerly known as 'Rabbits' (Regional Benefit Investigation Teams), utilize techniques broadly similar to those of SCCs. As a result they have attracted similar complaints: according to a dossier compiled by the CPSA their techniques of investigation have caused 'real distress to members of the staff and the public' in local offices and in local offices and in claimants' homes (*Guardian* 10.11.86). The complaints dossier includes allegations of investigators making uncorroborated accusations of fraud against an 'educationally sub-normal' claimant, the covert use of tape recorders when interviewing claimants, and accusing a young man, recovering from a hernia operation, of working while claiming (ibid.).

In a fraud drive against motor-cycle dispatch riders in central London, techniques used by investigators involved comparing names on employers' wage records with the unemployment register, noting the registrations of riders and obtaining the names and addresses of the owners (through the DVLC at Swansea), and cross-checking these details with the unemployment register (*Guardian* 16.9.87). By contrast, the drive against workers involved in the construction and running of the NEC involved 'seven months of surveillance' (ITV *Central News* 16.9.87). But the themes of targeting, proactive investigation and high-profile publicity are common characteristics in both instances.

The methods employed in fraud drives and manner in which they are represented in the public rhetoric derive from essentially political decisions to prioritize the issue of 'scrounging' at particular points in time. (It is significant that the two fraud drives mentioned here were not publicized at the time of the June 1987 election, when unemployment and 'caring government' were important issues.) In order to understand the techniques and rationales of the departments engaged in these activities it is necessary to locate departmental fraud policy in a wider economic and political framework (see Chapters 1 and 8). The relationship between departmental practice and political objectives is nowhere more evident than in the case of operation of SCCUs from 1981 to 1986.

'Super-snoopers': Special Claims Control Units

Following their introduction in 1980, SCCUs immediately attracted strong criticism. This was principally directed against the 'bullying' tactics which they allegedly used in order to get claimants 'off the books' (Moore 1981; R. Smith 1985; NACRO 1986). But their investigatory techniques were merely a logical consequence of the departmental policies of a government committed to combatting social security fraud while at the same time seeking to reduce public expenditure significantly. The (confidential) fraud investigators' guide in use at that time emphasized a shift in departmental policy geared to meeting these objectives:

> In the past, as many cases as possible were pursued to prosecution but, in future, while the deterrent effect of successful prosecutions will continue to be borne in mind, the cessation of a claim might be regarded in appropriate cases as the most cost-effective way of dealing with the matter.
>
> (Moore 1981: 138)

As will be seen below, techniques such as the 'non-prosecution interview' were used by investigators to achieve benefit savings through the 'cessation of a claim' (OWS 1983).

Social Security minister Reg Prentice had asserted in February 1980 that 'Efforts to control fraud and abuse have been inadequate for several years' (*Hansard* vol.798 no.118 col.710) and, as mentioned above, a commitment to stop the 'fiddling' was made at the Conservative conference that year. Having announced that up to £50 million *could* be saved as a result of new anti-fraud efforts, it is hardly surprising that the investigatory techniques of the new SCC squads were geared to meeting those ministerial targets of expected 'benefit savings'. According to DHSS staff 'unofficial league tables were rife' as SCC officers worked to meet their personal 'targets' of benefit savings (OWS 1981). The methods they adopted to that end will now be examined.

SCC techniques included many of those employed by SIs and already described above: targeting, surveillance and utilization of information from other sources. The Fraud Investigators' Guide (FIG) also encouraged the building of links with local police in the pursuit of social security fraud (*The Times* 2.5.81). However, what distinguished the character and techniques of SCCUs from other anti-fraud staff was their relative independence from local office control and their 'special squad ethos' (OWS 1981). SCCUs based at regional offices undertook 'swoops' on local offices where they selected certain cases from the 'live load' for investigation (according to criteria to be outlined below). But the very organization of these units set them apart from other departmental staff:

> Considerable effort was put into a team approach by SCC, who tried to create the esprit de corps of an elite.
>
> (R. Smith 1985: 118)

This factor, coupled with grave misgivings about SCC 'strong arm' methods, led Civil Service trade unions to advise their members to refuse to cooperate with SCCUs in local offices:

> The charge [the unions] ... brought specifically against SCC teams was that the techniques they employed involved essentially random investigation of claimants, using questionable interrogation techniques and unacceptable pressure to produce dubious savings, all in an atmosphere overcharged with the desire to meet targeted savings and root out fraud.
>
> (R. Smith 1985: 118)

Certainly there is much evidence to support these allegations: the NACRO working party studying the enforcement of Social Security law received similar complaints about SCC from organizations such as the National Association of Citizens Advice Bureaux and the Association of Directors of Social Services (NACRO 1986: 46).

The selection of cases for investigation by SCC was based upon official guidelines which implicitly allowed for the random investigation of any unemployed claimant who was not ill, and lone mothers with dependent children (R. Smith 1985; OWS 1982). DHSS investigation staff translated these broad categories into typical operative reasons for SCC case selection: these criteria included

> No recent requests for exceptional needs payments (ENPs), claimants suspected of being 'on the game', claimants living in luxury . . . and 'smoothies'.
>
> (OWS 1982)

There was, therefore, considerable room for personal and subjective judgements on the part of SCC staff in requesting certain categories of claimant for investigation:

> It seems that single women are particularly vulnerable to pressure, despite [circulars emphasizing] the very sensitive nature of some MC [mothers with children] cases. . . . This situation is compounded by the predominance of male SCC investigators . . . this also applies to general SI work.
>
> (OWS 1982)

Despite a re-write of instructions to SCC investigators in June 1983 which stressed the need to prevent distress (or duress) to claimants, the same vulnerable groups were targeted in a subsequent SCC drive planned for Scunthorpe in 1984. Here local officers were asked to take out the files of 7,000 of the 12,000 claimants in the town in preparation for the SCC drive, and investigators were asked to 'look closely at single parents and the able-bodied unemployed' (*Guardian* 24.1.84). Confidential evidence from DHSS officials indicated that SCC investigation often proceeded on the basis of 'a hunch' or 'smelling a rat'. As already discussed, broader prejudices and stereotypes (particularly concerning lone mothers, ethnic minorities and able-bodied unemployed people) may influence the interactions between staff and claimant. Such negative attitudes were, moreover, actually fostered in the targeting of those groups for SCC investigations. For instance the National Association of Probation Officers (NAPO) alleged that they had evidence of SCC being directed to investigate claimants with the surname Singh 'as this was a fertile area for investigation' (NCASSC 1985: 10). Interestingly, other critics compared the loose criteria for the selection of claimants for SCC investigation with the 'SUS' laws (CPSA/SCPS 1984). A conference on the Policing of Welfare Benefits suggested that 'SCC is part of a rigid authoritarian, anti-woman, anti-minority elite within the welfare system' (CPSA/SCPS 1984).

In relation to the treatment of female claimants by SCC, the evidence of other DHSS officials was damning:

> At least half the time and energy of SCC is devoted to accepting the order books voluntarily surrendered by women with children who are persuaded they are in fact living with men as members of a single household.
>
> (OWS 1981)

The methods used by SCC teams to persuade claimants to relinquish their claim to benefit allegedly included intimidation and inducement:

> Women interviewed in locked rooms by, sometimes, two SCC team members. Late afternoon is a favourite time, with mothers pre-occupied about their children at school, home or in waiting rooms.....Evening home visits by two SCC team members....Threats to women about their children will be taken into care by Social Services because they are unfit mothers. But, if they hand over their order books....Presentation of non-existent evidence (telephone directories in manilla folders), false stories of having watched and followed claimants for days and having obtained evidence of working or cohabitation. Threats to prosecute if order books not handed over or if claimants do not sign off....Inducements – Extra needs payments for working clothes used to be a favourite...now we find that single payments for children's clothing are used.
>
> (OWS 1981)

Revised instructions (circular Fig/21: DHSS 1983) to investigators marked a response by the then Social Security minister Rhodes Boyson to criticisms of SCC techniques: the instructions warned against 'unacceptable techniques' such as harassment, falsely alleging that evidence of fraud is in hand, falsely alleging that a third party has cast doubt on the claimant's entitlement to benefit or 'trying to gain the claimant's confidence by claiming to be a single parent' (*Guardian* 11.7.83; DHSS 1983). But clearly the aims of SCUUs, determined as they were by political and ideological principles, remained the same: to take the initiative against fraud and abuse (Fraud Investigators Guide 1983),to avoid prosecution, as there was 'no additional cash return' for a prosecution (Moore 1981), to favour the achievement of 'benefit savings' through the 'non-prosecution interview', and to be cost-effective in terms of manpower used and 'savings' achieved (ibid.).

The watchwords 'cost-effectiveness' and 'cash return' are in keeping with a political philosophy concerned with results in cash terms. The evidence presented here of the results when such principles are put into practice indicates that claimants' rights may have suffered at the expense of (dubious) savings to the Treasury. But the ideological role served by such rigorous policing of certain sectors of the poor was the reinforcement of the 'scrounger' mythology and negative stereotyping of the 'undeserving poor'.

However, the official discourses which were replicated in much of the mass media were not universally accepted. Pressure groups, such as the Child Poverty Action Group (CPAG), the National Association of Citizens Advice Bureaux (NACAB) and the National Council for Civil Liberties (NCCL), and trade unions representing civil servants protested both at SCC techniques and the political principles which underpinned them. In May 1986 Norman Fowler announced that SCCUs were to be abolished. But the announcement itself centred on the deployment of an *additional* 500 staff to anti-fraud work in the DHSS: 180 of the extra staff were to be placed in

> selected offices, specifically to reinforce their efforts to combat benefit fraud by claimants resident in hotels and other bed and breakfast accomodation.... The other 320 extra staff will be added to the regionally based teams: these teams will be regrouped into 31 benefit fraud teams.... They will help the local office in fully investigating allegations of fraud and bringing prosecutions where justified.
>
> (*Hansard* 15.5.86, col. 322)

SCC has therefore been abolished in theory, but it remains to be seen whether the abuses of claimants' rights by SCCUs have been halted, or whether the 'special squad ethos' and tactics remain effective in practice. Certainly the political priority of 'cost-effectiveness' is still dominant, and the abolition of SCC may well be merely a reflection of this policy goal: it was in the area of demonstrable cost-effectiveness that SCC conspicuously failed (NACRO 1986; R. Smith 1985).

Summary

Supplementary benefit fraud investigations take place within a social context shaped by contradictory views of the modern Welfare State and its benefit recipients. On the one hand, the Welfare State's main function can be seen to be the payment of benefits as of *right* and the relief of need, with due attention to the dignity of the individual claimant (NACRO 1986). On the other hand, the Welfare State's main function can be seen in terms of protecting the public purse, discouraging 'avoidable' dependency and paying benefits to those who demonstrate *need*. Patrick Jenkin argued, according to this view, that

> The *honest* and the *innocent* have nothing to fear from the enquiries of our officials.... Helping *genuine* claimants to get their benefits remains the main function of the Social Security organization.
>
> (*Hansard* 6.5.81, vol. 4, no. 97, my emphasis added)

The pursuit of supplementary benefit fraud may serve to reinforce notions of the *dishonest* claimant, and ultimately reinforce nineteenth-century distinctions between the deserving and undeserving poor.

Since the mid-1970s economic recession has promoted the dominance of (monetarist) political policies stressing a curbing of public expenditure. It is in this context that the Welfare State has become a crucial target for cost-cutting initiatives. Between 1979 and 1984 DHSS staffing was cut by 8,000 (McKnight 1985), yet at the same time extra staff and resources were being directed against fraud and abuse. In this chapter such contradictions have been attributed to three main policy aims of the DHSS:

1 *The aim of cutting overall DHSS costs* by using fraud staff to obtain 'savings' of benefit through their investigatory efforts and in effect also achieving 'savings' by deterring individuals from claiming benefits to which they may be entitled, through the publicizing of fraud drives (Beltram 1984a; R. Smith 1985).

2 *The aim of promoting the ideal of a 'go-getting' entrepreneurial society:* for there to be winners there must be losers, and those losers are labelled and stigmatized as such (see Chapters 1 and 8). Equally, in such a society, self-reliance should be stressed, hence an ambivalence to mounting official take-up campaigns (NCASSC 1985).

3 *The aim of undermining faith in the Welfare State* by exposing its wastefulness in paying benefits to the undeserving and the 'scroungers'. These policy goals, taken together, signal the end of any 'Welfare State consensus' and instead pose alternative social market principles in the provision of relief for the poor (Mishra 1986; Loney 1986).

Underlying these policy aims are the vocabularies of the free market, effort and individualism (see Table 6). New Right political philosophy has therefore intensified earlier critiques of welfare: for example, the notion of the undeserving poor has been utilized to incorporate additional claimant groups who are reconstituted as 'avoidably' dependent (Minford 1987). Single-parent families are thus represented as 'undeserving' if they have 'chosen' not to be members of a patriarchal nuclear family. The New Right's version of morality encompasses other culpable poor groups – young people who 'do not *want* to work' or unemployed people who place an excessive burden on the state by having 'too many' children.

As argued in Chapter 2, such moralizing attitudes towards the poor have a long history. But the crucial importance of such ideas is that they have been successfully incorporated into a political philosophy of the 1980s. In this way the New Right has not only tapped into a vast historical reservoir of ideas about the 'undeserving poor', but also hijacked the vocabularies of 'freedom' and 'individualism'. The former has been used to justify curbs on the freedom of the poor in the name of freedom from excessive taxation for the better-off, and the latter to justify the dismantling of collectivist social provision in the name of greater individual responsibility. For the time being, at least, social policy is dominated by the ideologies of the free market (rather than social justice) and individualism (rather than collectivism). But, as will be argued in Chapter 8, there are possibilities for change through challenging what is now regarded as the 'common sense' of New Right ideology. One means of effecting such a challenge is through exposing the inconsistencies and contradictions of New Right discourse: these contradictions are realized in the differential social, political and judicial responses to tax and supplementary benefit fraud.

Summary of Part III

In Chapters 5 and 6 the departmental enforcement policies and investigation methods used by the DHSS and Inland Revenue have been described. Concomitantly the relationship between official policy and regulatory practice has been analysed: this is summarized in Tables 5 and 6.

The Inland Revenue's enforcement policy has often been presented as a logical departmental response to the material realities of enforcement:

Table 5 Rationales for tax investigations

OFFICIAL ENFORCEMENT POLICY RATIONALES
  to protect the public purse
  to ensure the compliance of the taxpayer to the Taxes Acts
  to ensure the rights of the taxpayer

EFFECTIVE RATIONALE, IN PRACTICE
  to minimize administrative hassle – get the job (of collecting taxes) done
  to operate as effectively as possible – given the practical constraints of manpower
    and resources
  to spare the taxpayers' feelings – seek compliance through negotiation,
    effectively under-classify offences to minimize taxpayers' resistance, obtain
    financial settlement wherever possible, prosecute very rarely (only in the most
    serious cases)

GUIDING PRINCIPLES
  pragmatism
  compliance
  tacit acknowledgement of the 'intrusive' view of personal tax

---

Table 6 Rationales for supplementary benefit investigations

OFFICIAL ENFORCEMENT POLICY RATIONALES
  to protect the public purse
  to ensure the efficient payment of benefit in accordance with the rights of the
    claimant
  to prevent fraud and abuse

EFFECTIVE RATIONALES, IN PRACTICE
  cost-effectiveness – demonstrated by departmental cost-cutting, reductions in
    routine staff (but not fraud staff) and 'benefit savings' achieved as the result
    of anti-fraud work
  the effective policing of welfare – in practice accomplished through the routine
    stigma of the claiming process, work-tests, and the surveillance and
    investigation of 'target' groups
  efficiency – get the job done, given the practical difficulties (arising from
    'cost-cutting') for routine DHSS staff and claimants

GUIDING PRINCIPLES
  detection and punishment of 'scroungers'
  means-testing, to establish *needs* (and desert)
  tacit acknowledgement of the distinction between the 'deserving' and
    'undeserving' poor.

---

hence the Revenue's 'softly, softly' approach to its regulatory duties is represented as the result of the practical constraints encountered in achieving the department's primary goal – the protection of the Taxes Acts and the public purse. According to this approach, tax evaders should be *persuaded* to comply and pay their taxes.

However, the rationale of protecting the public purse generates different policy and practice when applied to the enforcement of social security regulations (NACRO 1986). The overriding goal of cost-effectiveness (or cost-cutting?) and the rigorous policing of the supplementary benefits system have characterized departmental policy since 1979. Although 'scroungerphobia' was rife long before 1979 (Golding and Middleton 1982), New Right economic and social policy effectively intensified the routine regulation of the poor (for instance through the increasing use of work-tests), and at the same time promoted the proactive policing of claimant groups considered most 'at risk' of committing fraud.

These chapters have also examined the practical consequences of investigation policy for individual taxpayers and benefit claimants. Interactions between tax officials and taxpayers were found to be characterized by formality and due attention to the taxpayer's rights as outlined in the Revenue's 'Charter'. By contrast, interactions between DHSS officials and claimants were characterized by mutual distrust and by stress – both personal and environmental (Mandla 1987; PSI 1985). Although there were some similarities in the investigatory techniques used by the two departments (for instance the common use of surveillance, targeting and in-depth interviews), there were significant differences in the practical operation of such techniques: for instance, surveillance by Board Investigation Officers is undertaken only with prior evidence of fraud, whereas surveillance by SCC units could proceed on grounds of 'suspicion'. Similarly compliance officers target certain occupational groups for investigation, but this does not involve the degree of coercion that was apparent in the targeting of vulnerable claimant groups by SCC (OWS 1982; NACRO 1986). Although no longer in operation, SCUUs have left a legacy in terms of poorer relations between claimants and DHSS staff (and amongst DHSS staff themselves), and a proactive and intrusive approach to the policing of welfare recipients.

At the heart of the contradictions in policy and in practice which have been analysed here is the ideological representation of the taxpayer as a 'giver' to the state and the supplementary benefit claimant as a 'taker' from the state (and thus, ultimately, from compliant taxpayers). These representations, and the different judicial and social responses they give rise to, are the subject of Part IV.

Part IV
Different Responses

7

Penalties and Prosecution

The analysis of the enforcement policy rationales of the Inland Revenue and DHSS in Part II revealed that the responses of these enforcing departments to benefit claimants and taxpayers suspected of defrauding the public purse vary in key respects – both in policy and in practice. For instance, policy towards investigating benefit fraud is underpinned by notions of 'scroungers' and the 'undeserving poor' whereas policy towards the investigation of tax fraud is underpinned by coercive view of personal taxation, and by advocacy of entrepreneurialism and the accumulation of personal wealth. These political and ideological contradictions which shape official policy are similarly evident in departmental investigation practices.

The attitudes of departmental staff invariably reflect the ideological construction of their clients as 'winners or losers', 'givers' to the state or 'scroungers' taking from society. The tone of interactions between staff/claimant and staff/taxpayer and the quality of service and respect accorded to the taxpayer and the benefit claimant are clearly at variance. Differences are particularly evident in the policy on the prosecution of tax and benefit fraud, and the use of financial penalties. But such policy differences are accentuated still further in the way in which penalties and prosecutions are imposed in practice. This chapter will therefore analyse, first, the penalty and prosecution *policy* of the Inland Revenue and DHSS respectively, and second, the punishment of tax and benefit fraudsters in *practice*.

Penalty and prosecution policy: tax

> The first responsibility of the Revenue is to get money in and not to lock people up in prison and prosecute them.
>
> (OVS 1985)

According to this official, the Inland Revenue's primary task is the collection of the taxes which Parliament says are due. This, the Revenue argues, may be more effectively accomplished through seeking the compliance of the taxpayer and, in the case of default or fraud, through seeking financial penalties in all but the most serious cases. The senior official quoted above reflects this view which may appear essentially pragmatic, yet effectively produces a 'non-prosecution' policy where most tax evasion is concerned. But there are several contradictions which render this policy open to question, on grounds of both equity and efficiency. Some of these doubts were raised in evidence to the Keith Committee:

> There are millions of tax evaders in the UK and over 100,000 are detected each year, yet only a handful are prosecuted (and fewer still convicted). Could this handful legitimately complain that they are suffering from the arbitrary exercise of an administrative whim?
>
> *(Cmnd 8822 1983: 457)*

The criteria used by the Revenue when deciding whether to prosecute do not vindicate the notion of an administrative 'whim', but do show a high degree of selectivity in the (few) cases proceeding to prosecution. The criteria for selection of cases for prosecution include

1 'Heinous cases'
2 Cases where individuals have already enjoyed a negotiated settlement
3 Cases where taxpayers have made incomplete disclosures (as, for instance, in the recent case of former jockey Lester Piggot)
4 'Status' prosecutions, for instance where accountants have been involved in fraud and public confidence in the tax system needs to be ensured.

(ibid: 22.1.9)

The common themes underlying these prosecution criteria are to prosecute where financial settlement or negotiation has not ensured the full compliance of the taxpayer, in cases where the Revenue's (and taxpayers') trust in professional advisers has been breached and in highly organized (or 'heinous') cases.

The Revenue's policy is to 'prosecute in some examples of all classes of fraud...because it is the possibility of prosecution which prevents the spread of tax fraud to unacceptable limits' (ibid: 378). This policy immediately poses three questions:

1 What is considered to be the boundary beyond which tax fraud is said to reach an 'unacceptable limit'?
2 Do such small numbers of Revenue prosecutions justify the claim implicit here, that they provide an effective 'deterrent' to the spread of unacceptable levels of fraud?
3 Is this selective (and subjective) approach to prosecutions equitable in practice if, for instance, a large fraud in respect of trading profits is likely

to result in a cash settlement whereas if a payable order made out by the Revenue is stolen, the thief is likely to be prosecuted?

The Centre for Policy Studies appeared to have similar questions in mind when they commented that the 'ease of presentation of the prosecution case has been a more important factor in the decision to prosecute than it should be', and furthermore that 'a bigger proportion of the more socially harmful kinds of offences tends to be the subject of negotiated settlement' (ibid: 22.1.3). A case of theft of a payable order is relatively easy to prove and is recognizable as 'real crime' – theft. However, to prove wilful default on the part of a businessman who understates trading profits is extremely difficult, and such frauds do not equate with what is publicly perceived as 'crime': after all, who is the victim? What is the boundary between tax fraud and shrewd business practice in common-sense terms (Pearce 1976; Chambliss 1978)? The prosecution policy of the Revenue is therefore not determined solely by pragmatism and the desire to collect tax efficiently, though this does play a significant part in the decision *not* to prosecute cases which are difficult to prove. Prosecution policy is also underpinned by notions of what constitutes socially acceptable financial practice (within the logic of a capitalist economy), and by ideological stereotypes of 'crimes' and criminals.

It is significant that of the 459 cases of criminal proceedings brought by the Revenue in 1986/7, the vast majority would fall into the descriptive category referred to above as 'real crime' and do not, for the most part, relate to business fraud at all: 274 of those prosecutions related to sub–contractor frauds and 138 to the theft of payable orders and girocheques (Board of Inland Revenue 1987). As the analysis of investigation techniques above indicated, such frauds are usually uncovered by the Revenue's 'police' (the BIO) and investigated by them or the police proper (see Appendix 1 for details of Revenue prosecutions since 1975/6 and breakdown of convictions obtained by the police).

Where the Revenue seeks financial settlement rather than prosecution, negotiations between taxpayer (and his/her advisers) aim to arrive at a mutually agreed figure of tax which has been underpaid. Where there is evidence of 'fraud, wilful default or neglect' on the part of the taxpayer, additional financial penalties may be imposed, on top of the repayment of the agreed figure of tax owed and the interest that would have accrued (to the Revenue) on that amount (Inland Revenue IR 73, 1987). Normally six previous years may be investigated and so interest is calculated from the date that the tax *should* have been paid up to the date that it actually *is* paid. Penalties are calculated as a percentage of the tax unpaid: in strict law penalties could be over 100 per cent of the amount of tax owed, or in cases of fraud 200 per cent, but in practice the Revenue does not seek penalties exceeding 100 per cent (ibid.). That figure is further reduced significantly according to the degree of the taxpayer's co-operation, the relative gravity of the offence and the fullness of any voluntary disclosure made.

Once again the policy is geared to compliance and the apparent goal is the collection of tax, but the qualitative treatment of taxpayers accused of fraud, wilful default or neglect in relation to their tax affairs goes beyond the immediate requirements of obtaining tax: their treatment by officials is far more respectful and mindful of individual rights than is evident in the case of benefit fraudsters. For instance, in seeking agreement on tax owed and in calculating any penalties due, the Revenue encourages discussion with taxpayers and their professional representatives, and all procedures for dealing with settlements are outlined in official leaflets. This contrasts starkly with the lack of respect, official knowledge and professional representation which characterizes the treatment of many benefit claimants accused of omissions from their statements of circumstances (see below). Yet despite the fact that financial penalties are a lenient option when compared with criminal prosecution, they are frequently represented (by both offenders and in the public rhetoric) as draconian and unjustly punitive. For instance, one article in a series on taxation opened with the following accusations in relation to the Revenue's financial penalties:

> An increasing number of tax inspectors are becoming 'trigger happy' about trying to invoke penalties against people whom they suspect of being defaulters; against people who make innocent errors; and also against people who are merely late in dealing with their tax returns.
>
> (Horner in *Guardian* 29.8.87)

But Revenue leaflets clearly state the precise meaning of the guidelines in operation:

> you may have done nothing more than make an innocent mistake. In that case, no penalty would arise. You may, however, have paid too little tax, or paid it late, as a result of fraud, wilful default or neglect. 'Wilful default or neglect' can include sending in your tax return late.
>
> (Inland Revenue IR 73, 1987)

The mythology surrounding the allegedly 'draconian' powers of the taxman derives essentially from the view of taxation as coercive, and the submission of income tax returns as an unwelcome intrusion into the taxpayer's private and business affairs: the intolerable inquisition school of thought. This view was articulated by one taxpayer I spoke to who had been charged financial penalties, following Revenue investigations into property holdings. He maintained that the Revenue routinely charged penalties at the rate of 200 per cent. This assertion is belied by evidence (ibid.) that the effective *maximum* penalty of 100 percent is further reduced according to the degree of mitigating circumstances already described – co-operation, gravity and full disclosure. But none the less, such accounts of tax investigations do illustrate the popular view that Revenue penalties are excessively punitive. In practice, the characteristics of coercion and intrusion are more applicable to supplementary benefit investigations, yet the regulation of the poor (who are financially supported by the state) does not attract the vehement disapproval which is expressed when the state attempts to regulate the 'rich'.

Penalty and prosecution policy: supplementary benefit

During the period of intense 'scroungerphobia' in the late 1970s the DHSS mounted increasing numbers of prosecutions for supplementary benefit fraud. Prosecutions reached a peak in 1980/81 with criminal proceedings taken against 20,105 supplementary benefit claimants (personal communication, DHSS 1985). This policy of 'prosecution where appropriate' was held to be a deterrent against fraud and abuse. But in keeping with emergent New Right ideology, calls for greater departmental cost-effectiveness led to a reappraisal of this policy following the Rayner team's inquiry in 1980. The official departmental policy from 1980 favoured the use of 'non-prosecution' interviews leading to benefit 'savings', a policy which was spearheaded by SCC units and fraud drives. Critics of this policy pointed out that encouraging claimants to withdraw their claim to benefit may lead to situations where investigators may conduct a non-prosecution interview and achieve the cessation of a claim, where a formal prosecution would have failed – for instance through lack of evidence, delay in proceedings or improper methods of investigation:

> A decline in the emphasis on prosecution could mean a decline in the adequacy of the evidence on which benefit is withdrawn.... In some circumstances benefit can be withdrawn on the basis of evidence which would not stand up in a court.

> (Moore 1981)

Although such commentators do not advocate the use of criminal proceedings against benefit fraudsters, they were fearful that 'non-prosecution' was potentially a greater evil: it entailed the possibility of coercing claimants and a potential slackening of standards by investigators eager to achieve savings targets, without the constraints of gaining the evidence necessary for court proceedings (Moore 1981; OWS 1982).

Numbers of prosecutions for supplementary benefit fraud did show a substantial decrease as a result of this shift in policy, dropping from 20,105 cases in 1980/81 to 8,090 cases in 1986/7 (see Appendix 2). None the less, these figures still demonstrate the relative prevalence of the use of criminal proceedings against benefit fraudsters in comparison with the infrequency of criminal proceedings against those who defraud the Inland Revenue (Appendix 1.). It is noteworthy that justifications in terms of the deterrent value of prosecution are not applied equally in the case of tax and benefit fraud: the prosecution of a small selection of the most serious cases of tax fraud is considered an adequate deterrent to the unacceptable spread of tax evasion, yet almost twenty times that number of prosecutions seem to be required in order to deter the supplementary benefit fraudster.

Clearly the differential prosecution of tax and benefit fraud is facilitated by the contradictory principles underlying taxation and the provision of state welfare. The apparent *rights* of equal citizenship afforded to welfare recipients are dissipated by the requirement to prove the *need* (and the personal worthiness) for state support, and by the political demands for departmental cost-effectiveness. Paradoxically it would be far more cost–effective to devote resources to the investigation of tax fraud which is, according to best estimates, far more costly and more prevalent than benefit fraud (see Chapters 1 and 5).

But differential responses to tax and benefit fraud also reflect the contradictory values of social justice and of the free market: as already argued, the relative dominance of the latter enables leniency towards the economically successful, but a punitive approach to the economic 'failures' who are dependent upon the state. The policy of 'sparing the taxpayer's feelings' therefore represents not only a pragmatic approach to the collection of tax, but also an acknowledgement that tax evaders are not 'criminals' in merely failing to give the appropriate slice of *their* income to the state. By contrast the benefit fraudster is 'criminal' in the sense that s/he is stealing the *taxpayer's* money. The prosecution policies of the two enforcing departments are therefore explicable in terms of these ideological contradictions and cannot be explained in terms of departmental cost–effectiveness and pragmatism alone.

The DHSS's approach to financial reparation also reflects these ideological distinctions between recipients of state benefits and those who are perceived as financing those benefits – the taxpayers. In the case of tax fraud (or 'default'), financial penalties are the preferred form of punishment on the grounds of sparing the taxpayer's feelings, pragmatism and the need for compliance. In the case of supplementary benefit claimants, all overpayments of benefit not arising from departmental error are recoverable, either through repayment in a lump sum or by instalments (if the claimant is no longer in receipt of benefit) or by deduction from benefit payments if they are still in receipt (Lynes 1985). Although *additional* financial penalties cannot be levied by the DHSS (as they *can* by the Revenue), claimants are more likely to face criminal proceedings in which the imposition of fines and court costs have precisely that effect. It is often argued that the rationale behind the use of financial penalties for tax fraud is the offender's ability to pay coupled with the need for compliance. But regardless of their poverty (and thus, theoretically, their inability to pay), benefit claimants *are* indeed required to pay, both through repayments to the DHSS and through financial penalties levied by the courts (see discussion of recovery practice and the 'ability to pay', pp. 165–7).

The key difference in departmental policies regarding financial penalty therefore lies in the context and manner of their imposition: for the tax fraudster financial penalties are civil matters dealt with by mutual agreement with officials of the Revenue. In the case of supplementary benefit fraud, financial penalties are imposed by courts and so involve the criminalization of the fraudster. As argued above, penalty policy also reflects ideological distinctions between the allegedly non-criminal nature of 'fiddling taxes' and the essentially criminal nature of stealing from the state (and taxpayers) through benefit fraud. The perceived relationship between the offender and the state is therefore crucial in explaining the differences in punishments and penalties imposed on tax and benefit fraudsters.

Prosecution and penalty: in practice

The punishment of tax and benefit fraudsters is in part determined by legal considerations: the differences of prosecution and penalty described above reflect disparities in the legal definitions of offences relating to tax and to supplementary benefit. The form of law itself can be seen in turn as indicative of different societal responses to those who defraud the public purse by failing to pay taxes or by falsely claiming state benefits (Uglow 1984). Disparities also emerge when examining the practice of departmental and judicial officials who administer the law and the punishments it prescribes. Differential practice in these respects will be analysed along the following lines:

1 Legal issues – intent and proof
2 Advice and representation
3 Sentencing offenders
4 The 'ability to pay' – the appropriateness of punishments

Legal issues: intent and proof

> Briefly, the offences available to the Inland Revenue are ones which require proof of *mens rea* in the form of dishonesty or intent to defraud.... The DHSS prosecutor has only to show knowledge of the falsity of the statement and does not have to show dishonesty in any wider sense. Are policies stressing the criminal aspect encouraged by the relatively easier task of prosecuting strict liability ofences?
>
> (Uglow 1984: 130)

Evidence provided to the Keith Committee and to the NACRO working party on the enforcement of Social Security law would indicate that, as Uglow suggests, policies stressing the criminal nature of social security offences and the 'non-criminal' nature of tax offences are generated and sustained by the availability of the substantive charges used against the different types of offender. For instance, according to the Keith Committee Report,

The Department commented 'Prosecution is a very drastic step which of its nature ought to be reserved, as a general proposition, to the really serious cases'. They frankly acknowledged, however, that significant practical considerations are also present which tended against a large number of prosecutions, namely 'the burden of preparing cases to the standard required in court and of seeing them through the courts'.

(*Cmnd 8822* 1983: 379)

By contrast, the task facing solicitors prosecuting on behalf of the DHSS is far less daunting; they must prove only the following: that the claimant made a 'representation' (statement), that it was false when made, that the claimant knew the purport of the representation and that it was false. There is no requirement to prove deliberate dishonesty or intention to defraud the department (OWS 1984; NACRO 1986). If prosecutions are brought under the Theft Act 1968 S.15 (obtaining property by deception), the prosecution must prove dishonesty and the wrongful obtaining of benefit, but these acts are used only in 'serious' cases (ibid.). The vast majority of prosecutions for supplementary benefit fraud are therefore brought under departmental regulations which require no proof of intent to defraud. The availability of easily prosecutable offences makes a vigorous anti-fraud policy, involving the relatively frequent use of (or threat of) prosecution on the part of the DHSS, more likely and more attractive (Uglow 1984).

The Inland Revenue adopts the principle that 'tax law is not something apart' and so it is usual to charge taxpayers with offences under the Theft Act. Effectively, then, it is necessary to prove *intention* to defraud in Revenue prosecutions, which perhaps contributes to their effectively non-prosecution-oriented approach (*Cmnd 8822*: 378). As one tax official commented, 'Revenue prosecutions tend to be for things that are readily provable. How do you prove deliberate intent to defraud by under-estimating profits?' (OVS 1985). In addition, many tax frauds involve a good deal of duplicity: they are by no means easily investigated, proved or understood. Evidence provided to the Keith Committee acknowledged the difficulties of mounting a successful Revenue prosecution, particularly in view of the technical complexities which both judge and jurors must understand:

> The difficulties of presentation of fraud cases to juries mean that too many fraudsters are being acquitted, or never prosecuted in the first place.
> (*Cmnd 8822* 1983: 165–6)

The Roskill Committee, set up in 1983, went so far as to recommend the use of a 'Fraud Trials Tribunal' as a potential solution, advocating that they be used instead of juries in the most lengthy and complex cases of fraud (Zander 1986). By contrast, in cases of supplementary benefit fraud the offence, of knowingly making a false statement for the purposes of obtaining benefit, is both easily provable and easily understood by magistrates and juries. This offence in itself is therefore perceived as less ambiguous than tax fraud and consequently more likely to be considered as straightforward 'crime'.

The relative ease of presentation of supplementary benefit fraud cases may, however, lead to a certain complacency on the part of DHSS investigators and prosecutors. According to one prosecuting solicitor, the case against supplementary benefit claimants is often 'full of holes'. He argued that in many instances he could 'get them off on technicalities'. This raises the important issues of the adequacy of the legal and procedural advice made available to claimants accused of fraud, and their access to legal representation.

Advice and representation

In the course of my research I undertook a study of cases of supplementary benefit fraud prosecuted in one Magistrates' Court (in a town of about 110,000 inhabitants) in the West Midlands. I examined official records relating to a selection of 206 prosecutions which proceeded through that court over a period of almost six years, between October 1981 and August 1987 (see Appendix 3 for details of full findings and statistical data collected). Of the 201 claimants who were convicted, 88 (42 per cent) had no legal representation in court. This factor may well have produced a 'communication gap' between defendant and magistrates which may have affected both verdict and sentence (Carlen 1976). Recent research on unemployment and Magistrates' Courts indicates that unrepresented defendants were 'inhibited from giving a fair account of themselves' (NACRO 1987: 17). In the words of one magistrate

> Some defendants don't know how to reply to magistrates' questions in court. Their perceptions are woolly; they only focus later on, outside the courtroom.
>
> (ibid.)

My own observations of several supplementary benefit fraud hearings in Magistrates' Courts confirm this view. For instance, one unrepresented defendant 'Bert' (accused of working as a builder's labourer while claiming supplementary benefit) seemed uncommunicative when questioned about his means and circumstances by the magistrate, despite the fact that there seemed to be a variety of factors which may have been considered in mitigation: his marriage had recently broken down, and setting up home elsewhere had proved costly and difficult for him. At the time of the hearing he was living in board-and-lodging accommodation and was unemployed. When asked if he wanted to say anything, Bert merely shrugged his shoulders and with head bowed said, 'It was one of those things I suppose'. This apparently flippant comment was clearly the result of nervousness, and demonstrated Bert's lack of knowledge concerning how to conduct his case. He was fined a total of £180 with costs of £35 (deductions were already being made from his supplementary benefit payments to recover the benefit he had fiddled by working and claiming). Yet once out of the courtroom, he seemed confident and articulate: for instance, referring to the magistrates and solicitors around him he commented wryly,

> This lot go on about scrounging, but who do they go to when they want an extension built? They come to us because we're cheap. How's that!
>
> (Bert)

Although Bert would clearly not have gained added sympathy by expressing these views to the magistrate, our conversation in itself did illustrate the 'communication gap' that had existed in court. The duty solicitor scheme should, in theory, prevent this problem (NACRO 1987), yet a significant proportion of defendants (42.7 per cent in my sample) remained unrepresented. In addition, 93 per cent of the sample pleaded guilty, despite the comments made by a prosecuting solicitor (noted above) suggesting the likelihood of weaknesses in the cases prepared by the DHSS.

The duty solicitor scheme should, then, enable defendants to obtain legal counsel, but the quality of the advice they may receive from these hard-pressed solicitors is questionable. For instance, one duty solicitor whom I observed evidently did not understand the regulations governing entitlement to supplementary benefit, particularly in relation to wife's earnings. As a result the defence he offered was both irrelevant and counter-productive. It is hard to imagine tax lawyers making such errors in defending their (high-paying) clients, and even harder to imagine an individual accused of tax fraud being unrepresented in court!

Analysis of Revenue and DHSS investigatory techniques has indicated significant disparities in the conduct of interviews with fraud suspects. For instance, the practice whereby Revenue investigation specialists supply a record of proceedings to interviewees are evidence of a 'professional' approach to investigation (Cmnd 8822 1983). They also, perhaps, reflect the Revenue's respect for the rights of taxpayers who have the financial and legal 'muscle' to insist upon those rights. By contrast, supplementary benefit claimants have less official knowledge of their rights and no means with which to purchase the best professional advice and representation. Agencies such as Citizens Advice Bureaux (CAB) and local government financed Welfare Rights Centres offer invaluable assistance to claimants, in obtaining their benefit entitlement and in dealing with investigations (OWS 1986). CAB advisers I interviewed said that claimants felt that they 'had a better deal' from the DHSS when advisers were present at interviews.

The possible consequences for claimants who do not receive advice (professional or voluntary) is evident in the experiences of Caroline and Barry, both of whom were unrepresented when facing supplementary benefit fraud charges in court. Caroline was not advised by the DHSS or the court to seek representation, and Barry was told by a DHSS official that there was 'no need to get a solicitor' because his case would probably not go to court, and if it did he would probably receive a conditional discharge. Barry was prosecuted, convicted, sentenced to a fine (plus costs), and told by the magistrate that he would have received a custodial sentence but for his being the father of four small children. He felt that he had been misled by departmental officials and had been unaware of the gravity of the sentence which the offence (working while claiming) was likely to attract. Caroline received a custodial sentence (see discussion of sentencing, pp. 160-5).

It is conceivable that the first indication a claimant suspected of fraud has that something may be 'wrong' could be the cessation of their benefit payments and a request that they attend the local office for interview. At this stage claimants are invariably unrepresented and so may face the official accusation (and presentation of 'evidence') of fraud without guidance on their legal rights or the possible implications of statements they may make. Prior to the Police and Criminal Evidence Act (PACE) in 1984, the DHSS did not advise claimants suspected of fraud to seek legal help: with the advent of PACE there is now a requirement to inform all persons interviewed under caution 'that they may obtain legal advice if they wish to do so' (personal communication, DHSS 1986).

Research has indicated that most claimants who have engaged in fiddles do admit their offences when confronted by DHSS officials. But it is significant that several claimants, who were interviewed by investigators and admitted their offences, were unaware of the possibility of prosecution, believing that when they agreed to repay the amount of benefit overpaid to them, the matter would be resolved. In addition, many claimants are not fully aware of how their overpayments are determined, and feel that they are bound to accept 'official' figures, whether they understand them or not. As NACRO aptly commented, 'it would be regarded as intolerable that a demand for tax should be made without an explanation of how it is calculated' (NACRO 1986).

The issue of claimants' access to representation and advice raises important questions concerning their ability to exercise the same rights as taxpayers when accused of fraud. Yet when knowledge of the benefit system is made more freely available to claimants, the assertion that such knowledge is tantamount to 'abuse' is frequently made: this was the case when welfare rights agencies promoted claimants' rights to exceptional needs payments prior to the 1986 reform of these single payments (see Chapter 6). The word abuse is, however, not used to describe the activities of advisers who help taxpayers gain their 'rights' in terms of minimizing tax liability: phrases with positive connotations, such as 'tax planning', are used instead. These differences in vocabulary are indicative of more fundamental differences in attitudes towards claimants and taxpayer: those who are perceived as takers from the state are effectively denied the knowledge, the confidence and the opportunity to assert their full rights of citizenship. Those who are perceived as 'givers' are seen as engaging in a contract with the state in which the taxpayers' compliance is essential: compliance, is, in great measure, won through ensuring the rights of individual taxpayers (Board of Inland Revenue 1986b).

Sentencing

> In 1984, the ratio of prosecutions brought by the Inland Revenue to that brought by the DHSS was 1:30. . . . The ratio of unsuspended prison sentences was about 1:10 and of all prison sentences, including some suspended ones, was 1:14. The greater proportionate severity of sentencing revenue law offenders reflects the fact that prosecution is so very much more exceptional and more strictly reserved for very serious cases.
>
> (NACRO 1986: 70)

In 1983, 268 Social Security offenders were imprisoned compared to 32 tax law offenders, and this despite the Revenue's aim of seeking harsh deterrent punishments for its most severe fraudsters (ibid.). But it should also be stressed that over 8,000 benefit fraudsters also acquired criminal records in that year. Even though significant numbers of tax defaulters are dealt with through the imposition of compounded financial penalties, this does not involve the publicity and effective criminalization suffered by benefit fraudsters, who are far more likely to undergo court proceedings.

The analysis of the sentencing of tax and benefit fraud presented here will seek to identify the rationales behind certain disposals, and to analyse the discourses used in criminal proceedings. Because of the small number of Revenue prosecutions, and consequent lack of opportunity to observe proceedings, official commentaries on selected court cases will form the empirical basis for this section. Observations of supplementary benefit fraud cases in a Magistrates' Court (together with additional local press coverage) will form the basis of the analysis of sentencing rationales for benefit fraud cases.

The Revenue's prosecution criteria (analysed above) are revealed in the types of cases selected for proceedings, which involve, for instance, failure to make full disclosures, particularly 'heinous' cases and those involving professional advisers. In one case Mr and Mrs A had substantially underestimated farming profits and enjoyed a 'tax holiday' for almost a decade, after which they failed to make a full disclosure. The tax thereby lost together with the interest on it amounted to £14,923. They were each sentenced to six months' imprisonment on each of three charges, suspended for two years, to run concurrently. Additional fines totalling £1,000 were imposed, the judge saying that the courts had 'no sympathy' in such serious cases. Harsher sentences are often imposed upon professional advisers who engage in fraud, and the nature and scale of the frauds involved also appear to play a part in determining sentences. For instance, Mr B was a chartered accountant who was found guilty of conspiring to defraud the Revenue of tax amounting to £500,000. He was sentenced to nine months' imprisonment and was referred to by the judge as a 'gamekeeper turned poacher'.

But even the sentencing of dishonest tax advisers may be influenced by 'mitigating circumstances': Mr C was an accountant who pleaded guilty to three charges of falsifying accounts. In mitigation it was argued that

> his professional career had been shattered... he had been a busy professional man, of high reputation in the local community, who had now lost everything through what were admitted as serious irregularities on his part.
>
> (OWS 1982)

He was sentenced to pay fines of £500 on each charge. Similarly Mr D, who was found guilty of Common Law cheat (in relation to the submission of false accounts), was not given a custodial sentence in view of his age, 'previous good character... the anxiety and general disgrace caused' and was sentenced to a £1,000 fine. The social disgrace suffered by the offenders in these cases was being presented as a form of punishment in itself, yet similar rationales are not used in mitigation where supplementary benefit fraudsters are concerned. The fact that the latter are almost by definition poor appears effectively to preclude the 'loss of status' plea in mitigation. In addition, the degree of punishment which the sentence of a fine inflicts is relative to the wealth and income of the offender: despite financial penalties imposed by the Revenue and fines imposed by the courts, many tax fraudsters are well able to pay. The same cannot be said in relation to fines imposed on offenders who already live on the official 'poverty line' (see pp. 165–7).

In the case of Mr E, a chartered accountant found guilty of defrauding the Revenue of £8,322, defence counsel emphasized Mr E's 'poor financial circumstances and the effect that the trial would have on the future income from the practice'. The judge took note of this and other mitigating factors and imposed a fine of £2,000 rather than a custodial sentence. Once again it appears that the status of the offender and the effects that court proceedings will have upon their future employment and earnings is taken into account when determining sentence. As will be seen below, being in regular employment may prove a similarly influential factor where benefit fraudsters are concerned, but for very different reasons: the view that the offender should no longer be financially dependent upon the state appears to be more influential than the notion that they have 'suffered enough' as a result of criminal proceedings, this notion being implicit in the sentencing of some tax offenders.

A particularly serious case of tax fraud involved Mr F, a successful salesman who falsely claimed to have emigrated to the USA and therefore evaded UK tax. Two days before he completed a written declaration to the Revenue (stating that he visited the UK only on business), he had agreed to purchase a £200,000 home in Chelsea (in his wife's name): his claim to non-residence was bogus. When arrested Mr F was intending to go to the Bahamas 'on a one-way air ticket'! The Revenue estimated that tax and interest lost could amount to over £300,000. Mr F was sentenced to eighteen months' imprisonment, twelve months of which were suspended, and fined £6,000. He was also ordered to pay costs of £9,000 and a criminal bankruptcy order was granted. However, arguments used by his defence counsel were that Mr F's current UK company employing 50 people would collapse without him, and that 'the atmosphere of corporate tax manipulation within a multinational group' contributed to the offences. Although an extremely serious offence, the bogus non-residence claim was being represented as the product of the pressures of the corporate business world.

By prosecuting 'a selection of the most serious cases' the Revenue seek to deter future possible offences. But the selection chosen still appears to concentrate upon *provable* cases which often involve *relatively* small-scale frauds (as discussed above, large-scale corporate tax fraud is beyond the scope of this study). But the status of the offender within the business community may be seen as another factor influencing sentencing, together with the desire of the Revenue to promote the compliance of individual taxpayers. For example, Mr G was a secondhand car dealer in the Liverpool area who, following VAT offences, was also found to have substantially under-estimated his trading profits. But his fraud was lacking in sophistication compared, for instance, with Mr F's international fiddle: Mr G had submitted accounts which, when analysed by investigators, 'indicated that ... he and his wife and three children had lived on £273 during a period of 11 years', and this despite his admitting to owning homes in Liverpool and Alicante! He was sentenced to imprisonment for one year, a heavier sentence than Mr F received at Knightsbridge Court for a substantially larger fraud (OWS 1981 and 1983).

Without drawing too firm conclusions from a small sample of tax prosecutions, it is fair to say that the Revenue seeks custodial sentences for those most serious cases which are selected for prosecution (OVS 1987). However, suspended prison sentences and fines are often imposed instead. I do not argue that it is desirable to *imprison* more tax fraudsters, but would rather argue that the differences in prosecution policy and judicial response to tax and to supplementary benefit fraud indicate gross social inequality. This is particularly evident in the case of Caroline.

Caroline was the subject of a DHSS investigation in 1978 when, following an anonymous tip-off from her employer, she was interviewed under caution. She admitted working part-time in a pub earning a total of £58, although by the time of the court hearing she no longer worked there. Caroline was 20 years old and living with her boyfriend. Because the tenancy of the flat in which they lived was in her name, she was regarded as the claiming partner and so was the subject of the prosecution. Caroline was from a middle-class background and had received a public-school education, but she had 'been in trouble with the police' for minor offences. Her address, given in court, was in a 'bad' area renowned for poverty and for crime. A social enquiry report was 'favourable' towards Caroline, but was largely ignored and she was given a custodial sentence, according to the magistrate, 'to teach you a lesson'. As already discussed, she was unrepresented in court and was completely unprepared for the possibility of imprisonment: the first three weeks of that sentence (she served three months in all) were served at Risley Remand Centre. It is almost inconceivable that an individual who defrauded the Inland Revenue to the tune of £58 should receive a custodial sentence to teach them 'a lesson'. It is also highly unlikely that such patronizing comments would be passed by the judiciary in cases of tax fraud (see also the cases of Bert and Jim discussed below). Ironically the Revenue now write off up to £70 tax underpaid by PAYE taxpayers as 'not worth collecting', yet supplementary benefit claimants who fiddle amounts *less* than £70 (for instance by fiddling and altering giros) may still be prosecuted (OVS 1987; NACRO 1986).

In the case of Caroline, issues relating to her class and gender may well have influenced the sentence passed. She felt that the magistrate regarded her as too independent for a 'young woman' of 20: she was living with a man and held the tenancy of a flat. Furthermore, she worked as a part-time barmaid, the job in itself evoking stereotyped sexualized images, which were particularly false in her case: she rejected her boss's advances and ironically it was this that led to a tip-off and her being investigated by the DHSS. Caroline also felt that she was regarded as doubly deviant because of her apparent rejection of her middle-class family background.

Bert reacted to the realities of supplementary benefit prosecution in a philosophical way, yet asserted, 'It's not as if we've beaten up old ladies and stolen their handbags, is it? We've not *hurt* anyone.' But in sentencing one offender, a magistrate referred to benefit fraud as 'one of the worst forms of stealing there is'. This discrepancy in the perceptions of the relative seriousness of benefit fraud perhaps confirmed an assertion made by another offender, Jim, who referred to the magistrate as being 'On another planet to us'. Another claimant similarly told me, 'They don't live in the same world as us; they don't know what our life is like'. If there is a relationship between perceptions of the seriousness of certain offences and the degree of personal empathy with the likely offenders, then this may affect the prosecution and sentencing of tax and benefit fraud: 'If the wrongdoer is someone like themselves and the situation a familiar one, people tend to be less censorious' (Jowell and Witherspoon 1985). The judges and magistrates who sentence tax and benefit fraud are far less likely to be familiar and sympathetic with the experiences of supplementary benefit claimants.

Jim was prosecuted for failing to declare his wife's earnings over a one-year period, during which time they were attempting to pay off accumulated debts of over £1,000. Jim had admitted the offence and agreed that the benefit overpaid be deducted from his weekly supplementary benefit payments at the rate of £1.65 per week. In sentencing Jim the magistrate said, 'This country's fed up to the teeth with people like you scrounging from fellow citizens'. He was sentenced to fines totalling £210 and ordered to pay costs of £34. It is difficult to see the logic of a sentence which inflicts further financial penalties upon a family (with three school-aged children) who effectively live below the poverty line because of deductions made for a £996 overpayment, and whose offence was itself motivated by an attempt to clear debts of a further £1,000. Under such circumstances Jim's 'joke' to his friends after the hearing was a sad indication of the family's plight: 'Ah well,' he said, 'I suppose it's the red light under the porch now'.

The proportion of indictable offences dealt with by fines is declining: in the 1970s 50 per cent of such offences were dealt with by fines compared with 40 per cent in 1985 (NACRO 1987). This shift has been linked with rising unemployment, although research has indicated that magistrates' sentencing patterns vary according to an area's history of unemployment and the existing unemployment rates (NACRO 1987). None the less, courts were less likely to modify financial penalties for those on low incomes where supplementary benefit fraud was concerned (ibid: 48). This view is consistent with my own research in which 40 per cent of offenders in the sample were sentenced to pay fines and 78 per cent were ordered to pay costs (see Appendix 3). But over the six-year period covered in this study there was a discernible increase in the use of conditional discharges and comparable reduction in the use of fines: during the period 1981-3 22 per cent of offenders were sentenced to a conditional discharge and 44 per cent to fines. In the year 1986-7 the same proportion of offenders (37 per cent) were sentenced to conditional discharges and to fines; this trend perhaps reflects a growing acknowledgement of the inappropriateness of fines in dealing with the crimes of the poor.

As evident in the case of Caroline, magistrates can be both punitive and patronizing in their attitudes towards benefit fraudsters: one magistrate used the same phrase on three occasions when sentencing supplementary benefit offenders: 'You are old enough to know better'. One offender reprimanded in this manner was 42 years old. Another was told when sentenced to 'pull himself together', and references was made to his 'deceiving society'. But one offender who was sentenced to a community service order was told that although he was 'in great danger of going to prison today, there is one plus in your favour – at least you're working'. The worst 'crime' is evidently to be financially dependent on the state.

One issue raised when analysing the sentencing of tax and benefit fraudsters is the tendency of a 'ratchet effect' to be operative in the case of unemployed offenders:

> an offender who has had, say, fines and a probation order is more likely, other things being equal, to be considered for a higher tariff disposal next time, and being unemployed may accelerate this process.
>
> (NACRO 1987: 25)

As many tax defaulters are likely to be dealt with by the Revenue policy of financial settlement (and penalties as appropriate), they are not subject to the ratchet effect: tax fraud is usually dealt with by 'civil' proceedings within the department, supplementary benefit fraud, despite an avowed non-prosecution policy by the DHSS, is more likely to result in 'criminal' proceedings. These in turn may have the cumulative effect of moving the offender's sentencing tariff upwards. This factor may accentuate the already unequal departmental and judicial response to those who defraud the Revenue and those who defraud the DHSS.

The ability to pay

There is a common assumption that the differential treatment of tax and benefit fraud derives from disparities in the offenders' relative 'ability to pay', in terms of repayment of money lost to the public purse or in terms of added financial penalty. It is often asserted that this explains both the high rate of prosecution of poorer fraudsters by the DHSS and the comparably low rates of prosecution (coupled with emphasis on financial settlement) by the Inland Revenue where richer fraudsters are concerned. However, this argument ignores the fact that the poorest members of society *do* pay for their fiddles, both in reparation to the DHSS through deductions from benefit, and in reparation to society through the courts, where in 1983 62 per cent of benefit fraudsters were also ordered to pay fines (NACRO 1986 – but see discussion of sentencing above for recent shifts). What follows will examine the contradictory rationales which underpin departmental and judicial assumptions concerning the individual taxpayer's or claimant's ability to 'pay' for their fiddles.

The DHSS has the power to recover over-payments resulting from fraud in four ways: by deduction from future benefit (the most common method, accounting for two-thirds of all recoveries), by lump sum payment, by instalments or by compensation order. Until 1980 departmental practice followed the rule that any deductions from benefit made in respect of over-payments should not reduce the claimant's income to below the basic supplementary benefit level, regarded as the 'poverty line'. But current regulations enable up to £6.80 to be deducted from the weekly benefit of (Income Support) claimants admitting fraud, and £5.10 in any other case

(CPAG 1988). As mentioned above, claimants are not always fully aware of how their over-payments have been calculated (NACRO 1986: 65). Moreover, it is difficult to see how benefit fraud is deterred by the use of recovery methods which can reduce a claimant's income to £6.80 below the poverty line and, if criminal proceedings ensue, possibly involve a fine imposed by the courts in addition: under such circumstances fiddling benefits or other crimes may ironically become the only means of financial survival.

Taxpayers are almost by definition better able to pay financial penalties than benefit claimants: at the very least they have sufficient earned or unearned income to be liable to pay tax. For this reason, as we have seen already, the taxpayers' ability to repay tax lost and to pay additional compounded penalties (if appropriate) is used as a justification for 'sparing the taxpayer's feelings' and for the adoption of an essentially non-prosecution policy. Most tax officials I have spoken to have a sympathy for this approach on practical grounds, but none the less they object to the 'double standards' evident where benefit fraudsters are concerned. This applies not only to disparities in prosecution policy, but also to some of the justificatory rationales used in respect of those policies.

Officials were particularly aware of the relatively extensive publicity which 'scrounging' attracts in comparison to tax evasion. But publicity is inextricably linked to the reporting of criminal proceedings in the courts, and if tax fraud cases do not reach the courts, then public awareness of the extent and costs of the problem will be minimal. To justify this 'softly softly' approach to publicizing tax evasion, it is sometimes argued that it promotes taxpayers' co-operation:

> The Inland Revenue argues that people will be prepared to co-operate more if they 'settle out of court', as it were, with no fuss. I think that is probably correct, but there is a need to weigh up the relative value of publicity as a deterrent, in relation to the *lack* of publicity being helpful in a handful of investigations.
>
> (OVS 1985)

This rationale for the relatively 'quiet' treatment of the tax fraudster is closely linked to the mitigation offered in court (as discussed in 'Sentencing' above), that social disgrace is in itself sufficient punishment for tax evaders. The notion that a fraudster has 'suffered enough' merely through the public exposure of his/her crimes is one which is not applied to supplementary benefit fraudsters. Indeed, the media treatment of them suggests just the opposite! It seems that in order to 'pay' for one's crimes through personal suffering and disgrace, one has to have some social standing to lose: hence these discourses are not available to justify lenience towards benefit fraudsters.

Although differences in the ability to pay offer a simple justification for the differential official and judicial responses to tax and benefit fraud, such justifications are themselves a product of particular sets of beliefs about the relative personal and economic worth of citizens who claim money *from* the state and citizens who pay money *to* the state. These beliefs are evident in discourses used in courts, by departmental officials (see Part III) and in popular rhetoric (see Chapters 1 and 8).

In summary, the poor who defraud the DHSS *are* required to pay, to the department and to society, as a punishment for their crimes. Those who defraud the Revenue may well pay financial penalties, but these are more likely to be civil, in nature and in tone: they are less likely than benefit fraudsters to suffer criminalization and public vilification.

Summary

This chapter has examined the official policy discourses relating to the prosecution and punishment of tax and supplementary benefit fraud. In addition, the practical outcome of these policies has been analysed and several contradictions have emerged. For example, although the DHSS at present officially operates a policy designed to *reduce* numbers of prosecutions and seek 'benefit savings', effectively it still prosecutes over 8,000 supplementary benefit claimants per year; this is in stark contrast to the official 'selective' approach to Revenue prosecutions which effectively resulted in only 459 prosecutions in 1986/7 (see Appendices 1 and 2). Moreover, the justificatory rationale behind both policies – deterrence – is not applied equally to tax and benefit fraudsters.

Judicial responses (and sentencing practice) towards tax and supplementary fraud are based on entirely different premises: the analysis of discourses used in court demonstrated crucial differences in the assumptions being made about claimant and taxpayer. In some cases it seemed that tax evaders were presumed to be victims – either of the ethos of the business and corporate world, or victims of the disgrace of their fellow citizens – as a result of Revenue prosecution. According to magistrates observed in this study, in cases of supplementary benefit fraud the victim is the taxpayer (who was seen to finance benefit payments), not the benefit fraudster. The tax fraudster is represented as at best folk-hero, at worst a victim of the taxman.

At the heart of the contradictions in policy and in practice which have been analysed here is the ideological representation of the taxpayer as a 'giver' to the state and the supplementary benefit claimant as a 'taker' from the state (and thus, ultimately, from the compliant taxpayer). These representations are the product of the particular histories of tax and welfare (Chapter 2). These histories are characterized by a traditional resistance to taxation, save in times of national crisis (for instance, during war or post-war reconstruction), and a parallel struggle over collective welfare provision, which was similarly and grudgingly accepted after the crises of two world wars. Specific economic, social and political pre-conditions therefore underpin attitudes to tax and welfare at particular times. Contradictions in the political, social and judicial responses to tax and welfare rest upon combinations of beliefs about the nature of the relationship between the state and the individual, and the desirability of social justice or economic growth as the primary goal of modern mixed economies. These combinations of beliefs, the vocabularies they invoke and the policies which they generate are summarized in Table 7.

Table 7   The ideological bases of differential response

Tax	*Welfare*
ECONOMIC IDEOLOGIES	
Free market	Social justice
Individualism	Collectivism
POLITICAL IDEOLOGIES	
Liberal minimalist state	Democratic interventionist state
LEGAL IDEOLOGIES	
Mens rea	Strict liability
('sporting' view of law,	('punish scroungers'
tax frauds as 'fiddling')	benefit fraud as 'crime')
ORGANIZATIONAL IDEOLOGIES	
Compliance	Control
Spare the taxpayer's feelings	Police the poor
Fraud deterred by exemplary	Fraud deterred by prosecuting
prosecution of the few	some and policing many others

8

Social Justice, Taxation and the Welfare State

The notion that there is 'one law for the rich and another for the poor' is often implicitly invoked in critical social commentaries, but is denied in official and judicial discourses which stress equality in citizenship and before the law. This book has examined this slogan by analysing the legal, social, material and ideological responses to the economic crimes committed by individuals who approximate to the 'rich' and the 'poor' in contemporary Britain. In order to ensure meaningful comparisons between *individual* law-breakers, the 'relatively rich' taxpayers and the 'poor' supplementary benefit claimants were the chosen focus of study. This enabled the techniques and justifications of individual tax and benefit fraudsters to be directly compared. Similarly direct comparisons could also be made between the departmental techniques used to regulate individual tax and benefit fraudsters, and the stated rationales of Revenue and DHSS enforcement policy and practice. The principal themes which emerged from these comparative analyses of fraudsters, investigators and of popular and judicial responses to tax and benefit fraud will now be summarized.

The 'deserving' and the 'undeserving' poor

The 1834 Poor Law left an important legacy which has influenced contemporary attitudes towards, and vocabularies used to describe, the poor. Implicit distinctions were made between those categories of poor who were seen to be 'deserving' of relief – aged, sick and infirm people, and children – and those who were regarded as 'undeserving' – unemployed people or 'idle' paupers. These distinctions still inform popular rhetoric and currently social policy towards unemployed people and new categories of claimants who could, it is argued, similarly 'avoid' poverty (Minford 1987).

The pillars of the 1834 Poor Law were the principles of less eligibility and the workhouse test. These principles remain operative in the 1980s, although in differing forms: for instance, pressure for unemployed benefit claimants to attend Job Clubs, the Restart interviewing programme and increasingly stringent tests of an individual's 'availability for work' all signify an intensification of the 'work-test', which now operates within the community, rather than within the walls of a workhouse. Such measures are, according to official pronouncements, designed to 'show people how to look for jobs more effectively' and to remotivate those who are unemployed. Yet an important latent function is to 'detect the "scroungers" and those not genuinely available for work' (*Guardian* 27.12.86 and 23.2.88).

Less eligibility still surfaces in arguments which invoke the notion of 'incentives to work' (discussed on pp. 171–2 and the 'anti-effort' (formerly 'unemployment') trap. Currently discourses centring on the implementation of the Social Security Act 1986 stress, amongst other issues, the officially stated goal of providing incentives for the unemployed to take low-paid jobs (BBC *Newsnight* 31.3.88). Such incentives will operate only if the claimant's lot is rendered 'less eligible' than that of the lowest paid worker (Rusche and Kirchheimer 1939).

Taken together, the principles of less eligibility and the work(house) test still exert important influences upon popular perceptions of, first, those who are by virtue of their age, health or 'unavoidable' misfortune regarded as *deserving* of state support, and second, those who are, because of their lack of effort (or their lack of adherence to the 'moral' nuclear family form) constituted as 'avoidably' poor and hence *undeserving* of state support.

Penality, welfare and taxation

An important theme which informs any analysis of welfare provision is the issue of penality: work-tests and less eligible levels of welfare benefits, inevitably result in the state functioning (through the claiming process and conditions and mechanisms of benefit payment) to instil discipline into welfare recipients. A generalized discipline may be seen to encompass the generation (through such processes) of sentiments of stigma and guilt, to which all claimants are exposed (Deacon and Bradshaw 1983; Foster 1983). But for the 'undeserving', an added obstacle course is presented by informal welfare rationing, 'mucking about' and attempts to maintain the work discipline through specific 'tests' (Deacon and Bradshaw 1983). These tests currently include a detailed seventeen-point questionnaire for all unemployed claimants, and ability-for-work testing in Restart interviews (despite the fact that fewer than 15 per cent of claimants 'end up with something positive as a result of Restart' – *Poverty* 1988a: 4). Work discipline may also be instilled through the threat of deductions from already-less-eligible levels of benefit for 'voluntary unemployment' (Deacon and Bradshaw 1983; Walker and Walker 1987). Around 400,000 claimants each year suffer a 40 per cent reduction in supplementary benefit for up to thirteen weeks on grounds of voluntary unemployment: from April 1988 this penalty may be continued for up to six months (*Poverty* 1988a).

Because welfare recipients are 'takers', the state may lay down conditions upon which their benefit is to be received. The state thus has the power to punish those who cannot, or will not, meet those disciplinary criteria: benefits can be reduced or withdrawn, and in some circumstances individuals penalized for failing to maintain their families financially (ibid; Lynes 1985). By contrast, taxpayers are 'givers' to the state and the discipline to which they are subjected is less rigorous and less direct – as a result, attempts to enforce the Taxes Acts frequently attract vociferous condemnation: for instance, a recent series of articles on Revenue investigation policy in *The Times* (February and March 1988) included those headlined 'Tax claw in the velvet glove', 'Shifting the burden of proof' and 'Targets for the hit squad'. In response to the aggressive anti-Revenue tone of these articles Bill Hawkes, Assistant Secretary of the Inland Revenue Staff Federation, commented,

> Every successful challenge or investigation which recovered tax, means that someone has lied to the Revenue – not just made a mistake. When the white middle classes lie it is seen as part of the game. If black working class people lie to the DHSS the morality of it is seen quite differently.
>
> (*Assessment* March 1988)

The vocabularies of the 'game' of tax evasion and the (lack of) 'morality' of benefit fraudsters are important themes in elucidating differential popular responses to tax and benefit fraud. But the complex problem of differential response cannot be 'read-off' as a product of structural inequalities of class and race *alone*: it can, rather, be seen as a product of the historical and ideological construction (*within* a structurally unequal society) of taxation as an intolerable inquisition to which the 'giving' taxpayer is subjected, in order to finance those who 'take' welfare benefits from the state. Thus the *differential powers* of the state (legal and administrative), and the disparate *political will* of the state to discipline and punish defaulting taxpayers and undeserving claimants are crucial in explaining differential response to tax and benefit fraud.

The incentives debate

Arguments which suggest that 'high' levels of welfare benefits act as an incentive to idleness, and 'high' rates of taxation act as a disincentive to effort remain ideologically powerful, despite their dubious empirical foundations (see Chapter 3). This version of the incentives argument enables tax fraudsters to be represented positively, often as enterprising individuals who are merely resisting 'excessive' personal taxation. Within this context tax evasion may be transformed from economic crime to a battle of wits to beat the taxman or as a 'part of the game' of capital accumulation, which is the taken-for-granted goal of a society geared to (capitalist) economic growth (see Chapters 1 and 3). Such representations of the incentives argument have important ideological effects:

> For success to glisten seductively at the winners, the failure of poverty must display its burden of guilt and shame.
>
> (Golding and Middleton 1982: 244)

The incentive to be a success in the 'enterprise culture' of the 1980s can be achieved only if the consequences of failure are the contempt and deprivation of the 'benefit culture'.

The right-wing view of incentives represents benefit claimants as welfare-drones or 'battery hens' who enjoy servitude and dependency (Boyson 1971; 1978). Their incentive to work is seen to be sapped by their very idleness and the 'moral hazard' of claiming state benefits (Parker 1982). Alternative discourses stress that the highest marginal rates of tax are not suffered by the enterprising middle classes but by the low paid, and go on to argue that unemployed people are not prevented from working by 'high' levels of state benefits but, rather, by mass unemployment and the chronic problem of low pay (Roll 1983; CPAG/Low Pay Unit 1986; CPAG 1987). None the less, these critical versions of the incentives argument fail to gain dominance within a capitalist economic framework, dominated by New Right discourse, wherein low wages are seen to mean higher profitability, workers allegedly need to 'price themselves into jobs', and lower expenditure on benefits (potentially) enables lower taxes (IEA 1977; Bosanquet 1983).

The pre-eminence of the ideology of what may be termed the 'effort' school of thought is particularly assured while political power rests with advocates of New Right politics. Their contemporary stress on the values of the 'enterprise culture' and parallel denunciation of the 'benefit culture' serves to polarize popular discourse on taxation and welfare. It is within this economic, historical and ideological context that differential responses to tax and benefit fraudsters are reproduced and justified.

The 'Robin Hood' myth

The 'Robin Hood' myth reflects the widely held belief that, since 1945, a fundamental redistribution of income and wealth has taken place in Britain. This belief is not supported by empirical evidence (Byrne 1987; CPAG 1987), yet remains ideologically powerful. The 'Robin Hood' mythology effectively presents the taxpayer as 'giver' to the poor (through progressive taxation), and the poor as 'takers' from the taxpayer and thus the state. This mythology serves two ideological purposes: first, it offers a justification for tax fraud in terms of resisting progressive taxation, which, it is alleged, has gone too far because 'making the rich poorer does not make the poor richer, but it does make the state stronger' (Joseph 1975). (This argument was much in evidence in Conservative defences of the 1988 Budget.) Second, the myth of redistribution effectively denies the principal motivation for benefit fraud – poverty – because, it is argued, the 'real' problem of poverty has been removed through the 'Robin Hood' activities of the state. And besides, according to Chancellor Nigel Lawson, '*everybody* ... is benefiting from the success of the economy' (Rentoul 1988: 12) in the 1980s. However, critics would argue that 'all that people on supplementary benefit or a state pension know of Lawson's "success of the economy" is the tail light of someone else's Porsche disappearing into the distance' (ibid.).

Differential attribution of motives for tax and benefit fraud

The myth of redistribution raises the issue of differential popular acceptance of justifications offered for tax and benefit fraud. For example, it has been argued that tax fraudsters may successfully justify their actions in terms of excessive state regulation and 'penal' rates of personal tax (Chapter 3). Their 'need' to be economically successful remains unquestioned, the accumulation motive taken for granted. However, supplementary benefit fraudsters are unable to invoke their main motivation (poverty) success-fully because they are perceived as committing fraud through 'greed' not 'need'. The attribution of this motive derives from concepts of the undeserving poor, coupled with an invocation of 'Robin Hood' myths which present benefit claimants as prime recipients of the 'gift' of state support, enabled by the selfless redistribution of the *taxpayer's* money.

Vocabularies of motive offered for tax fraud centre on resistance to pay over money legally due *to* the state, whereas the benefit fraudster attempts to justify taking money illegally *from* the state. The result is the same – loss to the public purse – and similar activities are engaged in by some tax and benefit fraudsters (for instance, working in the black economy, making false declarations to government departments). But differential attribution of motive essentially derives from the historical and ideological construction of the relationship between taxpayer and the state, and supplementary benefit claimant and the state: the vocabulary of 'givers' and 'takers' thus helps to explain why tax fraudsters may gain popular acceptance (and even muted praise) in defrauding both the state and the honest taxpayer; yet it is benefit fraudsters who are attributed the motives of greed, selfishness and 'immoral' lack of public spirit.

Freedom and social justice

As argued in Chapter 1, the social philosophies of individualism and liberalism cannot fully be reconciled as they are based upon entirely different premises concerning the relative role of the state and the individual in modern industrial societies: a struggle between these philosophies characterizes twentieth-century social policy, particularly in relation to taxation and welfare.

From 'The People's Budget' of Lloyd George and Beveridge's 'Social Insurance' to the concept of Social Security in the 1960s, the apparent object of social policy was the achievement of some measure of *social justice* through the taxation and welfare benefits systems. Yet the economic prosperity upon which such policies were based was seen as being dependent upon adherence to *free-market* principles. These principles involve the pre-eminence of competition, entrepreneurial spirit, minimal state regulation in the market and personal wealth creation. The ideologies of social justice, and of the free market, though fundamentally at odds, uneasily co-exist and are differentially invoked at particular times according to specific material and political conditions. Thus, for instance, in times of war the rhetoric of 'fair shares' was invoked to justify progressive taxation and a redistribution in favour of those who had been equal in war and in death. But the Butskellite 'consensus' upon which the post-war Welfare State rested was, rather, a grudging compromise (Deakin 1987).

The ideology of the free market has always epitomized the 'Old Right', and was revitalized by the political ascendancy of the New Right in the mid-1970s. It is, therefore, important to remember that the ideological contradictions which allow space for the practice and justification of differential response have a long history. The contradictions which enable differential responses to tax and welfare fraud derive from a struggle between the competing ideologies of social justice and free market individualism. Such key ideas have never 'disappeared', but have lost dominance at particular times: in this way the generation of knowledges and ideas has been examined here as a process of incorporation and transformation of existing discourses, rather than the creation of 'new' ones. To this extent the 'New' Right is not new: as Taylor-Gooby (1985) argues, this political philosophy weaves a variety of 'Old' Right arguments which, for example, derive from both the contradictions of the Butskellite era and the Victorian values of 'self-help' and 'morality'.

By the mid-1970s the material conditions created by economic recession particularly favoured two interlocking sets of beliefs which have firm roots in the histories of taxation and welfare:

1 the notion of the social security 'scrounger' which echoed nineteenth-century stereotypes of the undeserving poor, and which was similarly produced by a concern about the costs of 'poor relief' to the ratepayer/taxpayer;

2 a belief that allegedly 'progressive taxation' (raised in order to finance benefits to the poor) had gone too far in subsidizing the (idle) poor at the expense of the hard-working taxpayer: it was argued that incentives, entrepreneurial spirit and thrift had all been stifled as a result (Seldon 1979a; Joseph 1975).

These two sets of ideas fused in the growing concern expressed, from left- and right-wing perspectives, about the form and objectives of the tax-financed modern Welfare State (Mishra 1984). Advocates of social justice focused on the problems of inadequate levels of benefit, poor take-up of means-tested benefits, issues concerning claimants' rights and inefficient service-delivery to the poor. By contrast, the advocates of free-market individualism focused on the intrusive, stifling, inefficient and cossetting Welfare State which allegedly fails to 'help the poor to help themselves', while at the same time burdens the not-so-poor (taxpayers), who are faced with the spiralling costs of an allegedly unfair and inefficient state bureaucracy.

Taxation and welfare provision are therefore inextricably linked, in free market and social justice ideologies, though the nature of that 'link' hinges upon differing views on the respective roles of the individual and the state. But it is within the context of this historical, ideological and political struggle that the paradox of differential response must be understood and explained, rather than solely in terms of 'one law for the rich and another for the poor'.

The 1988 Budget and Social Security reforms

As research for this book was being completed, an opportunity arose to demonstrate the utility of its central themes by analysing contemporary discourses on taxation and welfare provision: this opportunity occurred because of a unique combination of 'reforms' of both tax and welfare announced in the 1988 Budget (presented on 15 March) and the Social Security Act 1986 (fully implemented in April 1988). The stated motives for both the Budget and the Social Security reforms were strikingly similar (see Table 8). The themes of reform, incentives, fairness, and the added impetus (according to Mrs Thatcher) to 'push the balance back in favour of the individual' characterize the rhetoric both of the Budget and the Social Security reforms. But the manner in which these vocabularies are applied in practice to taxpayers and to benefit claimants is entirely contradictory.

The 1988 Budget promised to put the values of 'incentives and opportunity in place of old fashioned egalitarianism' (*Financial Times* 16.3.88). According to *The Times* Britain had been brought closer to a 'low tax, high incentive economy' (16.3.88). When the New Right version of incentives is applied to taxpayers, they are seen to respond directly to reduced taxation by working harder and seeking out opportunities. In a similar vein, it is

Table 8   Rationales for the 1988 Budget and Social Security reforms

Motives for Budget reforms	Motives for Social Security reforms
Promote *incentives* to effort (for the wealth creators)	Promote *incentives* to work (for the unemployed, the young)
Radical reform, geared to *simplification* of the tax system (e.g. reduce the series of higher rate taxes to one rate – 40 per cent)	Radical reform geared to *simplification* of the benefit system (e.g. same means-testing rules to apply to all main benefits)
Greater *fairness* (e.g. taxing wives separately, stopping 'tax breaks')	Greater *fairness* (e.g. 'more help' for families, targeting the 'needy')

argued that dramatic reductions in higher rates of tax (from 60 per cent to 40 per cent) were justified by the need to maintain incentives for 'scarce talent' to remain in Britain. These interpretations of the incentives argument were questioned by critics who argued that there was no proven link between low top rates of tax and high economic growth:

> Anyone who tries to prove this first has to explain how countries varying from Japan (with a top rate of 78%) and Sweden (even higher) have achieved better prosperity than the U.K.... There has not been much evidence of an exodus of scarce talent from Japan or Sweden.
>
> (Keegan in *Guardian* 28.3.88)

None the less, tabloid press coverage centred on the 'high earners' who were allegedly being encouraged to greater effort in the Budget, and the popularization of this incentives argument proved bizarre as, for instance, when the *Sun* announced that

> Burton stores chief, Sir Ralph Halpern – famous for his sexploits – will get a bonking great boost of £5,097 a week.
>
> (*Sun* 16.3.88)

Official pronouncements were also evident in popular vocabularies: Nigel Lawson's assertion that 'Everyone will benefit' was reproduced on 16 March in the form of 'We're *all* in the money' (*Daily Express*) and 'Lotsa lovely lolly' (*Sun*). Although the language of *The Times* was less colourful, it was no less euphoric: 'Lawson's tax triumph'.

This powerful invocation of incentives clearly left behind all those who were unable to respond to tax cuts, either because their wages were too low (hence they remained stuck in the poverty trap), or because they paid no tax (unemployed people and pensioners). But those who disagreed with the 'official' justifications for tax cuts were likely to be branded 'humbugs', and the *Daily Mail* suggested that they should 'give the money back'. Crucial to an understanding of such popular sentiments is an ideological sleight of hand whereby the (largely working-class) readership of the *Sun* absorbs official pronouncements which justify £2 billion tax cuts to the top 5 per cent of wage-earners, while the lowest 30 per cent received virtually nothing (*Guardian* 17.3.88), all on the grounds of incentives to effort. Despite the dryness of much post-Budget media coverage, there is a common-sense notion amongst journalists that it is poverty and social security that are the 'boring' topics:

> Poverty may be a running phenomenon of our times, but it is not a news story and it can be pretty flat.
>
> (Hildrew 1988)

Certainly arguments about poverty and about fairness in the distribution of the 'lolly' were largely absent from official discourses on the Budget. But in any event, it was argued, 'Fairness is a vague term at the best of times' and to talk of 'distribution of wealth in a society is to borrow a word from statisticians: you might equally talk of the distribution of car-crashes or Cabbage Whites' (*Spectator* 26.3.88). The 'rubbishing' of egalitarianism became an intrinsic part of attempts to rejuvenate free market individualism and promote tax incentives to wealth creation:

> Nigel's Budget was the obituary for the doctrine of high taxation. . . . It was the epitaph for socialism.
>
> (Thatcher, quoted in Hall 1988)

As Stuart Hall (1988) pointed out, 'this budget was "about" the moral values and social principles on which the Thatcherite revolution is premised'. For this reason the comments of a 'Tory entrepreneur' are particularly significant:

> I think Nigel's taking the piss now. . . . I don't think anyone will work any harder. I certainly won't work harder, I'll just spend more . . . People will have three skiing holidays instead of one.
>
> (quoted in Rentoul 1988)

Such comments also indicate that the version of the incentives argument which sees higher-income earners motivated to greater effort by tax cuts (and hence still higher incomes) is a fallacious one.

Thatcherism has long held that the poor, by contrast, respond to the spur of their own poverty (Loney 1986). Therefore incentives are seen to operate entirely differently upon welfare recipients, who are presented as needing the 'incentive' of state work-tests and less eligible levels of benefit to persuade them to seek work. Incentives to effort are thus provided by, for example, the abolition of Exceptional Needs Payments: the finite Social Fund which replaces them will offer *loans* not grants and so, according to Social Security minister Nicholas Scott, 'will encourage claimants to take more responsibility for planning their own spending' (*Guardian* 25.3.88).

The ideology of individualism is once more evident, as individual 'responsibility' is advocated in order to counter the negative effects of the 'benefit culture' of dependency on the state. But such views also reflect nineteenth-century images of the culpable and indolent poor.

However, the *deserving* poor are allegedly 'targeted' for additional help in the Social Security reforms: Social Services secretary John Moore asserted that 'policy reforms will ensure a greater coherence, greater fairness and greater focusing of help to those in need' (*Guardian* 23.3.88). But representatives of 'Youth Aid' and of 'One Parent Families' argue that the young and lone parents (the new *undeserving* poor) will suffer disproportionately from the full implementation of the Social Security Act 1986.

Conclusion

The contradictions between free market and social justice ideologies are crucial in explaining the contemporary struggles over the meanings and motives of the Social Security reforms, and the 1988 Budget. These reforms will have very real effects on claimants and taxpayers, but whether these effects are the ones *apparently* intended by government is questionable. For instance, in theory the taxpayer, having been released from the burden of penal rates of taxation, will no longer be forced by the 'intolerable inquisition' to avoid paying taxes and, moreover, will be able to give more to charity to help the less fortunate. Whether tax evasion and avoidance (muted in the neutral term used by Mr Lawson – 'tax breaks'), will be reduced as a result of these extensive tax cuts for the rich remains to be seen: it will be the ultimate test of the shaky doctrine of incentives and a litmus test for the justification for tax evasion as a response to excessive taxation (Chapter 4). At the same time, the effective reduction in supplementary benefits (now 'Income Support') will test the justification that most fraud results from poverty: if this is true, then many claimants will increasingly find themselves before either the courts or the loan sharks.

Alternatively (or maybe concomitantly) one result of the 1988 Budget may be that if it can no longer be argued that the rich have valid *excuse* for tax evasion, then the New Right may indeed have gone a 'budget too far' and undermined the belief (even of *Sun* readers) that the rich are so hardworking and moral that they deserve even more 'lovely lolly'. For, as this book has suggested, discourses already exist that would make it possible to have very different responses to tax and social security fraud than those that currently prevail, responses that may even reduce the gross inequalities of regulatory practices. I have argued that differential response to tax and social security fraud is not determined by immutable economic relations; rather it is the product of certain combinations of material and ideological conditions. It follows, therefore, that change *is* possible as knowledges about taxation and welfare are forever open to deconstruction and to challenge.

Appendices

Appendix 1

Inland Revenue prosecutions

Nature of offence		1977/78	1978/79	1979/80	1980/81	1981/82	1982/83	1983/84	1984/85	1985/86	1986/87
					Number of persons convicted (acquittals shown in brackets)						
False accounts or returns of income		11(2)	33(4)	39	31(7)	27(9)	13(1)	28(2)	21(1)	22	17(2)
False claims to personal allowances, deductions for expenses and repayments		5	28(2)	19(2)	28	13(1)	7(1)	7(1)	4	3(3)	3
PAYE: False returns (offences by employers and pay clerks)[1]		14	11	12(1)	17	16	22(2)	20(3)	23(3)	19(2)	19(1)
PAYE: Forgery, impersonation by employees		—	—	5	1(1)	2	—	1	—	—	—
Sub-contractor exemption certificate frauds[2]		135(4)	108(2)	67(5)	94(9)	89(20)	92(4)	92(5)	184(2)	264(7)	274(9)
Theft of payable orders and giro cheques[3]		199(1)	261	174	227(2)	235	207(2)	84(10)	86	101	138
Assaults on Inland Revenue officers[4]		5(2)	1	2	—(1)	1	3	3	1	—	2(1)
Internal frauds[5]		4	4(1)	1	4	3	1(1)	9	12	4	5
Miscellaneous[6]		1	—	—	1	1	—	—	1	1	1
TOTALS		374(9)	446(9)	319(8)	403(20)	385(30)	345(11)	244(21)	332(6)	414(12)	459(13)

Notes: [1]Includes convictions obtained by the police for PAYE frauds: 1986/87 1.
[2]Includes convictions obtained by the police for sub-contractor frauds as follows: 1977/78 48: 1978/79 22: 1979/80 10: 1980/81 15: 1981/82 7: 1982/83 3: 1983/84 5: 1984/85 8: 1985/86 63: 1986/87 89.
[3]Includes convictions obtained by the police for theft of payable orders as follows: 1977/78 177: 1978/79 177: 1979/80 160: 1980/81 200: 1981/82 216: 1982/83 186: 1983/84 72: 1984/85 84: 1985/86 101: 1986/87 138.
[4]Includes convictions obtained by the police for assaults on Inland Revenue officers: 1986/87 1.
[5]Includes convictions obtained by the police for internal frauds as follows: 1983/84 2: 1984/85 6: 1985/86 Nil: 1986/87 1.
[6]Includes convictions obtained by the police for miscellaneous offences against the Inland Revenue: 1986/87 1.

Source: Board of Inland Revenue 1987. Reproduced by kind permission of Her Majesty's Stationery Office.

Appendix 2

Supplementary benefit prosecutions

1980/1	20,105	(includes 4,263 police prosecutions, 5 by the post office)
1981/2	16,423	(includes 4,146 police prosecutions, 17 by the post office)
1982/3	13,589	(includes 2,884 police prosecutions, 12 by the post office)
1983/4	9,101	(includes 3,346 police prosecutions, 2 by the post office)
1984/5	9,360	(includes 2,878 police prosecutions, 2 by the post office)
1985/6	8,902	(includes 2,364 police prosecutions, 0 by the post office)
1986/7	8,090	(includes 2,274 police prosecutions, 1 by the post office)

Source: personal communication, DHSS 1988

Appendix 3

Information from a study of 206 supplementary benefit fraud prosecutions in one Midlands Magistrates' Court (Oct. 1981 to Aug. 1987)

1 Gender
   Males – 145 (70%)   Females – 61 (30%)

2 Pleas
   Guilty – 191 (93%)   Not guilty – 15 (7%)

3 Verdicts
   Guilty – 201 (97.6%)   Not guilty – 5 (2.4%)

4 Legal representation
   Claimants represented – 118 (57%)   Not represented – 88 (43%)

5 Sentences passed
   Custodial   17 (8.4%)
   Community service   22 (10.9%)
   Probation   26 (12.9%)
   Fine   82 (40.8%)
   Conditional discharge   54 (27%)
   TOTAL   201

6 Social enquiry reports requested in 44 cases

7 Compensation orders made to the DHSS in 93 cases (46%)

8 Costs awarded to the DHSS in 156 cases (78%)

9 *Prosecutions by type of offence and gender*

Offence	No. of cases	Men	Women
Non-declaration of earnings	113	85	28
Non-declaration of wife's earnings	26	26	—
Giro/order book frauds	45	30	15
Non-declaration of capital	1	—	1
Other circumstances not declared	15	4	11
Cohabitation/ fictitious desertion	6	—	6
TOTAL	206	145	61

10 *Sentences passed, by gender*

Sentence	Total	Men	Women
Custodial	17	12	5
Community service	22	21	1
Probation	26	12	14
Fine	82	65	17
Conditional discharge	54	30	24
TOTAL	201	140	61

Bibliography

Allatt, P. (1981) 'Stereotyping: familism and the law', in B. Fryer, A. Hunt, D. McBarnett and B. Moorhouse (eds) (1981) *Law State and Society*. London, Croom Helm.

Annual Abstract of Statistics (1985) London, HMSO.

Atkins, S. and Hoggett, B. (1984) *Women and the Law*. Oxford, Basil Blackwell.

BBC *Grapevine* (1983) *The Oxfraud Incident*. BBC Community Programme Unit.

Beltram, G. (1984a) *Testing the Safety Net*. London, Bedford Square Press/NCVO.

Beltram, G. (1984b) 'Seeing it from the other side', *New Society* 16 August.

Beltram, G. (1985) 'A tough assignment', *Community Care*, 30 May.

Board of Inland Revenue (1986a) *128th Annual Report*. London, HMSO.

Board of Inland Revenue (1986b) *Taxpayer's Charter*. London, HMSO.

Board of Inland Revenue (1987) *129th Annual Report*. London, HMSO.

Bosanquet, N. (1983) *After the New Right*. London, Heinemann.

Box, S. (1987) *Recession, Crime and Punishment*. London, Macmillan.

Boyson, R. (1971) *Down With the Poor*. London, Churchill Press.

Boyson, R. (1978) *Centre Forward: A Radical Conservative Programme*. London, Maurice Temple Smith.

Bracewell-Milnes, B. (1977) 'The fisc and the fugitive', in IEA, *The State of Taxation*. IEA Readings 16. London, IEA.

Bracewell-Milnes, B. (1979) 'Is tax avoidance/evasion a burden on other taxpayers?' in A. Seldon (ed.) *Tax Avoision*. London, IEA.

Braithwaite, J. (1984) *Corporate Crime in the Pharmaceutical Industry*. London, Routledge & Kegan Paul.

Braybon, G. (1982) 'The need for women's labour in the First World War', in E. Whitelegg, M. Arnot, V. Beechey, L. Birke, S. Himmelweit, D. Leonard, S. Riehl and A. Speakman (eds) *The Changing Experience of Women*. Oxford, Martin Robertson.

Break, G.F. (1957) 'Income taxes and incentives to work: an empirical study', *American Economic Review* 47, 5.

Burghes, L. (1980) *Living From Hand to Mouth*. London, Family Services Unit/CPAG.

Burton, F. and Carlen, P. (1979) *Official Discourse*. London, Routledge & Kegan Paul.

Burton, J. (1985) *Why No Cuts?* Hobart Paper No. 24. London, Institute of Economic Affairs.

Byrne, D. (1987) 'Rich and poor: the growing divide' in A. Walker and C. Walker (eds) *The Growing Divide*. London, CPAG.

Campbell, B. (1984) *Wigan Pier Revisited*. London, Virago Press.

Carlen, P. (1976) *Magistrates' Justice*. London, Martin Robertson.

Chambliss, W. (1978) *On the Take*. Bloomington, Indiana, Indiana University Press.

CHAR (Campaign for Homeless People) (1986) *Benefits: A Housing and Supplementary Benefits Guide for People without a Permanent Home*. London, CHAR.

Chief Adjudication Officer (1987) *Annual Report for 1985/6*. London, HMSO.

Cmd 6404 (1942) *Social Insurance and Allied Services*. London, HMSO.

Cmnd 8822 (1983) *Keith Committee Report on the Enforcement Powers of the Revenue Departments*. London, HMSO.

Coetzee, S. (1983) *Flat Broke: How the Welfare State Collapsed in Birmingham*. Birmingham Welfare Rights Group.

Cohen, S. (1973) *Folk Devils and Moral Panics*. London, Paladin.

Cohen, S. and Young, J. (eds) (1973) *The Manufacture of News*. London, Constable.

Cook, D. (1987) 'Women on welfare – In crime or injustice?', in P. Carlen and A. Worrall (eds) *Gender Crime and Justice*. Milton Keynes, Open University Press.

Cooper, S. (1985) *Observations in Supplementary Benefit Offices. The Reform of Supplementary Benefit: Working Paper C*. London, Policy Studies Institute.

CPAG (Child Poverty Action Group) (1982) *Briefing on the Social Security Bill* (unpublished)

CPAG (1984) *Social Security Reviews 1984: Factpack*. London, CPAG.

CPAG (1987) *Poverty – The Facts*. London, CPAG.

CPAG (1988) *National Welfare Benefits Handbook*. London, CPAG.

CPAG/Low Pay Unit (1986) *Joint Briefing: The Rising Tide of Poverty* London, CPAG/LPU.

CPSA (Civil and Public Services Association) (1984) *Policing the Welfare – Benefits Under Attack*, Report of Special Conference, UCW Cardiff, 8 October 1983.

CPSA (1986) *Discussion Paper on Income Maintenance* (unpublished).

CPSA/SCPS (Society of Civil and Public Servants) (1984) *Note of a National Conference on DHSS Fraud* London, SCPS/CPSA.

David, M. (1986) 'Moral and maternal. The family in the right' in R. Levitas (ed.) *The Ideology of the New Right*. Cambridge, Polity Press and Blackwell.

Deacon, A. and Bradshaw, J. (1983) *Reserved for the Poor*. Oxford, Basil Blackwell and Martin Robertson.

Deakin, N. (1987) *The Politics of Welfare*. London, Methuen.

Dean, P., Keenan, T. and Kenney, F. (1980) 'Taxpayers' attitudes to income tax evasion: an empirical study', *British Tax Review* 1980 no. 1.

Deane, K.D. (1981) 'Tax evasion, criminality and sentencing the tax offender', *British Journal of Criminology* 21, 1, January.

DHSS (1979) *Annual Report of the Supplementary Benefits Commission*. London, HMSO.

Ditton, J. (1977) *Part-Time Crime*. London, Macmillan.

Donnison, D. (1982) *The Politics of Poverty*. Oxford, Martin Robertson.

Edgar, D. (1986) 'The free or the good' in R. Levitas (ed.) *The Ideology of the New Right*. Cambridge, Polity Press and Blackwell.

Ericson, R.V., Baranek, P.M. and Chan, J.B. (1987) *Visualizing Deviance*. Milton Keynes, Open University Press.

Esam, P., Good, R., and Middleton, R. (1985) *Who's to Benefit?* London, Verso.

Fairbairns, Z. (1985) 'The cohabitation rule: why it makes sense', in C. Ungerson (ed.) *Women and Social Policy*. London, Macmillan.

Field, F. (1979) 'Scroungers – crushing the invisible', *New Society*, 16 November.

Fitzgerald, T. (1983) 'The New Right and the family' in M. Loney, D. Boswell and J. Clarke (eds) *Social Policy and Social Welfare*. Milton Keynes, Open University Press.

Foster, P. (1983) *Access to Welfare*. London, Macmillan.

Franey, R. (1983) *Poor Law*. London, CHAR/CPAG/CDC/NAPO/NCCL.

Fraser, D. (1973) *The Evolution of the British Welfare State*. London, Macmillan.

Fraud Investigators Guide (1983) Unpublished DHSS Circular.

Furnham, A. (1985) 'The determinants of attitudes towards social security recipients', *British Journal of Social Psychology* February.

Gallie, W.B. (1976) 'Liberal morality and social morality', in A. Blowers and G. Thompson (eds) *Inequalities, Conflict and Change*. Milton Keynes, Open University Press.

Gamble, A. (1986) 'The political economy of freedom', in R. Levitas (ed.) *The Ideology of the New Right*. Cambridge, Polity Press and Blackwell.

Garland, D. (1985) *Punishment and Welfare*. Aldershot, Gower.

George, V. and Wilding, P. (1984) *The Impact of Social Policy*. London, Routledge & Kegan Paul.

Gershuny, J. and Pahl, R. (1980) 'Britain in the decade of the three economies', *New Society* 3 January.

Glasgow University Media Group (1982) *Really Bad News*. London, Writers and Readers.

Gofton, L. and Gofton, C. (1984) 'Making out in Giro City', *New Society*, 22 November.

Golding, P. and Middleton, S. (1982) *Images of Welfare*. Oxford, Martin Robertson.

Hall, S. (1988) 'Even worms turn', *New Statesman* 25 March.

Hall, S. and Jacques, M. (1983) *The Politics of Thatcherism*. London, Lawrence & Wishart.

Hall, S., Critcher, C., Jefferson, T., Clarke, J. and Roberts, B. (1978) *Policing the Crisis*. London, Macmillan.

Harrison, P. (1983) *Inside the Inner City*. Harmondsworth, Penguin.

HC 102 1983/4 (1983), *Committee of Public Accounts: Prevention and Detection of Evasion of N.I. Contributions and of Social Security Benefits*, London.

HC 123 1984/5 (1985), *Committee of Public Accounts: Control of Investigation Work, Board of Inland Revenue*, London.

Henry, S. (1978) *The Hidden Economy*. Oxford, Martin Robertson.

Henry, S. (1983) *Private Justice*. London, Routledge, Kegan & Paul.

Higgins, J. (1981) *States of Welfare*. Oxford, Basil Blackwell and Martin Robertson.

Hildrew, P. (1988) 'No news is bad news', *New Statesman Society* 10 June.

Holman, R. (1978) *Poverty*. London, Martin Robertson.

Houghton, Lord (1977) 'Administration, politics and equity', in IEA, *The State of Taxation*. IEA Readings 16. London, IEA.

Houghton, Lord (1979) 'The futility of taxation by menaces', in A. Seldon (ed.) *Tax Avoision*. London, IEA.

IEA (Institute of Economic Affairs) (1977) *The State of Taxation*. IEA Readings 16. London, IEA.

IEA (1979) *Tax Avoision*. London, IEA.

IEA (1980) *Prime Mover of Progress*, IEA Readings 23. London, IEA.

Inland Revenue form P11D (Guide) (1985) *Return of Expenses Payments and benefits etc. to or for Directors and 'Higher Paid' Employees*. London, HMSO.

Inland Revenue (Leaflets)

   IR 28 (1982) *Starting in Business*. London, HMSO.

   IR P7 (1983) and (1987) *Employer's Guide to PAYE*. London, HMSO.

   IR 72 (1987) *Inland Revenue Investigations: The Examination of Business Accounts*. London, HMSO.

   IR 73 (1987) *How Settlements are Negotiated*. London, HMSO.

   IR480 (1987) *Notes on Expenses, Payments and Benefits for Directors and certain Employees*. London, HMSO.

IRSF (Inland Revenue Staff Federation) (1982) 'Black Economy', *Taxes* July.

IRSF (1983) *Assessment* April.

IRSF/AIT (Association of HM Inspectors of Taxes) (1981) Submission to the Keith Committee (unpublished).

Jordan, B. (1973) *Paupers: The Making of the New Claiming Class*. London, Routledge & Kegan Paul.

Joseph, Sir K. (1974) Speech delivered on 19 October. London, Conservative Central Office.

Joseph, Sir K. (1975) in *Observer* 22 August.

Jowell, R. and Witherspoon, S. (1985) *British Social Attitudes – 1985 Report*. Aldershot, Gower.

Laurance, J. (1987) 'Avoidance tactics?', *New Society* 29 May.

Leigh, L.H. (1982) *The Control of Commercial Fraud*. London, Heinemann.

Levi, M. (1982) 'The powers of the Revenue agencies – An overview', *British Tax Review* 1982 no. 1.

Levi, M. (1987) *Regulating Fraud*. London, Tavistock.

Levitas, R. (ed.) (1986) *The Ideology of the New Right*. Cambridge, Polity Press and Blackwell.

Lewis, A. (1982) *The Psychology of Taxation*. Oxford, Martin Robertson.

Lewis, M. (1977) *British Tax Law*. Plymouth, MacDonald & Evans.

Lister, R. (1987) *There is an Alternative: Reforming Social Security*. London, CPAG.

Loney, M. (1986) *The Politics of Greed*. London, Pluto Press.

Loney, M. (ed.) (1987a) *The State or the Market?* London, Sage.

Loney, M. (1987b) 'A war on poverty or on the poor?', in A. Walker and C. Walker (eds) *The Growing Divide*. London, CPAG.

Loney, M., Boswell, D., and Clarke, J. (eds) (1983) *Social Policy and Social Welfare*. Milton Keynes, Open University Press.

Low Pay Unit (1986) *Low Pay Review No. 24*. London, Low Pay Unit.

Low Pay Unit/CPAG (1988) *An Abundance of Poverty*. London, LPU/CPAG.

Lynes, T. (1985) *The Penguin Guide to Supplementary Benefits*. Harmondsworth, Penguin.

MacGregor, S. (1981) *The Politics of Poverty*. London, Longman.

McKnight, J. (1985) 'Pressure points: the crisis in management', in S. Ward, (ed.) *DHSS in Crisis*. London, CPAG.

Mandla, D. (1987) 'War on the dole', *New Society* 26 June.

Mars, G. (1982) *Cheats at Work*. London, Allen & Unwin.

Marsden, D. (1982) *Workless*. London, Croom Helm.

Marwick, A. (1965) *The Deluge*. London, Macmillan.

Mesher, J. (1983) *C.P.A.G.'s Supplementary Benefits Legislation, annotated*. London, Sweet & Maxwell.

Minford, P. (1987) 'The role of the social services: a view from the New Right', in M. Loney, *The State or the Market?* London, Sage.

Mishra, R. (1977) *Society and Social Policy*. London, Macmillan.

Mishra, R. (1984) *The Welfare State in Crisis*. Brighton, Wheatsheaf Books.

Mishra, R. (1986) 'The Left and the Welfare State: a critical analysis', *Critical Social Policy* 15, Spring.

Monroe, H. (1981) *Intolerable Inquisition*. London, Stevens.

Moore, P. (1981) 'Scroungermania again at the DHSS', *New Society*, 22 January.

Myddleton, D.R. (1979) 'Tax avoision – its costs and benefits', in A. Seldon, (ed.) *Tax Avoision*. London, IEA.

NACRO (National Association for the Care and Resettlement of Offenders) (1986) *Enforcement of the Law Relating to Social Security*. London, NACRO.

NACRO (1987) *Unemployment and Magistrates Courts*. London, NACRO.

NAO (National Audit Office) (1987) *DHSS and Department of Employment: Incorrect Payments of Social Security Benefits*. HC 319. London, HMSO.

NCASSC (National Campaign Against Social Security Cuts) (1985) *Bulletin No 3* January 1985.

Network: the Quarterly Magazine of the Inland Revenue (1985) July, pp. 10–11. Burnham, Bucks, Creative Solutions.

Network: the Quarterly Magazine of the Inland Revenue (1986) January, pp. 4–5. Burnham, Bucks, Creative Solutions.

O'Connor, J. (1973) *The Fiscal Crisis of the State*. New York, St James Press.

O'Higgins, M. (1981) 'Tax evasion and the self employed', *British Tax Review* 1981 no. 6.

Parker, H. (1982) *The Moral Hazards of Social Benefits*. Research Monograph no 37. London, IEA.

Pearce, F. (1976) *Crimes of the Powerful*. London, Pluto Press.

Pearce, I. (1977) 'Taxing the dole' in IEA, *The State of Taxation*. IEA Readings 16. London, IEA.

Pearl, D. and Gray, P. (1981) *Social Welfare Law*. London, Croom Helm.

Piachaud, D. (1980) 'Taxation and social security' in C. Sandford, C. Pond and A. Walker, (eds) *Taxation and Social Policy*. London, Heinemann.

Piachaud, D. (1987) 'The growth of poverty', in A. Walker and C. Walker (eds) *The Growing Divide*. London, CPAG.

Pond, C. (1980) 'Tax expenditure and fiscal welfare' in C. Sandford, C. Pond and A. Walker (eds) *Taxation and Social Policy*. London, Heinemann.

Poverty (1987/8) no. 68, Winter. pp 20–1. London, CPAG

Poverty (1988a) no. 69, Spring. pp 4–5. London, CPAG

Poverty (1988b) no. 70, Summer. pp 20-1. London, CPAG.
PSI (Policy Studies Institute) (1985) *Observations in Supplementary Benefits Offices.* London, PSI.
Rawnsley, A. (1985) 'Well met by moonlight', *Guardian* 27 December.
Reid, I. (1981) *Social Class Differences in Britain.* London, Grant McIntyre.
Rentoul, J. (1988) 'The new idle rich', *New Statesman Society* 25 March.
Roll, J. (1983) *A Memorandum on the Incentives Issue.* London, CPAG.
Rowell, M.S. (1982) 'Erosion of discretion in supplementary benefits', *New Law Journal* 28 October.
Royal Commission on the Distribution of Income and Wealth (1979) *Cmnd 7595.* London, HMSO.
Rusche, G. and Kirchheimer, O. (1939) *Punishment and Social Structure.* New York, Columbia University Press.
Sabine, B.E.V. (1966) *A History of Income Tax.* London, Allen & Unwin.
Saville, J. (1983) 'The origins of the Welfare State' in M. Loney, D. Boswell and J. Clarke (eds) *Social Policy and Social Welfare.* Milton Keynes, Open University Press.
Scraton, P. and South, N. (1984) 'The ideological construction of the hidden economy', *Contemporary Crises* no. 8 1984.
Seldon, A. (ed.) (1979a) *Tax Avoision.* London, IEA.
Seldon, A. (1979b)' Avoision - the moral blurring of a legal distinction without an economic difference', in A. Seldon (ed.) *Tax Avoision.* London, IEA.
Shenfield, A.A. (1968) *The Political Economy of Tax Avoidance.* IEA Occasional Paper 24. London, IEA.
Sinfield, A. (1970) in P. Townsend (ed.) *The Concept of Poverty.* London, Heinemann.
Smart, C. and Smart, B. (eds) (1978) *Women, Sexuality and Social Control.* London, Routledge & Kegan Paul.
Smith, R. (1985) 'Who's fiddling? Fraud and abuse', in S. Ward (ed.) *DHSS in Crisis.* London, CPAG.
Smith, S. (1986) *Britain's Shadow Economy.* Oxford, Oxford University Press.
Social Security Consortium (1986) *Of Little Benefit: a Critical Guide to the Social Security Act 1986.* London, SSC.
Social Security Statistics (1986). London, HMSO.
Social Trends No. 15, (1985) London, HMSO.
Social Trends No. 16, (1986) London, HMSO.
Stockwell and Clapham Law Centre (1983) *Supplementary Benefit Fraud Manual.* London: Stockwell and Clapham Law Centre.
Sutherland, E. (1960) *White Collar Crime.* New York, Holt, Rinehart & Winston.
Taylor-Gooby, P. (1985) *Public Opinion, Ideology and State Welfare.* London, Routledge & Kegan Paul.
Thatcher, M. (1975) Speech delivered 15 September. London, Conservative Central Office.
Titmuss, R.M. (1963) *Essays on the Welfare State.* London, Allen & Unwin.
Titmuss, R.M. (1970) *The Gift Relationship.* London, Allen & Unwin.
Townsend, P. (ed) (1970) *The Concept of Poverty.* London, Heinemann.
Townsend, P. (1979) *Poverty in the United Kingdom.* Harmondsworth, Penguin.
TUC (Trades Union Congress) (1983) *Taxation.* Submission to Keith Committee (unpublished).

Uglow, S. (1984) 'Defrauding the public purse', *Criminal Law Review* March.

Ungerson, C. (ed.) (1985) *Women and Social Policy.* London, Macmillan.

Vincent-Jones, P. (1986) 'The hippy convoy and criminal trespass', *Journal of Law and Society* 13, 13 Autumn.

Vinson, N. (1980) 'Successful entrepreneurship based on inquiry and invention' in IEA, *Prime Mover of Progress*. IEA Readings 23. London, IEA.

Walker, A. and Walker, C. (eds) (1987) *The Growing Divide*. London, CPAG.

Walker, C. (1987) 'Reforming Social Security – despite the claimant', in A. Walker and C. Walker (eds) *The Growing Divide*. London, CPAG.

Walker, M. (1978) 'Measuring the seriousness of crimes', *British Journal of Criminology* 1978, 348–64.

Ward, S. (ed.) (1985a) *DHSS in Crisis*. London, CPAG.

Ward, S. (1985b) 'Flat broke: the Birmingham strike' in S. Ward (ed.) *DHSS in Crisis*. London, CPAG.

Welfare Rights Bulletin 83 (1988) April pp. 8–10. London, CPAG.

Welfare Rights Bulletin 84 (1988) June pp. 1–2. London, CPAG.

Williams, K. (1981) *From Pauperism to Poverty*. London, Routledge & Kegan Paul.

Wilson, E. (1977) *Women and the Welfare State*. London, Tavistock.

Wilson, E. (1980) *Only Halfway to Paradise*. London, Tavistock.

Wilson, E. (1983) 'Feminism and social policy', in M. Loney, D. Boswell and J. Clarke (eds) *Social Policy and Social Welfare*. Milton Keynes, Open University Press.

Wilkins, L.T. (1964) *Social Deviance*. London, Tavistock.

Zander, M. (1986) 'The Report of the Roskill Committee on fraud trials', *Criminal Law Review July 1986*.

Index